ADVANCES IN VOCATIONAL PSYCHOLOGY

Volume I:
The Assessment of Interests

Edited by

W. Bruce Walsh
Samuel H. Osipow
The Ohio State University

LEA LAWRENCE ERLBAUM ASSOCIATES, PUBLISHERS
1986   Hillsdale, New Jersey   London

Lawrence Erlbaum Associates, Inc., Publishers
365 Broadway
Hillsdale, New Jersey 07642

Library of Congress Cataloging-in-Publication Data
Main entry under title:

Advances in vocational psychology.

   Bibliography: v. 1, p.
   Includes indexes.
   Contents: v. 1. The assessment of interests.
   1. Vocational interests — Addresses, essays, lectures.
2. Vocational guidance — Addresses, essays, lectures.
I. Walsh, W. Bruce, 1936–   II. Osipow, Samuel H.
HF5381.5.A3   1986   158.6   85-18237
ISBN 0-89859-755-2 (v. 1)

Printed in the United States of America
10   9   8   7   6   5   4   3   2   1

Contents

List of Contributors

FRED H. BORGEN
Iowa State University
LINDA S. GOTTFREDSON
The Johns Hopkins University
JO-IDA C. HANSEN
University of Minnesota
JOHN L. HOLLAND
The Johns Hopkins University
FREDERIC KUDER
Educational and Psychological Measurement, Inc.
JACK R. RAYMAN
Pennsylvania State University
DONALD G. ZYTOWSKI
Iowa State University

Introduction: The Assessment of Interests

W. Bruce Walsh
Samuel H. Osipow
The Ohio State University

The systematic assessment of vocational interests can be traced to 1927 when E. K. Strong, Jr. published the Strong Vocational Interest Blank for Men (SVIB). The SVIB was an empirically based inventory that compared an individual's likes and dislikes to the likes and dislikes of people employed in a variety of different occupations. More than 50 years later, the *Eighth Mental Measurements Yearbook* (Buros, 1978) reported that the Strong Inventory was the fourth most frequently used assessment instrument in research, accounting for some 1,720 papers on empirical studies. In their survey of assessment instruments, Brown and McGuire (1976) found the Strong inventory to be the eighteenth most frequently used assessment inventory. Engen, Lamb, and Prediger (1982) surveyed test use at the secondary school level and Zytowski and Warman (1982) assessed the use of tests in private practice, colleges, and universities. The Strong Campbell Interest Inventory was high on both lists. There is no question that E. K. Strong's work has had a profound impact on interest measurement. The third and most recent edition of the SVIB was published in 1981 and is called the Strong Campbell Interest Inventory. A fourth edition was published in 1985. The advances made by the 1985 version of the Strong Campbell Interest Inventory are elaborately discussed by Hansen in chapter 1 of this volume.

A second milestone in the area of interest measurement was the work of G. F. Kuder. In 1934 Kuder introduced the Kuder Preference Record, made up of a series of content scales assessing preferences for specific activities. Kuder's early work was not empirically normed, but in 1966 he introduced the Kuder Occupational Interest Scale, which used empirically defined occupational scales. The most recent revision (second edition) of the Kuder Occupational Interest Survey occurred in 1979 (Kuder & Diamond, 1979). A third edition was developed and published in 1985. Advances in the 1985 version of the KOIS are presented by Zytowski and Kuder in chapter 2. Also of note is the fact that the surveys of Engen, Lamb, and Prediger (1982) and Zytowski and Warman (1982) found the KOIS to rank high in terms of use.

In 1959, John Holland theorized that behavior is a function of interests, personality, and social environments. In this context, Holland suggested that the choice of an occupation is an expression of personality and that interest invento- ries are therefore personality inventories. Holland was convinced that people entered vocational environments because of their interests and personalities. To measure the interest and personality types, Holland developed the Vocational Preference Inventory and more recently the Self-Directed Search. Other invento- ries that have drawn upon his theoretical concepts include the Strong Campbell Interest Inventory, the UNISEX edition of the ACT Interest Inventory, the Ca- reer Assessment Inventory, the Harrington and O'Shea System for Career Deci- sion Making, and the United States Employment Services Interest Inventory. It is clear that Holland's theory and subsequent assessment techniques have had con- siderable impact on the field of interest measurement over the past 2 decades. Again the Engen and Zytowski surveys previously mentioned have found the SDS to rank high in terms of use in secondary school systems, private practice, colleges, and universities. In chapter 3 of this volume, Holland and Rayman report the origin and development of the Self-Directed Search, its application to career counseling and other forms of career assistance, and an account of future research and development possibilities.

Chapter 4 by Borgin focuses on innovations in interest measurement. In this chapter, specific attention is directed to newer interest inventories (the Career Assessment Inventory, the Jackson Vocational Interest Survey, the UNISEX edition of the ACT Interest Inventory, and the Vocational Interest Inventory) and how they have built upon or gone beyond the Strong Campbell Interest Invento- ry, the Kuder Occupational Interest Inventory, and the Self-Directed Search. The focus is on conceptual and psychometric change and the implications of such change for counseling use. Borgin discusses how different inventories have handled issues in interest measurement, and how some of the newer inventories reflect innovative approaches or a continuation of established traditions.

Chapter 5 by Gottfredson examines the appropriateness of interest inventories in counseling members of special groups and explores how interest inventories might be beneficially used in the career counseling of both minority and majority populations. The first section of this chapter outlines recent concerns about special groups and the impact those concerns have had on the structure of interest inventories and on perceptions of the role that interest inventories do or should play in the counseling process. The second section suggests that the use of any counseling tool, including inventories, can be improved by a more analytical understanding of the career choice problems that people have. The third and final section of the chapter proposes nine principles for the beneficial use of interest inventories for both minority and majority populations.

Keeping up with new developments in vocational psychology is important to both psychological practitioners and researchers. This volume is devoted to presenting important advances in the field of interest assessment.

REFERENCES

Brown, W. R., & McGuire, J. M. (1976). Current psychological assessment practices. *Professional Psychology, 7,* 475–484.

Buros, O. K. (Ed.). (1978). *The eight mental measurements yearbook* (Vol. 1). Highland Park, NJ: Gryphon Press.

Engen, H. B., Lamb, R. R., & Prediger, D. J. (1982). Are secondary schools still using standardized tests? *Personnel and Guidance Journal, 60,* 287–290.

Kuder, G. F., & Diamond, E. E. (1979). *Occupational Interest Survey, general manual* (2nd ed.). Chicago: Science Research Associates.

Zytowski, D. G., & Warman, R. E. (1982). The changing use of tests in counseling. *Measurement and Evaluation in Guidance, 15,* 147–152.

1 Strong Vocational Interest Blank/Strong–Campbell Interest Inventory

Jo-Ida C. Hansen
Center for Interest Measurement Research
University of Minnesota

The current version of the Strong Interest Inventory, the Strong Vocational Interest Blank/Strong–Campbell Interest Inventory (SVIB-SCII), was completely revised in 1985. This edition features 264 scales including 6 General Occupational Themes (GOT), 23 Basic Interest Scales (BIS), 207 Occupational Scales, 2 Special Scales, and 26 Administrative Indexes. This compares to the earliest form of the Strong that included only 10 Occupational Scales on the profile. A sample of the 1985 edition of the profile is shown in Fig. 1.1.

MATERIALS FOR THE SVIB-SCII

The Strong Inventory booklet contains 325 items to which the respondent is asked to answer *like, indifferent,* or *dislike,* to indicate how she or he feels about each of the listed occupations, school subjects, occupational activities, leisure activities, types of people, and her or his own characteristics. Samples of the items are given in Table 1.1.

Because of the large number of scales on the Strong profile, and because many of the scales are more than 60 items long, templates are not available for handscoring, and this inventory must be scored by computer. The responses of the individual are analyzed, scores are computed for each of the scales, and the results are printed on a profile. The results also may be printed in the form of an interpretive report that provides the user with additional information about the relationship of the scores to one another. Interpretive reports are especially useful

1

FIG. 1.1. Profile for the Strong Vocational Interest Blank/Strong–Campbell Interest Inventory. Reproduced by special permission of the Publisher, Consulting Psychologists Press, Inc., Palo Alto, CA 94306, from Strong-Campbell Interest Inventory by Edward K. Strong, Jr., David P. Campbell, and Jo-Ida C. Hansen (c) 1933, 1938, 1945, 1946, 1966, 1968, 1974, 1981, 1983, 1985. Further reproduction is prohibited without the Publisher's consent.

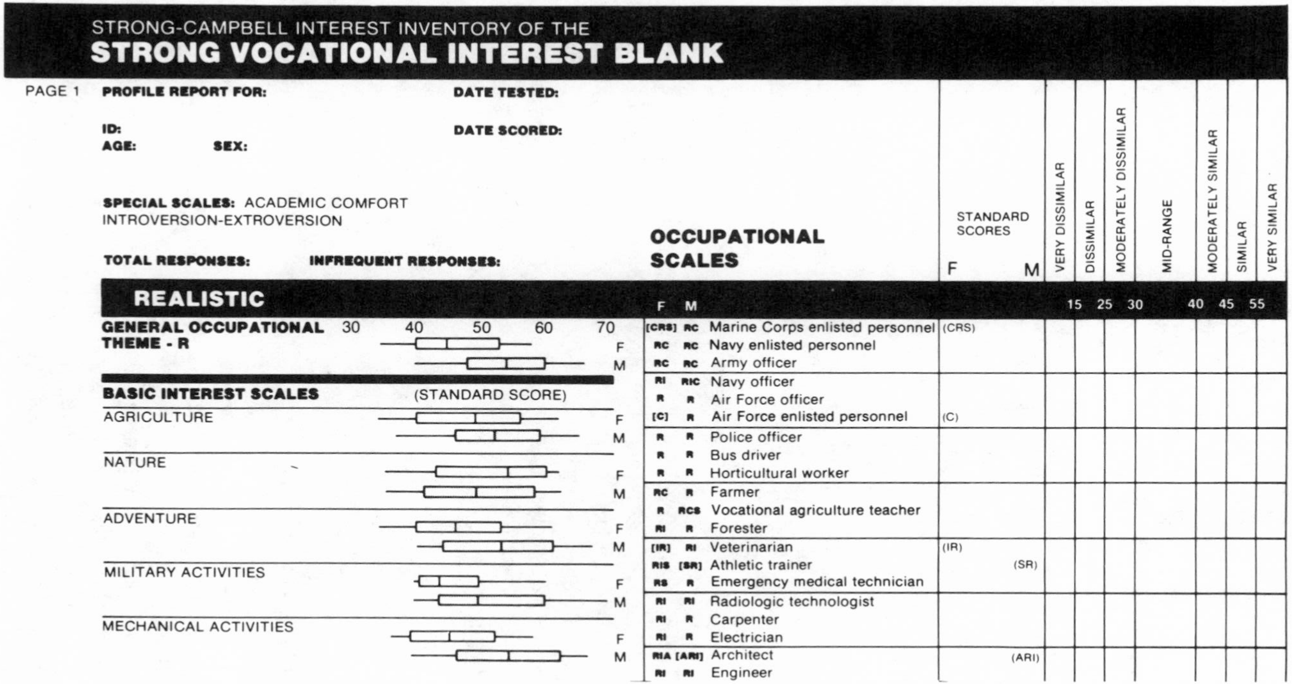

STRONG-CAMPBELL INTEREST INVENTORY OF THE
STRONG VOCATIONAL INTEREST BLANK

PAGE 1 **PROFILE REPORT FOR:**

ID: **DATE TESTED:**
AGE: **SEX:** **DATE SCORED:**

SPECIAL SCALES: ACADEMIC COMFORT
INTROVERSION-EXTROVERSION

TOTAL RESPONSES: **INFREQUENT RESPONSES:**

REALISTIC

GENERAL OCCUPATIONAL THEME - R 30 40 50 60 70
(STANDARD SCORE)

BASIC INTEREST SCALES

AGRICULTURE F / M

NATURE F / M

ADVENTURE F / M

MILITARY ACTIVITIES F / M

MECHANICAL ACTIVITIES F / M

OCCUPATIONAL SCALES

STANDARD SCORES F M

VERY DISSIMILAR 15 DISSIMILAR MODERATELY DISSIMILAR 25 30 MID-RANGE 40 MODERATELY SIMILAR 45 SIMILAR VERY SIMILAR 55

F M

(CRS) RC Marine Corps enlisted personnel (CRS)
RC RC Navy enlisted personnel
RC RC Army officer
RI RIC Navy officer
R R Air Force officer
(C) R Air Force enlisted personnel (C)
R R Police officer
R R Bus driver
R R Horticultural worker
RC R Farmer
R RCB Vocational agriculture teacher
R R Forester
(IR) RI Veterinarian (IR)
RIB (SR) Athletic trainer (SR)
RB R Emergency medical technician
RI RI Radiologic technologist
RI R Carpenter
RI R Electrician
RIA (ARI) Architect (ARI)
RI RI Engineer (ARI)

2

INVESTIGATIVE

GENERAL OCCUPATIONAL THEME - I

(STANDARD SCORE) 30 40 50 60 70

F
M

BASIC INTEREST SCALES

SCIENCE — F / M
MATHEMATICS — F / M
MEDICAL SCIENCE — F / M
MEDICAL SERVICE — F / M

			15	25	30	40	45	55
		F	M					
IRC	IRC	Computer programmer						
IRC	IRC	Systems analyst						
IRC	IR	Medical technologist						
IR	IR	R & D manager						
IR	IRI	Geologist	(I)					
IR	(I)	Biologist						
IR	IR	Chemist						
IR	IR	Physicist						
IR	(RII)	Veterinarian	(RI)					
IRS	IR	Science teacher						
IRS	IRS	Physical therapist						
IR	IRS	Respiratory therapist						
IC	IR	Medical technician						
IC	IE	Pharmacist						
ISR	(CSE)	Dietitian	(CSE)					
(SII)	ISR	Nurse, RN	(SI)					
IR	I	Chiropractor						
IR	IR	Optometrist						
IR	IR	Dentist						
I	IA	Physician						
(IRI)	I	Biologist	(IR)					
I	I	Mathematician						
IR	I	Geographer						
I	I	College professor						
IA	IA	Psychologist						
IA	IA	Sociologist						

ARTISTIC

GENERAL OCCUPATIONAL THEME - A

(STANDARD SCORE) 30 40 50 60 70

F
M

BASIC INTEREST SCALES

MUSIC/DRAMATICS — F / M
ART — F / M
WRITING — F / M

			15	25	30	40	45	55
		F	M					
AI	AI	Medical illustrator						
A	A	Art teacher						
A	A	Artist, fine						
A	A	Artist, commercial						
AE	A	Interior decorator						
(RIA)	ARI	Architect	(RIA)					
A	A	Photographer						
A	A	Musician						
AR	(EA)	Chef	(EA)					
(E)	AE	Beautician	(E)					
AE	A	Flight attendant						
A	A	Advertising executive						
A	A	Broadcaster						
A	A	Public relations director						
A	A	Lawyer						
A	AS	Public administrator						
A	A	Reporter						
A	A	Librarian						
AS	AS	English teacher						
(SA)	AS	Foreign language teacher	(SA)					

CONSULTING PSYCHOLOGISTS PRESS
577 COLLEGE AVENUE
PALO ALTO, CA 94306

STRONG-CAMPBELL INTEREST INVENTORY OF THE
STRONG VOCATIONAL INTEREST BLANK

PROFILE REPORT FOR:

ID:
AGE: SEX:

DATE TESTED:
DATE SCORED:

SOCIAL

GENERAL OCCUPATIONAL THEME - S

	30	40	50	60	70	
						F
						M

BASIC INTEREST SCALES (STANDARD SCORE)

TEACHING						F
						M
SOCIAL SERVICE						F
						M
ATHLETICS						F
						M
DOMESTIC ARTS						F
						M
RELIGIOUS ACTIVITIES						F
						M

OCCUPATIONAL SCALES

		STANDARD SCORES		VERY DISSIMILAR	DISSIMILAR	MODERATELY DISSIMILAR	MID-RANGE	MODERATELY SIMILAR	SIMILAR	VERY SIMILAR
		F	M	15		25	30	40		55
F	M									
SA	[AS]	Foreign language teacher	(AS)							
SA	SA	Minister								
SA	SA	Social worker								
S	S	Guidance counselor								
S	S	Social science teacher								
S	S	Elementary teacher								
SRI	SAR	Special education teacher								
SIA	SAI	Occupational therapist								
		Speech pathologist								
SI	[ISR]	Nurse, RN	(ISR)							
SCI	N/A	Dental hygienist	N/A							
SC	SC	Nurse, LPN								
[RIS]	SR	Athletic trainer	(RIS)							
SR	SR	Physical education teacher								
SRE	SE	Recreation leader								
SE	SR	YWCA/YMCA director								
SEC	SCE	School administrator								
SCR	N/A	Home economics teacher	N/A							

ENTERPRISING

GENERAL OCCUPATIONAL THEME - E

(STANDARD SCORE)

Scale: 30 40 50 60 70

BASIC INTEREST SCALES

Scale	F	M
PUBLIC SPEAKING		
LAW/POLITICS		
MERCHANDISING		
SALES		
BUSINESS MANAGEMENT		

Scale markers: 15 25 30 40 45 55

F   M

Code		Occupation	
E	ES	Personnel director	
ES	E	Elected public official	
ES	ES	Life insurance agent	
EC	E	Chamber of Commerce executive	
EC	EC	Store manager	
N/A	ECR	Agribusiness manager	N/A
EC	EC	Purchasing agent	
EC	E	Restaurant manager	
[AR]	EA	Chef	(AR)
EC	E	Travel agent	
ECR	E	Funeral director	
[CSE]	ESC	Nursing home administrator	(CSE)
EC	ER	Optician	
E	E	Realtor	
E	[AE]	Beautician	(AE)
E	E	Florist	
EC	E	Buyer	
EI	EI	Marketing executive	
EC	ECI	Investments manager	

CONVENTIONAL

GENERAL OCCUPATIONAL THEME - C

(STANDARD SCORE)

Scale: 30 40 50 60 70

BASIC INTEREST SCALES

Scale	F	M
OFFICE PRACTICES		

Scale markers: 15 25 30 40 45 55

F   M

Code		Occupation	
C	C	Accountant	
C	C	Banker	
CE	CE	IRS agent	
CES	CES	Credit manager	
CES	CES	Business education teacher	
[CS]	CES	Food service manager	(CS)
[ISR]	CSE	Dietitian	(ISR)
CSE	[ESC]	Nursing home administrator	(ESC)
CSE	CSE	Executive housekeeper	
CS	[CES]	Food service manager	(CES)
CS	N/A	Dental assistant	N/A
C	N/A	Secretary	N/A
C	[R]	Air Force enlisted personnel	(R)
CRS	[RC]	Marine Corps enlisted personnel	(RC)
CRS	CR	Army enlisted personnel	
CIR	CIR	Mathematics teacher	

ADMINISTRATIVE INDEXES (RESPONSE %)

OCCUPATIONS	%	%	%
SCHOOL SUBJECTS	%	%	%
ACTIVITIES	%	%	%
LEISURE ACTIVITIES	%	%	%
TYPES OF PEOPLE	%	%	%
PREFERENCES	%	%	%
CHARACTERISTICS	%	%	%
ALL PARTS	%	%	%

Strong-Campbell Interest Inventory of the Strong Vocational Interest Blank, Form T325.
Copyright © 1933, 1938, 1945, 1946, 1966, 1968, 1981, 1983, 1985 by the Board of Trustees
of the Leland Stanford Junior University. All rights reserved. Printed and scored under license
from Stanford University Press, Stanford, California 94305.

CONSULTING PSYCHOLOGISTS PRESS
577 COLLEGE AVENUE
PALO ALTO, CA 94306

TABLE 1.1
Samples of Items in the Strong Inventory Booklet

Part I. Occupations	Response Choice		
Actor/Actress	L	I	D
Sports Reporter	L	I	D

Part II. School Subjects			
Agriculture	L	I	D
Geometry	L	I	D

Part III. Activities			
Making a Speech	L	I	D
Cabinetmaking	L	I	D

Part IV. Leisure Activities			
Golf	L	I	D
Planning a Large Party	L	I	D

Part V. Types of People			
Highway Construction Workers	L	I	D
Prominent Business Leaders	L	I	D

Part VI. Preferences			
Airline pilot vs. Airline ticket agent	L[a]	=	R
Going to a play vs. Going to a dance	L	=	R

Part VII. Your Characteristics[b]			
Usually start activities of my group	Y[b]	?	N
Have patience when teaching others	Y	?	N

[a]Respondent indicates if the choice on the left is preferable (L), if the choice on the right is preferable (R), or if the two choices are equally attractive or unattractive (=).

[b]Respondent indicates whether the item is true for her or himself (Y), not true (N), or if she or he does not know if the characteristic applies (?).

in group interpretations when the time the counselor has to explain the results individually may be somewhat limited; the interpretive report helps respondents to refresh their memories as they review the results later on their own.

Two manuals are available to assist users in learning the intricacies of the Strong profile: *The Manual for the SVIB–SCII* (Hansen & Campbell, 1985) is the technical resource and includes data on the construction and validation of all of the scales; the *User's Guide to the SVIB–SCII* (Hansen, 1984) is the interpretive resource and includes theoretical possibilities, research findings, clinical knowledge and occupational information along with case studies illustrating the interpretive nuances of the inventory.

USES OF THE STRONG

The earliest versions of the Strong (1927, 1933, 1938, 1946) were designed to measure how similar a person's interests were compared to those of people in specific occupations; this was done using the empirically constructed Occupational Scales. But with the addition of the Basic Interest Scales (BIS) in the 1960s and the General Occupational Themes (GOT) in the 1970s, the uses for the instrument were greatly expanded. Now the inventory is used to identify not only an individual's occupational interests, but also her or his: (a) interest in being around different types of people; (b) interest in various leisure activities; and (c) interest in working or living in a variety of environments. However, career counseling of students and employees continues to be the major use of the inventory.

Within the career counseling context, the instrument is employed with several possible goals that depend to a large extent on the individual's motivation for exploring careers. Some clients wish to expand their career considerations by identifying interests that they may not have explored in the past; other individuals merely are interested in confirming a choice that they already have made; still others are at the stage in their career identification that requires reduction of the number of possibilities that they are considering. In all of these cases, the Strong serves as a method for efficiently identifying the person's interests and then for organizing them into a world-of-work structure that helps the person to integrate the new interest information with what she or he already knows about herself or himself from past experiences.

The Strong also is used in some settings as a selection and placement tool for making employment and training decisions. Typically, the inventory would be one of several assessment devices used to gather information about the individual and would be only one part of the entire package used to make decisions.

Finally, the Strong is used in research as the instrument employed to measure interests. For example, recent studies have used the Strong to look at: (a) general societal trends (Hansen, 1982a); (b) the interests of people in other cultures

(Fouad, 1984); (c) the structure of interests of minorities (Fouad, Cudeck, & Hansen, 1984); and (d) constructs of Holland's theory of interest types (Swanson & Hansen, in press).

ADMINISTERING THE STRONG INVENTORY

The reading level of the Strong Inventory is about the sixth grade level. However, it usually is not administered before the eighth or ninth grade (ages 13 to 15), because most people's interest patterns have not developed enough to be identified before that age. The GOT scales and BIS especially are useful with young individuals who are just beginning to think about careers. These scales provide an introduction to the world of work and indicate where interests are beginning to emerge even if complete patterns of interests have not developed yet. The appropriate age for using the Strong Inventory actually spans 50 years, because the inventory is used with high school and college students, with people considering midcareer changes and occupational or career reentry, and with people preparing for retirement.

The Strong Inventory can be administered individually or in groups by following the simple instructions found on the item booklet. It takes about 20–30 minutes to complete.

HISTORICAL BACKGROUND

The long line of Strong Interest Inventories was first published in 1927, but its history extends farther than even that early date suggests. As with all interest inventories, the instrument depends on its item pool for its psychometric integrity; within the item pool lies the power of the instrument to differentiate the interests of occupations, to identify clusters of interests and, ultimately, to predict occupational choice which, of course, is the primary application of interest measurement.

The Strong Inventory's item pool had its beginning in a seminar conducted at Carnegie Institute of Technology under the direction of Clarence S. Yoakum in 1919. That initial pool of 1,000 items found its way into many different published inventories over the subsequent 10 years (e.g., Occupational Interest Inventory, Freyd, 1923; Interest Report Blank, Cowdery, 1926; General Interest Survey, Kornhauser, 1927; Purdue Interest Report, Remmers, 1929; and Interest Analysis Blank, Hubbard, 1930).

The Strong, however, is the one inventory of all of those that used some portion of that early item pool still in use today. One of the reasons for the instrument's survival over so many years and for its salvation from obsolescence is that the Strong has been updated periodically, and the updates have occurred frequently in recent years.

Forms of the Strong

The first form of the Strong developed by E. K. Strong, Jr., to measure the interests of men and based on norms only for men, was published in 1927. The first form for women was developed in 1933, also by E. K. Strong, Jr. This early work set the precedent for future revisions of the Strong. The men's form always was revised first, and eventually, the women's form was revised. For example, the men's form was revised in 1938 (called *Form M*) and the women's form in 1946 (called *Form W*). The men's form was revised again in 1966 (*Form T399*) and the women's form again in 1969 (*Form Tw398*). The consequence of this sequence of revisions is that the women's form always has been psychometrically superior to the men's form; new techniques and analyses were tried with the men's form, evaluated for a year or two, and then, modifications to improve the new additions were made at the time of the revision of the women's form.

In 1974 the first merged–sex inventory, meaning one form for both females and males, was published. The publication of this version of the Strong, called the Strong–Campbell Interest Inventory (SCII), marked the beginning of a concerted effort by the publisher of the Strong to produce an inventory that provided equal career exploration opportunities for both women and men. Subsequent revisions, in 1981 and 1985, were directed toward increasing the breadth of occupations represented on the profile to include those in areas previously considered untraditional for one sex or the other. For example, the profile now includes Occupational Scales that measure the interests of women who are carpenters, electricians, and police officers as well as Occupational Scales that measure the interests of men who are nurses, flight attendants, and occupational therapists.

Popularity of the Strong

The Strong is one of the most widely used, if not *the* most widely used, of all interest inventories. The latest studies exploring use of interest inventories in college counseling centers indicated that the Strong leads all others (Sell & Torres–Henry, 1979; Zytowski & Warman, 1982); about 1 million profiles are scored annually. Not only is the Strong used widely with a varied clientele (including high school and college students, adults considering midcareer changes or doing preretirement planning, minorities, cross-cultural populations and the disabled) in a variety of settings (educational, industrial, military, business, social service, consulting, rehabilitation and community service), but it also is used extensively in research efforts as the instrument chosen to operationalize occupational interests. For example, the eighth edition of the *Mental Measurements Yearbook* (Buros, 1978) lists 1,521 references for the SVIB-SCII.

THE 1985 VERSION OF THE SVIB-SCII

The 1985 version of the SVIB–SCII (Hansen & Campbell) has two major features that make it different from earlier forms of the inventory. First, the emphasis of the Occupational Scales was broadened from one that offered predominantly professionally oriented occupations to one that offers a mix of professional occupations along with nonprofessional or vocational–technical occupations. Second, the General Reference Sample used for scale construction and standardization was updated.

Adding Nonprofessional Occupational Scales

The new focus makes the inventory useful with clients who have a wide range of occupational and educational goals. It should increase the utility of the inventory when it is employed, for example, in prison release programs, Job Corps programs, or in retraining programs in industry or manufacturing. The profile now includes 34 occupations (65 Occupational Scales) that may be categorized as nonprofessional or vocational–technical according to education level required for entering the occupation or the mean educational level of the sample used for scale construction. It also includes an additional 72 occupations (142 Occupational Scales) categorized as professional (those requiring a college degree for entry into the occupation).

The vocational-technical occupations added to the profile were selected to represent each of the six areas of interest proposed in Holland's Theory of Careers (Holland, 1973): *realistic, investigative, artistic, social, enterprising,* and *conventional.* For example, the profile includes female- and male-normed *carpenter* scales, coded *RI* and *R,* respectively; female- and male-normed *medical technician* scales coded *ICR* and *IR;* female- and male-normed *photographer* scales coded *A* for both sexes; female- and male-normed *licensed practical nurse* scales coded *S* for both sexes; female- and male-normed *travel agent* scales coded *EC* and *E;* and female- and male-normed *army enlisted personnel* scales coded *CRS* and *CR.*

One important consideration in selecting nonprofessional occupations to add to the profile was the employment outlook for each. All of the jobs added have at least an average or above average outlook. Another consideration was whether enough women and men were employed in the occupation to collect a Criterion Sample that was sufficiently large to construct a reliable and valid Occupational Scale.

Developing Matched-Sex In-General Samples

Another feature of the 1985 version was the development of a new General Reference Sample composed of 300 Women-in-General and 300 Men-in-General. These samples are used to standardize the GOT and BIS and to contrast samples in the empirical construction of the Occupational Scales. In previous editions of the Strong, Women- and Men-in-General Samples were constructed independently, and no effort was made to match the occupations represented in each sample. Also, the In–General samples used for the first merged-sex form of the Strong (1974), as well as the 1981 edition, were based essentially on the response rates of women and men collected in the 1960s (Campbell, 1974; Campbell & Hansen, 1981). Thus, the possibility existed that societal changes in interests—and consequently in response rates—had occurred during the 1970s and early 1980s, making imperative the need for research on change of interests.

The 1985 General Reference Sample was drawn from a pool of 1,588 subjects (794 females and 794 males) all of whom were employed adults, between the ages of 25 and 60, who liked their occupations. The pool represented 93 different professional and nonprofessional occupations. The selection procedure involved identifying, from the original pool of 794 females, 150 professional and 150 nonprofessional women (for a total Women-in-General sample of 300) using a random numbers table. Then, the 300 Men-in-General were identified by randomly selecting male subjects from the same occupations as those already represented in the Women-in-General sample.

Comparison of the 1974 and 1985 General Reference Samples.   Comparisons can be made between the 1974 General Reference Sample, which was based on response rates collected in the 1960s, and the 1985 General Reference Sample by comparing the item response rates for the two groups. Because one might expect more changes in the interests of women during this period than in the interests of men, the Women-in-General and the Men-in-General were examined separately. The surprising result was close compatability of interests between the decades. The 1974–1981 and 1985 Women-in-General differed significantly in their response rates on only 18 of the 325 items, and the 1974–1981 and 1985 Men-in-General differed significantly on only five items.

The stability of interests of these four samples is especially noteworthy because different methods were used by Campbell in 1974 and Hansen in 1985 to develop the General Reference Samples. One might anticipate that technique differences alone would contribute to more change than appeared.

In spite of the similarity between the interests of the 1974 and 1985 samples, the new General Reference Sample represents a tremendous step forward for research that focuses on comparison of the interests of women and men.

Occupational Scales

The Occupational Scales on the Strong Interest Inventory always have been the foundation of the inventory; they were the first scales presented on the profile by E. K. Strong, Jr., and with 106 occupations represented by 207 Occupational

Scales on the 1985 Strong, they continue to be predominant in the presentation and use of the inventory.

The Occupational Scales are empirically constructed using the method of contrast groups. This method, developed by Strong in the 1920s and modified to its present form in the interim, involves contrasting the item response rates of a Criterion Sample, in this case an occupational sample, with the response rates of a Contrast Group, in this case either a Women-in-General sample or a Men-in-General sample.

Separate-Sex Occupational Scales.   Although the Strong now has only one item booklet for women and men, and all respondents are scored on every scale, separate-sex Occupational Scales and norms remain necessary because women and men respond differently to the items. Efforts have been made during the last decade to develop valid combined-sex Occupational Scales for the Strong (Campbell & Hansen, 1981; Hansen, 1976; Hansen & Campbell, 1985; Webber & Harmon, 1978), as well as for other inventories such as the Kuder Occupational Interest Survey (Kuder, 1977), but all have been unsuccessful because of sex differences in interests of women and men that appear at an early age and last into adulthood (Hansen & Campbell, 1985; Riley, 1981).

The differences in interests are obvious when Women-in-General are compared to Men-in-General, but more important to the decision to retain separate-sex Occupational Scales is that the sex differences are apparent between women and men in the same occupations. These differences in interests have been very persistent over the decades; 50 years ago they occurred in the same interest areas as they do now and were as large in the 1920s as they are now (Hansen, 1981, 1982a). The stability of sex differences in interests appears to be a function of the overall stability of interests described earlier for Women- and Men-in-General and is illustrated in Fig. 1.2 for three samples of male foresters, who were studied over a period of 5 decades in the early 1930s, the mid–1960s, and the late 1970s.

Construction of the Occupational Scales.   The first step in empirical construction of an Occupational Scale for the Strong is to collect a Criterion Sample composed of subjects representing that occupation. Several selection criteria are used to determine who is eligible to be part of the Criterion Sample.

First, each individual included in the sample must be satisfied with her or his occupation. All respondents are asked to indicate how they feel about their work: *I couldn't be more satisfied; I like it; I am indifferent to it; I dislike it.* Anyone indicating indifference or dislike is excluded from the sample.

Second, the samples are composed of people who are between the ages of 25 and 60; these lower and upper limits are used to identify subjects whose interests, because of their young age, may not have stabilized and to identify subjects whose interests, because of their older age, no longer reflect the interests of the occupation.

General Occupational Themes

Theme	30s 60s 70s
R-Theme	55 56 56
I-Theme	51 54 52
A-Theme	44 45 43
S-Theme	48 48 44
E-Theme	46 49 47
C-Theme	53 50 49

Basic Interest Scales

Scale	30s 60s 70s
NATURE	55 56 56
ADVENTURE	51 54 52
MECHANICAL ACTIVITIES	53 56 55
SCIENCE	51 53 51
MATHEMATICS	53 55 53
MEDICAL SERVICE	49 49 48
MUSIC/ DRAMATICS	44 45 43
ART	44 45 43
WRITING	45 46 45
TEACHING	44 48 45
SOCIAL SERVICE	46 45 44
ATHLETICS	53 52 49
PUBLIC SPEAKING	47 52 49
LAW/ POLITICS	48 51 49
MERCHANDISING	47 48 46
SALES	47 49 49
BUSINESS MANAGEMENT	50 50 48
OFFICE PRACTICES	50 48 47

FIG. 1.2.   Mean interest profile for male Foresters tested in the 1930s (●), 1960s (x), and 1970s (○).

Third, inclusion in a Criterion Sample is restricted to those people who have at least 3 years of experience in the occupation. This criterion helps to screen participants on two dimensions: 3 years of experience gives the subjects an opportunity to assess how they feel about the occupation and also gives their employers an opportunity to assess their competence. Thus, those subjects included in the sample have at least a minimal level of achievement in their occupation, reflected by 3 years of experience.

Fourth, the subjects are screened to ensure that they are performing the job in a typical manner. For example, in almost every occupation there are individuals who spend more time involved in administration than in job activities related to the occupational title. Subjects such as these would be eliminated from the Criterion Sample because the objective in developing the Occupational Scales is to have measures that identify the interests typical of the occupation.

The second step in Occupational Scale construction is to develop the General Reference Sample (development of the 1985 sample was described earlier), which actually is two samples: one composed of 300 Women-in-General and one composed of 300 Men-in-General. Because items differ in their popularity, these samples are necessary to determine the base rate of popularity of each item. If a contrast sample such as these Women- or Men-in-General was not used the result would be scales that were dominated by a large popularity factor. The women and men in the General Reference Sample represent all of the Holland areas of interest; the average age for both women and men is 38 years; half of the subjects work in professional occupations and the other half in nonprofessional occupations.

The third step (see Table 1.2) is to compare the item response rates of the Criterion Sample to the response rates of the Contrast Samples—Women-in-General if a female-normed scale is constructed, and Men-in-General if a male-normed scale is constructed. This is accomplished by computing the percent of each sample answering *like, indifferent,* or *dislike* to each of the 325 items and, then, by identifying those items that differentiate the Criterion and the Contrast

TABLE 1.2

Response Comparison for Female Architects and Women-in-General (Step 3) and Item Weighting (Step 4) for the Items *Geometry* and *Meeting and Directing People*

Sample	Item-response percentages		
	Like	Indifferent	Dislike
Geometry			
f Architects	84%	16%	0%
Women-in-General	44%	24%	32%
(Step 3) Difference	+40%	− 8%	−32%
(Step 4) Weighting	+ 1	0	− 1
Meeting and Directing People			
f Architects	47%	38%	15%
Women-in-General	73%	21%	6%
(Step 3) Difference	−26%	+17%	+ 9%
(Step 4) Weighting	− 1	+ 1	+ 1

Samples at a significant level. Years of analyses have shown that a 16% difference between the response rates of the two samples will identify valid and reliable items. Collectively, these items produce an Occupational Scale that will discriminate between people in different occupations and that will be resistant to cross-validation shrinkage. The goal is to select 60–70 items that differentiate the two samples at the 16% level or higher. If more than 60–70 items are available at the 16% level, the cutoff percentage is raised to 17%, 18%, and so on, until the number of items selected for the scale drops approximately to 60. For example, the minimum response percent difference for the female *architect* scale is 23%; thus, 66 items are selected for the scale at this or a higher percent of difference.

The fourth step (see Table 1.2) is to weight the items selected for the Occupational Scale. This is done by identifying the *like* or *dislike* response choice showing the largest difference between the Criterion and Contrast Samples and, then, assigning weights of +1 or −1 depending on the direction of the difference. If the Criterion Sample responded *like* significantly more often than did the Contrast Sample, the weight is a +1; if the Criterion Sample responded *dislike* more often, the weight is a −1. The opposite response choice, which is unweighted at this point in the scale construction, then is assigned a weight of 1 in the opposite direction.

Once the *like* and *dislike* response choices are weighted, the *indifferent* response is weighted if the difference between the two samples is 10% or larger. If the minimum *like* and *dislike* response difference cutoff is raised to 21% or higher, then, the *indifferent* cutoff for weighting is raised to 13%. Table 1.2 illustrates the selection (Step 3) and weighting (Step 4) of two items for the female *architect* scale.

The fifth step, once all the items are selected and weighted, is to norm the scale. This is accomplished by scoring the Occupational Criterion Sample on the scale and using the resulting raw-score mean and standard deviation in a linear standard score conversion formula, with the standard score mean for the Criterion sample set equal to 50 and the standard deviation at 10.

Reliability and Validity of the Occupational Scales.   The most important reliability check for the Strong Interest Inventory is test–retest reliability to verify that the scales themselves are stable measures over time. Once the test–retest reliability of the scales is determined, then, users can be assured that changes in an individual's profile are in fact real changes in interests and not just changes that are a function of the unreliability of the inventory being used to assess the interests.

To minimize the influence of interest instability, which is more characteristic of the interests of young people than of adults, on test–retest reliability coefficients, adult populations generally are used to study an inventory's reliability. For the Occupational Scales on the 1985 profile, the median test–retest coefficient over a period of 2 weeks is .92, over a period of 30 days is .89, and over a period of 3 years is .87. All of these correlations are high for their respective elapsed periods of time between test and retest indicating that the Strong can be used with confidence that the scales are reliable.

Both concurrent validity, which assesses the power of a scale to discriminate between people concurrently in different occupations, and predictive validity, which assesses the scale's power to distinguish between people who eventually will enter different occupations, are relevant for interest inventories. Concurrent and predictive validity are especially relevant for the Occupational Scales of the Strong because these scales are used for making educational and occupational decisions.

The statistic most frequently used to measure the concurrent validity of the Occupational Scales is Tilton's percent overlap (Tilton, 1937), which identifies how well the Occupational Scales discriminate between subjects in the Criterion Sample and subjects in the Contrast (Women- or Men-in-General) Sample. The overlap in scores can range from 100% of the two samples, indicating that the scale does not discriminate between the two samples at all, to 0% indicating that the two samples are separated completely by the scale. Figure 1.3 illustrates the distribution and overlap of scores for Women-in-General and female Athletic Trainers on the female *athletic trainer* scale; the overlap is 19%, which is roughly a separation of $2\frac{2}{3}$ standard deviations between samples.

The median overlap for the Occupational Scales is 36% or about two standard deviations, an enormous separation in psychological research. The best female-normed scale based on this measure of validity is *physicist*, which has an overlap of only 13% between the Criterion Sample of female Physicists and Women-in-General; the best male-normed scale is *medical illustrator*, which has an overlap of 15% between the Criterion Sample of male Medical Illustrators and Men-in-General.

Scales with the best concurrent validity (lowest percent overlap) generally are those that represent occupations that are well-defined and homogeneous in interest. Those with low validities typically represent occupations that are more heterogeneous in interest and that are more likely to attract people for a variety of reasons, such as the male *college professor* scale with an overlap of 46%.

One of E. K. Strong, Jr.'s earliest concerns in the development of the Strong Interest Inventory was predictive validity of the instrument. This remains an important consideration in assessing the usefulness of any interest inventory. Predictive validity data for the SVIB–SCII are available beginning with Strong's research in the 1930s.

The usual procedure for a predictive validity study is to test a group of high school or college-aged subjects, put the profiles and answer sheets away for a few years (usually between 4 and 10 years), locate the original subjects at a later date, and determine their current occupation or occasionally their educational activities (such as college major), and examine the correspondence between their original measured interests and a criterion such as their current occupations. The correspondence between the subjects' interest scores and the criterion usually is

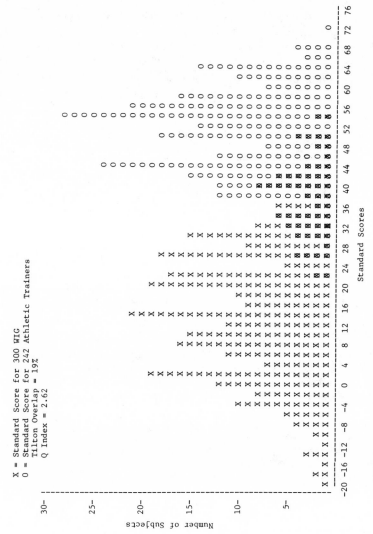

FIG. 1.3. Distribution and overlap of standard scores for 300 Women-in-General and 242 female Athletic Trainers scored on the female *athletic trainer* scale.

17

reported as the percent of the subjects who have excellent correspondence, moderate correspondence or poor correspondence and is referred to as a hit rate.

As Table 1.3 indicates for a number of predictive validity studies for the SVIB and SVIB–SCII, the excellent and moderate hit rate generally is between 60% and 75% of college-aged subjects entering occupations or college majors that were predictable from their earlier scores.

The level of predictive accuracy is affected by external factors as the data in Table 1.3 suggest. For example, McArthur (1954) found that students from homes of high socioeconomic status have less predictable profiles than do those from moderate or low socioeconomic status, probably because the former are more

TABLE 1.3
Summary of SVIB and SVIB–SCII Predictive Validity Studies

| | | | | | Hit Category (%) | |
| | | | | | Excellent and Moderate Hits | Poor Hits |
Study	Form	Sex	N	Study span (yrs)	(≥ 40)	(≥ 39)
McArthur (1954) (total sample)	SVIB	m	60	14	65	35
McArthur (1954) (public school)	SVIB	m	31	14	74	26
Brandt and Hood (1968) (total sample)	SVIB	m	259	7	67	33
Brandt and Hood (1968) (normals)	SVIB	m	129	7	72	28
Spokane (1979) (total sample)	SCII	f	120	3 1/2	59	41
Spokane (1979) (total sample)	SCII	m	236	3 1/2	71	29
Hansen and Swanson (1983) (total sample)	SCII	f	245	3 1/2	58	42
Hansen and Swanson (1983) (total sample)	SCII	m	183	3 1/2	64	36
Hansen and Swanson (1983) (satisfied)	SCII	f & m	130	3 1/2	71	29
Hansen and Swanson (1983) (unsatisfied)	SCII	f & m	298	3 1/2	53	47
Hansen and Swanson (1983) (stable profiles)	SCII	f & m	95	3 1/2	66	34
Hansen and Swanson (1983) (unstable profiles)	SCII	f & m	88	3 1/2	40	60
Swanson and Hansen (1985) (high AC scores)	SCII	f & m	115	3 1/2	67	33
Swanson and Hansen (1985) (low AC scores)	SCII	f & m	64	3 1/2	36	64

likely to enter occupations dictated by family fortunes and tradition rather than to follow their interests as the latter group is inclined to do.

Swanson and Hansen (1985) found that academic comfort is a moderator variable of predictive validity of the Strong for choosing college majors; they also found that predictive validity increases if the students are satisfied with their college experience and if their interests are stable during college (Hansen & Swanson, 1983). Brandt and Hood (1968) found the Strong to be less predictive for students with severe emotional problems than for normal students.

Other studies with the Strong have shown that it is valid to use with special populations such as international groups (Fouad & Hansen, 1984; Lonner, 1968); minority groups (Borgen & Harper, 1973; Fouad, Cudeck, & Hansen, 1984); and spinal cord injured patients (Rohe & Athelstan, 1982). This assortment of positive results for use of the Strong in a variety of settings with a variety of populations suggests that the instrument is robust, and that it can be used with confidence in most career counseling situations that require measurement of interests.

Coding the Occupational Scales.   As shown on the profile in Fig. 1.1, the Occupational Scales are assigned codes representing Holland's six occupational types. The codes are assigned and the occupations ordered on the profile based on four sets of data. Most important are the mean scores of each Criterion Sample on the GOT Scales; next are the correlations between the GOT scales and the Occupational Scales, then the mean scores of each Criterion Sample on the BIS, and last, the overall rank-order of the scores of all of the Criterion Samples on each of the Occupational Scales. Based on these data, each Occupational Scale is assigned from one to three codes, for example, female *mathematician* is coded *I*, male *engineer* is coded *RI*, and female *nursing home administrator* is coded *CSE*. Once codes are assigned, the Occupational Scales are ordered on the profile in the *R–I–A–S–E–C* hexagon order proposed by Holland (1973). The codes are extremely useful in interpretation of the Occupational Scales and provide: (a) insight into the item content of the scales; (b) information about the similarities and dissimilarities between occupations; and (c) data for generalizing to occupations not listed on the Strong profile.

General Occupational Themes

The GOT are rationally constructed scales developed to measure the six occupational types hypothesized by Holland's theory (1973)—*realistic, investigative, artistic, social, enterprising,* and *conventional.* They were added to the profile to give a global view of an individual's interests. The scales are useful for identifying occupational interests and also for identifying interests in various living and occupational environments, interest in different types of people, and leisure interests. Thus, the GOT provide a useful starting point for discussing not only vocational interests but an individual's entire lifestyle.

Item Selection.   Items were selected for each GOT by examining definitions of the types and then identifying items in the Strong booklet that represented each of the types (Campbell & Holland, 1972; Hansen & Johansson, 1972). Twenty items are included in each homogeneous GOT Scale; the same items are used for both women and men, and *like, indifferent,* and *dislike* responses are weighted +1, 0, and −1, respectively.

Norming the General Occupational Themes.   Three different types of normative information are provided on the profile for the GOT Scales. (See profile in Fig. 1.1.) The same data are provided for the BIS scales, which are described later.

First, a standard score is derived by a raw-score–to–standard-score conversion based on the General Reference Sample (300 Women-in-General and 300 Men-in-General) described earlier. All scores are converted into distributions with standard-score means for the General Reference Sample set equal to 50 and standard deviations set equal to 10.

The second type of normative information for the GOT Scales is Interpretive Comments, ranging from *very low* to *very high,* that compare the respondent's scores to the scores of a sample of the respondent's sex, either Women-in-General or Men-in-General. Interpretive Bars are the third type of normative data that visually display the distribution of scores for Women-in-General (open bars in Fig. 1.1) and Men-in-General (closed bars in Fig. 1.1); these bars allow comparison of the individual's scores to those of their own sex or the opposite sex.

The Interpretive Comments and Interpretive Bars are an important feature of the Strong profile, because women and men have different distributions of scores on the GOT and BIS. Interpretation of scores based on the person's own sex will provide the most options for exploration in areas traditionally dominated by one sex or the other. For example, a standard score of 58 for a man on the *artistic* GOT is 11 points above the *artistic* mean score (47) for Men-in-General but only 5 points above the mean score for Women-in-General (53). Compared to Men-in-General, the Interpretive Comment for a score of 58 on the *artistic* Theme is *moderately high;* compared to Women-in-General this same score of 58 would be assigned an Interpretive Comment of *average.* The more similar the distributions of scores are for women and men on the GOT, the greater the agreement between the female- and male-normed Interpretive Comments.

Reliability and Validity of the General Occupational Themes.   The median test–retest reliability coefficients of the GOT over three different intervals are high—2 weeks, .91; 30 days, .85; and 3 years, .81—indicating that Theme scores generally are stable over short and long periods of time (Hansen & Campbell, 1985). The coefficient alphas also are high ranging from .90 to .95

with a median of .92 for a sample of males and from .90 to .93 with a median of .91 for a sample of females (K. Larkin, personal communication, April 1984).

Several types of data indicate the concurrent validity of the GOT. First, correlations between same-named SVIB–SCII Themes and Vocational Preference Inventory (VPI) scales are high ranging from .72 to .79 with a median of .765 (Hansen, 1983) indicating that the two inventories are measuring similar interest traits. Second, the range of scores for more than 500 occupational samples scored on the Themes is 2 to 2½ standard deviations, indicating that the Themes do separate occupations. And, third, the rank ordering of the 500 occupational samples on each Theme meets theoretical expectations.

Contribution of the Themes to the Profile.   In addition to providing a global measure of interests, the GOT contribute to the Strong profile in two important ways. As described earlier, scores of each of the Occupational Criterion Samples on the Themes are used as part of the procedure for assigning Theme codes to each of the Occupational Scales. In turn, the codes are used to order the Occupational Scales on the profile in the *R–I–A–S–E–C* order beginning with Scales which have Realistic codes, then those with Investigative codes, Artistic codes, and so on.

The GOT also are used to order the BIS on the profile. Each BIS is correlated with each GOT and then clustered under the appropriate Theme according to its highest correlation. For example, the *science* BIS has its highest correlation (.91) with the *investigative* Theme and, therefore, is clustered with other *I-Theme* BIS (Hansen & Campbell, 1985).

Other Uses of the General Occupational Themes.   In addition to measuring vocational interests, avocational interests, work environment, and preferences for different types of people, the Themes can be used to help the counselor or interviewer to choose counseling techniques that match the preferences of the client (Hansen, 1984). Such matching strategies have been shown to improve counseling outcomes (Kivlighan, Hageseth, Tipton, & McGovern, 1981). For example, Realistic people typically have trouble expressing their feelings and talking about themselves with others. As a consequence, counselors may wish to spend more time building rapport with Realistic types than would be necessary with a Social type who typically would have verbal skills. Realistic types also may prefer counseling that is structured, practical, and concrete rather than sessions that are nondirective or overly philosophical.

Basic Interest Scales

The BIS preceded the GOT and followed the Occupational Scales chronologically in the development of the Strong. They originally were constructed to improve the understanding of the Occupational Scales which, because of their heterogeneous item content, may be difficult to interpret especially for the novice.

Scale Construction.   The method used to develop the 23 homogeneous BIS (Campbell, Borgen, Eastes, Johansson, & Peterson, 1968) was modeled after the cluster analysis technique used to develop the BIS of the Minnesota Vocational Interest Inventory (MVII; Clark, 1961). The procedure involved two major steps: first, correlation coefficients were generated between all possible pairs of items in the Strong Inventory booklet; and second, those items with large intercorrelations were gathered.

The items on the BIS are weighted in the same way as the items on the GOT: *like* responses +1, *indifferent* responses 0, and *dislike* responses −1. The same items are used for both women and men.

Norming the Basic Interest Scales.   The BIS were normed using the General Reference Sample (300 women and 300 men) which also was used for construction of the Occupational Scales and standardization of the GOT. Three types of normative information are provided on the profile. (See profile in Fig. 1.1.) First, is a standard score based on the General Reference Sample with mean set equal to 50 and standard deviation of 10; then, an Interpretive Comment based on a sample composed of the respondent's own sex (either Women-in-General or Men-in-General); and finally, Interpretive Bars illustrating the distribution of scores for both Women- (open bars) and Men-in-General (shaded bars).

The BIS are clustered on the profile into the six GOT categories. The clustering, as described earlier, is based on high correlations between the GOT and the BIS.

Reliability and Validity of the Basic Interest Scales.   The median test–retest reliability coefficients of the BIS, over the same three time periods as those coefficients reported for the Occupational Scales and the General Occupational Themes, are .91 (2-week test–retest interval), .88 (30-day interval), and .82 (3 years). Correlations of this magnitude over these time periods indicate substantial reliability of the scales. Coefficient alphas ranged from .77 to .96 with a median of .90 for a sample of 1,445 males and from .77 to .95 with a median of .90 for a sample of 1,410 females (Larkin, 1984). These data indicate the high degree of internal consistency of the BIS.

The concurrent validity of the BIS has been examined by studying the scores of more than 500 occupational samples on each scale. The occupations' scores are spread over $2–2\frac{1}{2}$ standard deviations, or a range of 20–25 points. Those occupations scoring highest on each Scale are the ones whose interests are relevant to that area; for example, broadcasters, elected public officials, lawyers, ministers, public administrators, and public relations directors all score high on the *public speaking* scale and agribusiness managers, farmers, foresters, horticultural workers, and vocational agriculture teachers all score high on the *agriculture* scale.

The use of the BIS with the Occupational Scales enhances the predictive validity of the Strong Inventory (Johnson & Johansson, 1972). The more consistent the scores are across the entire profile—for example, high scores on both the *sales* scale and a sales-area Occupational Scale such as *life insurance agent*—the more likely the person is to enter sales work.

Uses of the Basic Interest Scales.   The BIS provide more specific information about interests than do the global GOT and add to the understanding of the underlying interests that are measured by the Occupational Scales. They can be used in a manner similar to the GOT to identify a person's interests in activities, jobs, environments, hobbies, and types of people.

Academic Comfort Scale

Undoubtedly, the most important remark to make about the *academic comfort* scale is to emphasize that it is not a measure of ability. Rather, it is an indicator of interests that typically predict persistence in an educational environment (Swanson & Hansen, 1985).

Constructing the Academic Comfort Scale.   The *academic comfort* scale was constructed using the same empirical method of contrast groups used to develop the Occupational Scales. In this case the two groups, whose item responses were contrasted, were good and poor university students defined by an index based on their high school rank and college grade point average. The items favored by the high academic comfort group cover a range of academic topics with a focus on science and the arts and are weighted +1. Items favored by the low academic comfort group cluster around interests in the sales and realistic areas and are weighted −1.

Norming the Academic Comfort Scale.   The scale was normed using three samples of PhDs—college professors, psychologists, and mathematicians ($N = 494$ women and 421 men). The raw score means and standard deviations for these three samples were averaged, and the results were used in a raw-score–to–standard-score conversion formula that placed these samples at a standard score mean of 60 with a standard deviation of 10.

The metric, after standardization, for interpreting the *academic comfort* scale is generally: (a) people with PhDs score between 56 and 65; (b) with professional degrees between 50 and 55; (c) with master's and bachelor's degrees between 45 and 55; (d) with associate or vocational/technical degrees between 35 and 44; and (e) with high school diplomas 34 or lower.

Reliability and Validity of the Academic Comfort Scale. The test–retest reliability coefficients for the *academic comfort* scale are high. The 2-week test–retest correlation coefficient is .91, for 30 days it is .86, and for 3 years it is .85.

Swanson and Hansen (1985) studied the construct of academic comfort as measured by the *academic comfort* scale and found several results that contribute to its validity. First, they found that the correlation between mean *academic comfort* scores and mean years of education for the Strong Inventory Occupational Criterion Samples is high—.79 for females and .73 for males. Second, the Scale is related to educational expectations of college freshmen; those who indicated that college was preparation for further education scored, on the average, 13 points (1⅓ standard deviations) higher on the *academic comfort* scale than did those who indicated that they were in college for a good time. The same group also scored higher by 6 points, or over ½ a standard deviation, than did those students who indicated that they were in college for career training.

Introversion–Extroversion Scale

The *introversion–extroversion* scale is another empirically constructed scale using two contrast samples to select the items. The subjects for the contrast samples were identified by their scores on the Social Introversion Scale on the Minnesota Multiphasic Personality Inventory. Items favored by the subjects in the introverted sample emphasize ideas or things and are weighted +1, and those favored by the extroverted sample focus on people and are weighted −1.

Norming the Introversion–Extroversion Scale. The *introversion–extroversion* scale was normed so that a standard score of 50, with standard deviation set equal to 10, would represent those occupations that have a combination of interests in introverted as well as extroverted domains. Thus, occupations with the most introverted interests score about 60 (1 standard deviation above the mean), and occupations with the most extroverted interests score about 40 (1 standard deviation below the mean).

Reliability and Validity of the Introversion–Extroversion Scale. As has been reported for the other scales on the Strong Inventory, the test–retest reliability coefficients for the *introversion–extroversion* scale are high, showing that it is stable over short and long periods of time. The 2-week test–retest reliability coefficient is .91, the 30-day coefficient is .90 and the 3-year coefficient is .82.

To examine the concurrent and construct validity of the *introversion–extroversion* Scale, more than 250 occupational samples were scored on the Scale. The samples are spread over a range of about 2 standard deviations (20 points) indicating that the Scale does differentiate occupations. Those occupations scoring in the introverted direction (high scores) are the ones that work with ideas or things as theory would predict—for example, farmers, mathematicians, sewing machine operators, physicists, computer programmers, and geologists all score high. Those occupations with low or extroverted scores are the ones that work with people especially in sales-oriented occupations—for example, stockbrokers, auto sales dealers, elected public officials, life insurance agents, sales managers, and Chamber of Commerce executives.

Administrative Indexes

The Strong Inventory has three indexes that provide a cursory check of the validity of a profile. First, is the *total response* index, which simply indicates how many of the 325 items in the booklet the respondent has answered. Most people answer every item, but occasionally one or more items will be missed. As long as the number of items answered does not drop below 305, the profile will not be affected adversely.

Second, is the *infrequent response* index that was developed by identifying those items that are either very popular or very unpopular with the majority of people. For example, the item *taking responsibility* is an extremely popular item to which most women and men respond *like*. If an individual responds *dislike* to the item, that is an unusual or infrequent response compared to most people, and the person's score would be lowered on the *infrequent response* index. A large number of atypical responses to the items on the *infrequent response* index, resulting in a negative score, indicates a potential problem somewhere. In some cases, the respondent has not understood the directions for completing the inventory; in other cases, the respondent may be trying to sabotage the career-counseling process.

Third, the profile reports 24 *response percentage* indexes. These Indexes indicate the percent of *like, indifferent,* and *dislike* responses given to each of the seven parts of the inventory described earlier as well as to the entire item pool. Most people choose about an equal number of *likes, indifferents,* and *dislikes.* Deviations from that norm can provide insight into the respondent and signal a warning if response rates are extremely skewed in one direction or the other. If the "*like*" *response percentage* for the entire item pool exceeds 55% or drops below 20%, special care should be taken in interpreting the scores.

The Administrative Indexes can be used to identify the rare occurrence of a scoring service error. Over the years, improvements in the machinery used to score the Strong Inventory have increased the consistency and reliability of profile reports (Hansen, 1977, 1982b). However, periodic checks still are made to ensure that no systematic or random errors have entered the scoring system.

The Administrative Indexes, especially the *infrequent response* index, also may be used to identify respondents who have deliberately attempted to alter their scores. Most people answer the Strong Inventory honestly (Campbell, 1971), however, the GOT and BIS are susceptible to attempts to fake an interest in a certain area. This is true because of the homogeneity of the items in each GOT and

BIS, which results in the content being more obvious than is the case with the heterogeneous Occupational Scales.

INTERPRETATION

The main purpose of the Strong Inventory is to stimulate respondents to think about occupations and activities that match their interests. The Strong helps the individual to objectively identify her or his interests, provides a framework for organizing those interests and for relating them to career possibilities, and encourages the individual to identify occupations, relevant to her or his interests, that previously have not been considered.

In addition to the information provided on the profile and the many occupations listed there, the Strong profile can be used to suggest other occupations not on the profile to maximize the number of opportunities that a respondent can explore. The *Manual* (Hansen & Campbell, 1985) and the *User's Guide* (Hansen, 1984) provide two sets of materials for identifying relevant occupations not listed on the profile through use of the codes assigned to each Occupational Scale. The first set of materials includes a description of every Occupational Criterion Sample used to develop the Occupational Scales as well as a descriptive summary of the occupation from the *Dictionary of Occupational Titles*. This information, used along with the second set of materials, which is a listing of occupations related to the Occupational Criterion Samples, helps to link the Strong Inventory to the world of work and helps to provide wide-range vocational exploration.

CROSS-CULTURAL USE OF THE STRONG

One area of development in the application of the Strong Inventory is its increasing use in other cultures. Translations currently are available in French Canadian (Chevrier, 1979), Hebrew, and Spanish (Hansen & Fouad, 1984). And the version used in Great Britain has been adapted to accommodate British and United States differences in English (M. Cook, personal communication, July 1982).

Translation and validation typically involves a four-step process: (a) the translation; (b) a back translation from the translation language into English to identify discrepancies in meaning between the two versions; (c) bilingual testing to identify the comparability of the two forms; and (d) testing a population in another country to determine the predictive accuracy of the Strong in that culture compared to the accuracy with a similar population in the United States.

To date, the Spanish version of the Strong is the translation that has been most thoroughly validated. The results are extremely positive showing that the Spanish translation based on United States normative data and developed with U.S. Occupational Criterion Samples can be used with predictive accuracy comparable to that found for the English version when it is used in the United States (Fouad & Hansen, 1984).

In a more theoretical vein, the Spanish version of the Strong also has been used to study the generalizability of Holland's theory to other cultures with results that support the hypothesis that the theory is cross-culturally robust (Fouad, Cudeck, & Hansen, 1984).

SUMMARY

The 1985 revision of the Strong Interest Inventory extends the long history of research begun by E. K. Strong, Jr. in the 1920s. The widespread use of the inventory and the feedback from counseling and research psychologists have led to continued development of the inventory and to refinements in the guidelines for interpretation.

The Occupational Criterion Samples and Women- and Men-in-General Samples, used to construct and standardize the 1985 scales, are the best that ever have been collected for the development of Strong Inventory scales. Characteristics of the samples were studied carefully to ensure that they are representative, and each occupation is represented by a national sample. The extension of the Occupational Scales to include more nonprofessional or vocational/technical occupations should make the Strong Inventory useful with a broad spectrum of the population. The carefully developed General Reference Sample (Women- and Men-in-General) will allow more conclusive research to be conducted on the similarity or dissimilarity of interests of women and men. And most importantly, the 1985 revision meets the guidelines established by the National Institute of Education (NIE) for sex fairness in career interest inventories (Diamond, 1975).

REFERENCES

Borgen, F. H., & Harper, G. T. (1973). Predictive validity of measured vocational interests with black and white college men. *Measurement and Evaluation in Guidance, 6,* 19–27.

Brandt, J. E., & Hood, A. B. (1968). Effect of personality adjustment on the predictive validity of the Strong Vocational Interest Blank. *Journal of Counseling Psychology, 15,* 547–51.

Buros, O. K. (Ed.). (1978). *Mental measurements yearbook* (8th edition). Highland Park, NJ: Gryphon.

Campbell, D. P. (1971). *Handbook for the Strong Vocational Interest Blank.* Stanford, CA: Stanford University Press.

Campbell, D. P. (1974). *Manual for the SVIB-SCII* (1st Edition). Stanford, CA: Stanford University Press.

Campbell, D. P., Borgen, F. H., Eastes, S., Johansson, C. B., & Peterson, R. A. (1968). A set of Basic Interest Scales for the Strong Vocational Interest Blank for Men. *Journal of Applied Psychology Monographs, 52,* No. 6, part 2.

Campbell, D. P., & Hansen, J. C. (1981). *Manual for the SVIB-SCII* (3rd Edition). Stanford, CA: Stanford University Press.

Campbell, D. P., & Holland, J. L. (1972). Applying Holland's theory to Strong's data. *Journal of Vocational Behavior, 2*, 353–376.

Chevrier, J. M. (1979). *Test de preferences professionnelles Strong-Campbell manuel.* French translation of D. P. Campbell *Manual for the Strong-Campbell Interest Inventory.* Montreal: Institut de Recherches Psychologuiques, Inc.

Clark, K. E. (1961). *Vocational interests of nonprofessional men.* Minneapolis: University of Minnesota Press.

Cowdery, K. M. (1926). Measurement of professional attitudes: Differences between lawyers, physicians, and engineers. *Journal of Personnel Research, 5*, 131–141.

Diamond, E. E. (Ed.). (1975, Spring). *Issues of sex bias and sex fairness in career interest measurement.* Washington, DC: Department of Health, Education, and Welfare, National Institute of Education, Career Education Program.

Fouad, N. A. (1984). Comparison of interests across cultures. *Dissertation Abstracts International,* 4503A, (84–13): 777.

Fouad, N. A., Cudeck, R., & Hansen, J. C. (1984). Convergent validity of the Spanish and English forms of the Strong-Campbell Interest Inventory for bilingual Hispanic high school students. *Journal of Counseling Psychology, 31*, 339–348.

Fouad, N. A., & Hansen, J. C. (1984). *Cross-cultural predictive accuracy of the SCII: An example of psycho-technological transfer.* Minneapolis: Center for Interest Measurement Research, University of Minnesota.

Freyd, M. (1923). *Occupational Interests.* Chicago: C. H. Stoelting.

Hansen, J. C. (1976). Exploring new directions for Strong-Campbell Interest Inventory occupational scale construction. *Journal of Vocational Behavior, 9*, 147–160.

Hansen, J. C. (1977). Evaluation of accuracy and consistency of machine scoring the SCII. *Measurement and Evaluation in Guidance, 10*, 141–143.

Hansen, J. C. (1981, August). *Changing interests: Myth or reality?* Paper presented at the meetings of the American Psychological Association, Los Angeles.

Hansen, J. C. (1982a, July). *The effect of history on the vocational interests of women.* Paper presented at the meetings of the International Congress of Applied Psychology, Edinburgh, Scotland.

Hansen, J. C. (1982b). *Scale score accuracy of the 1981 SCII.* Minneapolis: Center for Interest Measurement Research, University of Minnesota.

Hansen, J. C. (1983). *Correlation between VPI and SCII scores.* Minneapolis: Center for Interest Measurement Research, University of Minnesota.

Hansen, J. C. (1984). *User's Guide for the SVIB-SCII.* Stanford, CA: Stanford University Press.

Hansen, J. C., & Campbell, D. P. (1985). *Manual for the SVIB-SCII* (4th edition). Stanford, CA: Stanford University Press.

Hansen, J. C., & Fouad, N. A. (1984). Translation and validation of the Spanish form of the Strong-Campbell Interest Inventory. *Measurement and Evaluation in Guidance, 16*, 192–197.

Hansen, J. C., & Johansson, C. B. (1972). The application of Holland's vocational model to the Strong Vocational Interest Blank. *Journal of Vocational Behavior, 2*, 479–493.

Hansen, J. C., & Swanson, J. L. (1983). Stability of interests and the predictive and concurrent validity of the 1981 SCII for college majors. *Journal of Counseling Psychology, 30*, 194–201.

Holland, J. L. (1973). *Making vocational choices: A theory of careers.* Englewood Cliffs, NJ: Prentice-Hall.

Hubbard, R. M. (1930). Interest Analysis Blank. In D. G. Paterson, R. M. Elliott, L. D. Anderson, H. A. Toops, & E. Heidbreder (Eds.), *Minnesota Mechanical Ability Tests* (p. 280). Minneapolis: University of Minnesota Press.

Johnson, R. W., & Johansson, C. B. (1972). Moderating effect of basic interests on predictive validity of SVIB occupational scales. *Proceedings of the 80th Annual Convention, American Psychological Association* (pp. 589–590). American Psychological Association, Washington, DC.

Kivlighan, D. M., Jr., Hageseth, J. A., Tipton, R. M., & McGoven, T. V. (1981). Effects of matching treatment approaches and personality types in group vocational counseling. *Journal of Counseling Psychology, 28,* 315–320.

Kornhauser, A. W. (1927). Results from a quantitative questionnaire of likes and dislikes used with a group of college freshmen. *Journal of Applied Psychology, 11,* 85–94.

Kuder, G. F. (1977). *Activity interests and occupational choice.* Chicago: Science Research Associates.

Lonner, W. J. (1968). The SVIB visits German, Austrian and Swiss psychologists. *American Psychologist, 23,* 164–179.

McArthur, C. (1954). Long-term validity of the Strong Vocational Interest Blank in two subcultures. *Journal of Applied Psychology, 38,* 346–354.

Remmers, H. H. (1929). The measurement of interest differences between students of engineering and agriculture. *Journal of Applied Psychology, 13,* 105–119.

Riley, P. J. (1981). The influence of gender on occupational aspirations of kindergarten children. *Journal of Vocational Behavior, 19,* 244–250.

Rohe, D. E., & Athleston, G. T. (1982). Vocational interests of persons with spinal cord injury. *Journal of Counseling Psychology, 29,* 283–291.

Sell, J. M., & Torres–Henry, R. (1979). Testing practices in university and college counseling centers in the United States. *Professional Psychology, 10,* 774–779.

Spokane, A. R. (1979). Occupational preferences and the validity of the Strong-Campbell Interest Inventory for college women and men. *Journal of Counseling Psychology, 26,* 312–318.

Strong, E. K., Jr. (1927). *Vocational Interest Blank.* Stanford, CA: Stanford University Press.

Strong, E. K., Jr. (1933). *Vocational Interest Blank for Women.* Stanford, CA: Stanford University Press.

Swanson, J. L., & Hansen, J. C. (1985). Relationship of the construct of Academic Comfort to educational level, performance, aspirations, and prediction of college major choices. *Journal of Vocational Behavior, 26,* 1–12.

Swanson, J. L., & Hansen, J. C. (in press). Holland's theory of vocational interests: Re-analysis of the undifferentiated profile. *Journal of Vocational Behavior.*

Tilton, J. W. (1937). The measurement of overlapping. *Journal of Educational Psychology, 28,* 656–62.

Webber, P. L., & Harmon, L. W. (1978). The reliability and concurrent validity of three types of occupational scales for two occupational groups. In C. K. Tittle & D. G. Zytowski (Eds.), *Sex-fair interest measurement: Research and implications.* Washington, DC: National Institute of Education.

Zytowski, D. G., & Warman, R. E. (1982). The changing use of tests in counseling. *Measurement and Evaluation in Guidance, 15,* 147–152.

2

Advances in the Kuder Occupational Interest Survey

Donald G. Zytowski
Iowa State University

Frederic Kuder
Educational and Psychological Measurement, Inc.

In the nearly half century since the first Kuder Preference Record was conceived, many changes have been made in the inventories that have emerged from it. Some of them are genuine advances:

- Almost exclusive reliance on activities for item content.
- Triad item format with most/least preferred responses.
- Application of activity preferences to the measurement of personal characteristics (Form A).
- Development of the 10 interest areas of Form C, serving as an organizational structure for interests and occupations.
- Development of a unique methodology to score the criterion group scales of the Kuder Occupational Interest Survey (KOIS).

This chapter begins with a recapitulation of Kuder's (1966, 1977) lambda score method to highlight the advance represented by the KOIS itself; this is not elsewhere presented in a single source. The chapter continues by describing recent changes in the reporting and the content of the KOIS. Finally, it reports a novel application, which Kuder (1977, 1980) has called *Person-Matching*.

THE KOIS AS AN ADVANCE

Interest (and personality) inventories that are criterion-group scaled generally are scored on the basis of the proportion of a given group that endorses (*like* or *prefer*) each of the items in the inventory. For the Strong–Campbell Interest

31

Inventory (SCII) (Campbell & Hansen, 1982), an occupational scale is formed from 40–60 items on which the proportions of an occupational group and an in-general reference group differ, usually by at least 16%. Inventory takers earn a unit weight on an occupational scale for every item they endorse. To make scores on all scales comparable, the total earned units are converted to T scores on the basis of the score distributions of the members of each occupational sample on their own scale.

Kuder (1977) takes a different tack. He observes that the proportion of a criterion group that endorses any most- or least-preferred response in his item triad can vary from 0–100%. He scores inventory takers by awarding them the proportion of the criterion group that endorses the same response the inventory taker does. If the proportions of a large group of architects responding to item 1 of the KOIS were as shown in Table 2.1, an inventory taker who endorsed alternatives 1 and 5 would score 1.60 for that item on the *architect* Scale, but the person who chose 3 and 4 would score just 0.20. If a group of journalists were to distribute their responses to the same item as shown in Table 2.2, then the endorser of 1 and 2 would earn a score of 0.80 on the *journalist* scale, less than that earned on the *architect* scale, and the endorser of 3 and 4 would earn 0.40 on the *journalist* scale, contrasting with the score of 0.20 that the same response pattern would earn on the *architect* scale. The sum of the proportions of each occupational or other group on the response patterns selected for all 100 items on the KOIS is the inventory-taker's score on that scale. No general reference or contrast group is used: Each occupation is in effect contrasted or differentiated from every other occupation for which the KOIS is scored.

It is evident that for our hypothetical item, the vast majority of architects (80%) tend to endorse the same two responses. Their interests, reflected in their responses to this single item, would be called *very homogeneous*. If one were to sum the proportions (squared) for one occupational group to all items of the KOIS, one would have an index of the homogeneity of interests of that group—a very valuable direct measure to decide whether a group has sufficient homogeneity to include it among the groups scored. Random responding or an utterly unhomogeneous group would result in a Sum p^2 of 66.67. If the pattern of the architects were repeated on all 100 items, the index would be 132. In practice,

TABLE 2.1
Architects' Responses to Items 1
on KOIS

M		L	
(1)	.80	(4)	.10
(2)	.10	(5)	.80
(3)	.10	(6)	.10

TABLE 2.2
Journalists' Responses to Item 1
on KOIS

M		L	
(1)	.50	(4)	.20
(2)	.30	(5)	.30
(3)	.20	(6)	.50

the Sum p^2 for the occupations presented scored on the KOIS varies between 87 and 101.

It can be seen that depending on how the proportions of any occupational group respond to each of the items that the highest raw score they can earn will vary. If the architects responded to all 100 items in the same proportions as they did in the sample item, their highest possible proportion score (HPPS) would be 1,600, but if the accountants responded as portrayed in the sample, their HPPS would be 1,000. If the final scores on each scale are to be comparable, the raw scores must receive some treatment to compensate for this difference. This is the function of the lambda coefficient, first suggested by Clemans (1958). When applied to the proportion scores of the KOIS, the formula is as follows:

$$\text{lambda} = \frac{\text{Sum of proportions} - 66.67}{\text{HPPS} - 66.67}$$

(A proportion score of 66.67, which is the equivalent of random responding, receives a zero in this formula.) Thus, a lambda score is similar to a ratio between the obtained raw score and the highest possible score for that scale. Because no one ever endorses exactly the same responses as are represented in the HPPS, all lambda scores are less than 1.00, and usually no higher than about the high 60s or low 70s.

Because no proportion of the response distribution of men- or women-in-general has been removed from the scoring, a lambda coefficient includes both the inventory-taker's similarity to people in general and to each occupational group. For this reason, scores are not directly comparable from one person to another, but are comparable for one person in terms of rank order. As the SCII attests, the in-general interests of men and women differ, but because these interests are not factored out of the KOIS scales, a person's scores on the male and female criterion groups are directly comparable, when taken in terms of their rank order.

The lambda coefficient, equalizing the effects of the proportions of responses by men- or women-in-general, also makes it possible to test the effectiveness of the KOIS in differentiating one occupational group from another. One can score a group of architects and a group of journalists on their own occupational scales, subtract the *journalist* score for each person from their *architect* score, resulting in a positive figure for architects and a negative figure for journalists. Comparing the distributions of these scores shows that 95.6% of the persons in each group were correctly identified by their own scale. One can calculate the difference between the means of the two groups, score distance, as an index of the differentiation achieved. For architects and journalists, the figure is .287. Kuder (1977) shows that differentiation achieved by the KOIS method is superior to that achieved when a reference group is used in a scoring procedure similar to that of the SCII.

In sum, Kuder's use of the lambda coefficient in the KOIS made it possible to dispense with the men- and women-in-general groups, to measure directly the homogeneity of interests of any group as an aid to deciding whether or not to include that group in the scoring of the KOIS, to make ranks of scales in the male and female normed criterion scales directly comparable, and to provide an effective measure of the differentiation of any given scale from all other scales.

THE 1985 REPORT FORM[1]

The Kuder Preference Records have long given inventory takers a measure of independence in understanding their results. The profile report for Form C gives a relatively complete explanation of the meaning of each of its 10 scales, plus material to identify high and low percentiles. The score report for the 1966 edition of the KOIS was accompanied by a four-page explanatory leaflet, detailing what lambda scores represent, the V- and experimental scores, occupation and college major scores, other things to consider, and sources of additional information (see Fig. 2.1).

All of this is consistent with the recent view that interest inventories should serve more purpose than simply predicting occupational entry. Tittle's (1979) review of studies of the effects of taking an interest inventory adds the following purposes:

1. Additional self-knowledge.
2. Exploration of more alternatives.
3. Exploration of a greater diversity of alternatives.
4. Exploration of nontraditional (sex-stereotyped) alternatives.
5. More frequent and varied information seeking.

---

[1]Material in this and the next part of this chapter recounting changes in the KOIS is adapted from the KOIS Manual Supplement, 1985, with permission of the publisher, Science Research Associates, Chicago, IL.

Accordingly, the 1985 report form for the KOIS was revised to try to meet many of these objectives, while at the same time offering those inventory takers who wished it maximum independence in assimilating their own results.

The inventory yields two copies of the report form, one for the inventory taker and one for the counselor, each with appropriate different explanatory material printed on the reverse side. The reports are computer written and entirely individualized. The inventory-taker's copy does not report any numbers (lambdas or percentiles), nor scores on the experimental scales. The counselor's copy includes all scores. The report is organized in four distinct sections, giving dependability information, Vocational Interest Estimates (VIEs), Occupational Scales, and College Major Scales, each keyed by number to the explanatory material on the back.

The Dependability Statement

The KOIS has relied on several indices to reflect on the dependability or trustworthiness of the results: The Verification, or V-score, the level of the highest occupational score, and the number of spoiled or unreadable responses. Previously, they have been reserved for counselor interpretation. In the 1985 report form, these scores are combined into one of several narrative statements that is computer-written for the individual inventory taker. Most will receive a "go-ahead," but some will receive one of the cautionary statements, or one that suggests the inventory be filled out again. The decision rules that govern each statement are given in Table 2.3.

When the V-score is between 42 and 44, especially among high school graduates, the problem is likely unusual interest patterns—strong preferences for activities that are unique, work roles that are not highly popular, or a unique cultural background. If the high-ranking occupational or college major scores are relatively in accord with the client's expectations, it is probably a valid report form.

When the caution message appears with a V-score of less than 42, it is probably the result of poor reading or inattention. Although the report form might be given cautious, limited use, it is probably better to ask the client to fill the answer sheet out again, paying closer attention to its verbal content.

When the V-score is acceptable, but the highest lambdas are low, between 31 and 39, the problem might be insufficiently developed interests. That is, although the person has interests, they probably have not developed a "patterning" that marks people who have attained occupational roles. In this situation, the high-ranking occupations and college majors may suggest possible plans, but should be taken as much more tentative than those derived from lambda scores of 40 or more.

Kuder Occupational Interest Survey Report Form

Name	R GRAINGER
Sex	MALE **Date** 12/20/84
Numeric Grid No. 0070342003 **SRA No.** 234567	

1 **Dependability:** How much confidence can you place in your results? In scoring your responses several checks were made on your answer patterns to be sure that you understood the directions and that your results were complete and dependable. According to these:

YOUR RESULTS APPEAR TO BE DEPENDABLE.

2 **Vocational Interest Estimates:** Vocational interests can be divided into different types and the level of your attraction to each type can be measured. You may feel that you know what interests you have already — what you may not know is how strong they are compared with other people's interests. This section shows the relative rank of your preferences for ten different kinds of vocational activities. Each is explained on the back of this report form. Your preferences in these activities, as compared with other people's interests, are as follows:

Compared with men

HIGH	
SCIENTIFIC	96
MUSIC	90
COMPUTATIONAL	84
AVERAGE	
MECHANICAL	72
ARTISTIC	64
OUTDOOR	48
LOW	
PERSUASIVE	24
LITERARY	18
SOCIAL SERVICE	10
CLERICAL	8

Compared with women

HIGH	
SCIENCE	90
MECHANICAL	86
COMPUTATIONAL	78
ARTISTIC	76
AVERAGE	
MUSIC	58
PERSUASIVE	36
LOW	
SOCIAL SERVICE	24
OUTDOOR	20
CLERICAL	18
LITERARY	6

3 **Occupations:** The KOIS has been given to groups of persons who are experienced and satisfied in many different occupations. Their patterns of interests have been compared with yours and placed in order of their similarity with you. The following occupational groups have interest patterns most similar to yours:

Compared with men

ENGINEER	.50
ARCHITECT	.49
CHEMIST	.48
STATISTICIAN	.47
BOOKSTORE MGR	.47
PSYCHOLOGIST	.47
LIBRARIAN	.46
MATHEMATICIAN	.46
PERSONNEL MGR	.45
RADIO STATION MGR	.44

Compared with women

COMPUTER PROGRMR	.47
INTERIOR DECOR	.47
PSYCHOLOGIST	.45
DENTIST	.44
PHYSICIAN	.42
THESE ARE NEXT	
MOST SIMILAR:	
DIETITIAN	.40

Compared with men
THESE ARE NEXT
MOST SIMILAR:

AUDIOL/SP PATHOL'	.43
INTERIOR DECOR	.43
METEOROLOGIST	.43
PHOTOGRAPHER	.42
TRAVEL AGENT	.42
OPTOMETRIST	.42
SCIENCE TCHR, HS	.41
ACCT, CERT PUB	.41
CLOTHIER, RETAIL	.41
FLORIST	.41
FORESTER	.40
PLANT NURSRY WKR	.39
ELEM SCH TEACHER	.39
LAWYER	.39
PHARMACEUT SALES	.39
COUNSELOR, HS	.38
JOURNALIST	.38
PRINTER	.37
PHYSICIAN	.37

THE REMAINING ARE
LISTED IN ORDER
OF SIMILARITY:

BUYER	.36
REAL ESTATE AGT	.36
MATH TEACHER, HS	.36
MINISTER	.36
SOCIAL WORKER	.35
PHARMACIST	.34
PODIATRIST	.32
SCHOOL SUPT	.30
TV REPAIRER	.29
X-RAY TECHNICIAN	.28
PHYSICIAN	.25
VETERINARIAN	.23
BLDG CONTRACTOR	.23
EXTENSION AGENT	.23
BANKER	.21
PLUMBING CONTRAC	.20
SUPERVSR, INDUST	.18
BRICKLAYER	.16
ELECTRICIAN	.15
FARMER	.14
MACHINIST	.13
AUTO MECHANIC	.13
BOOKKEEPER	.12
PLUMBER	.12
WELDER	.12
PAINTER, HOUSE	.12
POLICE OFFICER	.10
POSTAL CLERK	.10
CARPENTER	.08
DENTIST	.05
PHYS THERAPIST	.03

FIG. 2.1. Sample counselor's copy of the 1985 KOIS Report Form.

Compared with women NEXT SIMILAR, CON'T.		Compared with men REMAINING, CON'T.		Compared with women	
OCCUPA THERAPIST	.40	TRUCK DRIVER	.03		
BANKER	.40	FILM/TV PROD/DIR	.01		
SCIENCE TCHR, HS	.39	AUTO SALESPERSON	-.01		
BOOKSTORE MGR	.38	COMPUTER PROGRMR	-.02		
COL STU I ERS WKR	.37	INSURANCE AGENT	-.04		
BOOKKEEPI R	.37	NURSE	-.07		
NUTRITIONIST	.37				
PHYS THERAPIST	.37				
AUDIO/SP PATHOL	.35				
LAWYER	.35				
SOCIAL WORKER	.34				
EXTENSION AGENT	.34				

THE REMAINING ARE
LISTED IN ORDER
OF SIMILARITY:

4 College Majors: Just as for occupations, the KOIS has been given to many persons in different college majors. The following college major groups have interest patterns *most* similar to yours:

		Compared with men		Compared with women	
ACCT, CERT PUB	.33	ARCHITECTURE	.50	ART & ART EDUC	.46
RELIGIOUS ED DIR	.33	MUSIC & MUSIC ED	.48	DRAMA	.46
MATH TEACHER, HS	.33	ENGINEERING	.48	MATHEMATICS	.45
COUNSELOR, HS	.30	ART & ART EDUC	.47	BIOLOGICAL SCI	.45
FLORIST	.27	PHYSICAL SCIENCE	.46	MUSIC & MUSIC ED	.45
X-RAY TECHNICIAN	.26	FORESTRY	.46	PSYCHOLOGY	.44
ELEM SCH TEACHER	.24	SERV ACAD CADET	.46	ENGLISH	.42
NURSE	.22	BUSINESS ADMIN	.45	HISTORY	.41
DENTAL ASSISTANT	.22	MATHEMATICS	.45	HOME ECON EDUC	.41
SECRETARY	.20	PSYCHOLOGY	.44		
DEPT STORE-SALES	.20			THESE ARE NEXT	
BEAUTICIAN	.18	THESE ARE NEXT		MOST SIMILAR:	
BANK CLERK	.16	MOST SIMILAR:			
OFFICE CLERK	.15			FOREIGN LANGUAGE	.38
		FOREIGN LANGUAGE	.43	POLITICAL SCI	.37
		ECONOMICS	.41	HEALTH PROFESS	.36
		DRAMA	.40	PHYSICAL EDUC	.35
		BIOLOGICAL SCI	.40		
		SOCIOLOGY	.39	THE REMAINING ARE	
		ELEMENTARY EDUC	.37	LISTED IN ORDER	
				OF SIMILARITY:	
		THE REMAINING ARE			
		LISTED IN ORDER		ELEMENTARY EDUC	.30
		OF SIMILARITY:		SOCIOLOGY	.26
				NURSING	.22
		HISTORY	.36		
		PREMED/PHAR/DENT	.35		
		AGRICULTURE	.34		
		ANIMAL SCIENCE	.29		
		PHYSICAL EDUC	.22		
		POLITICAL SCI	.14		

Experimental Scales.			V-SCORE		46	
M	.36	MBI	.41	W	.34	WBI	.41
S	.33	F	.38	D	.27	MO	.28

7-3881

TABLE 2.3
Dependability Checks Instructions

Conditions	Section 1 Computer Adds	Action
V > 44 Unreadables < 15 Highest lambda > 39	Your results appear to be dependable	Print entire report
V = 42–44 Unreadable < 15 Highest lambda > 39	Caution: There is some indication that your interests are unusual.	Print entire report
V < 42 Unreadables < 15 Highest lambda > 39	Caution: Your response-patterns are very unusual. Your profile may not be accurate.	Print entire report
V > 44 Unreadables < 15 Highest lambda = 31–39	Caution: There are some indications that your interest patterns are not settled.	Print entire report
V > 44 Unreadables < 15 Highest lambda < 31	See comment in section 3.	Print only Section 2 results. Computer add in Section 3 "Your interest patterns appear to be insufficiently developed to score for occupations or college majors."
Unreadables > 15	Too many unreadables responses. Check or remark answer sheet.	No report. Return answer sheet to sender.

Vocational Interest Estimates

The VIEs are short versions of the scales from the Kuder Preference Records, Forms C and E. They are computer-written in rank order by percentile scores on both male and female norms, and marked as *high, moderate,* or *low.* Explanatory material gives scale descriptions. On the inventory-taker's copy there is an explanation of how one can score high on a given VIE and not score high on an obviously related occupational or college major scale. The counselor's copy gives information on how to convert VIEs to Holland codes.

Further description and data on the VIEs is given in the next section of this chapter.

Occupational and College Major Scales

The core of the KOIS, its criterion group scales, remains intact, with essentially one exception. Aside from some name changes (such as from Dean of Women to

College Student Personnel Worker), a major change has been made by merging many of the occupational specialties into single scales. Despite evidence (Kuder & Diamond, 1979) that, for instance, the *engineering* specialty scales do differentiate well within engineering, they do not add that much information for the vast majority of persons who are likely attempting to differentiate between engineering and perhaps several other occupational prospects.

Accordingly, the social worker and psychologist specialties for both norm groups have been merged into "generic" *social worker* and *psychologist* scales; within the female norm group dietitians and home economics college teachers have been made into a *dietitian* scale, and the *secretary* and *stenographer* scales have been combined into a *secretary* scale. Among the male normed scales, all engineers are combined into one occupational and one college major scale; osteopath, pediatrician, physician, and psychiatrist are combined into a *physician* scale, the three business college majors are made into a single *business administration* scale, and the two *service academy* scales combined into one.

Deleted for reasons of redundancy or low popularity are *teaching Catholic sister, general social sciences, law school grad* (college majors) and *YMCA secretary* (male occupational scale).

Occupational and college major scales are reported in rank order according to their lambda scores, separately for each sex. The introductory sentence is, "The following occupational (college major) groups have interest patterns *most* similar to yours:" Inventory takers are made the object rather than the subject to emphasize their central importance in the comparison. It is not implied that the inventory taker does or does not "measure up" to some standard, but rather that the inventory taker is there to discover who is similar to him or her.

Three levels of similarity are identified: Most similar are those scales which fall within .06 lambdas (3 standard errors) of the top score. "Next most similar" identifies the next .06 lambda range, and "The remaining groups are listed in order of similarity" heads the rest of the scales reported. Because no numbers appear on the inventory taker's report form, and rank order is the "scoring" information of importance, both male and female normed ranks start at the same level. Counselors may compare, if they wish, the relative lambdas for the male and female normed listings.

Inventory takers are invited to consider their ranking for both their own sex and the other sex. The explanatory material suggests that the rankings of some occupations represented by both sex groups may differ in their positions. This is explained as arising because men and women in the same occupations do not always do the same things, and that a discrepancy should suggest to them that they should investigate the occupation for these differences.

One of the unique aspects of the KOIS has been the absence of grouping or clustering schemes such as Holland's types or a factor analysis. This position has been adopted in order to underline the nuances of occupational life—a CPA who works for a large accounting firm (and whose high ranking occupational scales might include *lawyer*, and *banker*, for instance) might be different, to some extent, from a CPA who is a business manager for a medical clinic (and whose profile might show high ranks on *physician* and *pharmacist*). In order to help inventory takers form a concept of their own results, they are urged to "find the pattern" in their top ranking scales; that is, to identify a few words or a phrase that would represent the way they would describe their results to others. This is frankly an untested approach, and would merit inquiry in the future for accuracy, richness, and other dimensions of the concepts generated.

VOCATIONAL INTEREST ESTIMATES

Interest measurement has had two major lines of development. Fryer's (1931) account of the history of interest measurement documents them.

The method of homogeneous scaling, that is, clustering interest items that are empirically related, was first seen in Miner's 1918 Analysis of Work Interests. It grouped items into "interest areas," but was not scored in any conventional sense. Brainard's subsequent 1925 Activity Inventory was scored for 10 interest areas. From this approach came eventually the several Kuder Preference Records, beginning in the 1930s.

The other approach to interest measurement, criterion group scaling, was developed in C. S. Yoakim's graduate seminar at Carnegie Tech, and according to Campbell (1971), spawned quite a number of very similar inventories, culminating in Strong's Vocational Interest Blank of the late 1920s.

Interestingly, the two "descendant" inventories, the Strong–Campbell and the Kuder, have adopted each other's method over the years; Kuder (1956) producing his Occupational Interest Inventory (Form D) in 1956 to measure similarity of a person's interests with those characteristic of a number of occupational groups, and Campbell adding the Basic Interest Scales (BIS) to Strong's inventory in 1966 (Strong, 1966).

Kuder has now borrowed from himself. In the 1985 version of the KOIS, the occupational and college major scales are retained, but it now incorporates 10 VIEs derived from the scales of the well-known Kuder Preference Record, Form C (Kuder, 1948).

KOIS items were derived from the earlier Form A–Personal, and Form C–Vocational. It is possible to score the KOIS for scales from these forms, but they are quite short and the reliabilities too low for practical use. Recent development work has improved the reliabilities of the Form C scales in the KOIS to a level which permits limited use, especially for the purpose of illuminating the companion occupational and college major scales.

Kuder explains the scoring of the Preference Record scales in the Form E (1964) manual. To facilitate hand scoring, he uses just six scoring patterns—all possible combinations of *most* and *least* responses to the triadic items. Computer technology makes it possible to score for 48 patterns—all combinations of *most* and *least* responses to one, two, or three of the triad elements. This makes it possible to drop individual responses that detract from either the homogeneity of a scale or its correlation with other scales. The effect of applying the expanded scoring scheme on the Form C scales is revealed in Table 2.4.

The new scale reliabilities are in some cases considerably short of the high standard of Form C. It was considered appropriate to call these scales "estimates" of the more reliable Form C or E scales; thus the name Vocational Interest Estimates. The low homogeneity coefficients of several scales might be regarded as causing their meaning to be "cloudy" or "impure," and caution should be observed in their interpretation. Although homogeneity coefficients are not reported for the comparable scales of the SCII (Campbell, 1977), the relative shortness of some of them suggests the possibility of a similar problem. On the other hand, the VIEs' test–retest coefficients suggest they are producing relatively stable results.

The concept which underlies the reporting of occupational and college major scales of the SCII is the rank order in which they are placed by their scores. For consistency, VIEs are also reported in rank order, based on percentile scores, with those labelled high at the 75th percentile level or higher, and those identified as low, below the 25th percentile. The reliability of the rank orders can be represented as profile stability by calculating the rank order correlation between

TABLE 2.4
Reliabilities of Kuder Vocational Interest Scales

| | KPR | KOIS | | |
| | Form C | Original | VIEs | |
Scales	KR-20[a]	KR-20	KR-20[b]	Test–Retest
0. Outdoor	.90	.55	.64	.83
1. Mechanical	.90	.66	.77	.82
2. Computational	.86	.66	.66	.78
3. Scientific	.88	.66	.66	.83
4. Persuasive	.87	.47	.47	.73
5. Artistic	.89	.72	.72	.84
6. Literary	.88	.64	.66	.70
7. Musical	.87	.75	.75	.80
8. Social Service	.87	.75	.85	.83
9. Clerical	.88	.57	.63	.75

[a]Median figure for four groups.
[b]$N = 356$.
[c]$N = 192$.

profiles of the same person obtained at two different times. The median profile stability for the VIE scales has been found to be .80 (n = 192 college students; 2-week interval), a figure which is quite comparable with those reported by Hansen and Swanson (1983), and Jackson (1977).

Scale Intercorrelations

A hallmark of the Kuder inventories has been the relative independence of their scales. Table 2.5 shows the intercorrelations of the VIEs. All but 7 of the 45 are below .30. By comparison, Campbell (1977) makes no claim of independence for the SCII BIS, and there are many correlations in the matrix of the 23 scales in the .60s and .70s.

Of the VIEs, *outdoor* and *mechanical* show a relatively strong negative relationship with *social service,* reflecting probably one of the predominant dimensions of interests: things versus people. The strong negative correlation between *clerical* and *social service* may arise from a similar foundation. Overall, the correlation matrix appears to support the utility of the VIE scales.

Norms

The VIE scales were normed by selecting answer sheets submitted to the publisher for scoring from a wide geographic distribution, including three classes of users: high school, college, and private agencies, thus reflecting successively older populations. Table 2.6 gives means and standard deviations for men and women from each of the age groups. Men and women both show an increase

TABLE 2.5
Intercorrelations of Revised Scales

Scales	1	2	3	4	5	6	7	8	9
0. Outdoor	46	07	12	−26	−19	08	07	−48	17
1. Mechanical		10	11	−03	−35	−16	−04	−62	29
2. Computational			10	−07	−32	−11	−01	−29	27
3. Scientific				−09	−22	02	−01	05	−21
4. Persuasive					03	01	−19	−12	−11
5. Artistic						00	−02	28	−25
6. Literary							05	00	−31
7. Musical								00	−22
8. Social Service									−58
9. Clerical									

TABLE 2.6
Means and Standard Deviations of Three Groups on VIEs

| | High School | | | | College | | | | Adult | | | |
| | Male[a] | | Female[b] | | Male[c] | | Female[d] | | Male[e] | | Female[f] | |
Scales	M	S.D.	M	S.D.	M	S.D.	M	S.D.	M	S.D.	M	S.D.
Outdoor	9.16	3.40	8.46	3.18	9.53	3.63	9.25	3.31	10.35	3.72	10.25	3.30
Mechanical	11.90	3.37	7.56	2.82	10.49	3.52	7.56	2.89	11.30	3.75	7.83	3.04
Computational	8.09	3.15	7.38	3.20	7.83	3.08	7.15	3.46	7.77	3.26	6.66	3.40
Science	10.34	3.82	9.19	3.70	10.26	3.85	9.64	3.80	10.08	3.47	9.27	3.61
Persuasive	10.52	3.04	9.22	2.99	9.59	3.30	8.74	3.13	9.21	3.38	9.21	3.51
Art	5.01	2.32	6.62	2.55	5.11	2.76	6.19	2.79	5.08	2.63	6.23	2.78
Literature	7.36	3.19	7.94	3.16	8.17	3.38	8.43	3.34	8.35	3.45	8.73	3.43
Music	4.13	2.47	3.75	2.28	4.36	2.40	4.14	2.43	4.48	2.39	4.05	2.39
Social Service	9.71	3.69	13.60	3.72	11.21	3.96	13.88	3.74	11.15	4.02	13.01	3.97
Clerical	8.53	3.23	9.61	3.60	8.60	3.30	9.47	3.73	8.59	3.58	9.44	3.97

[a] n = 670.
[b] n = 653.
[c] n = 521.
[d] n = 620.
[e] n = 392.
[f] n = 358.

with age in interest in *outdoor*, men a slight decrease in *persuasive*, and men and women a slight upward trend in *literature* and *music*. The differences between men and women on some scales is substantially larger, as might be expected from experience with Forms C and E. Men score higher, on the average, on *mechanical* and *science*, and women score higher on *social service* and *art*. Younger men and women differ on *persuasive* interests, but this difference disappears with age. These findings are interpreted to mean that separate sex norms are useful, but age norms are not.

On the report form, VIEs are computer-written in rank order by percentiles (with the numbers absent on the inventory-taker's copy). The boundaries for the interpretive remarks of high and low are the 75th and 25th percentiles, respectively, as has been customary for Forms C and E.

VIE Content in Occupational Scales

Experienced interest inventory users know that some clients and students want to know how their high ranking occupations are similar to their interest patterns. Heretofore, counselors have had to tap their personal knowledge of occupational groups and make suppositions about the dimensions of similarity. Table 2.7 shows the highest three ranking VIEs for each of the occupations and college majors on the KOIS report form. For the most part, the high ranking scales agree with popular wisdom, especially in the first rank. Some, like the frequent appearance of music in the ranks for apparently unrelated occupations, invite systematic inquiry. Possibly music may be "standing in" for some personality characteristic which the occupational groups contain.

Converting VIEs to Holland Codes

Holland (1970) has indicated which of Kuder's vocational interest scales he considers equivalent to his six personality types, and has provided some supporting data (1970, 1979). Users who wish to employ Holland's extensive occupational coding system (Gottfredson, Holland, & Ogawa, 1982; Holland, 1977) may use Table 2.8 to convert VIE percentiles to a Holland code.

Interestingly, Athanasou (1982) compared the preferences and understanding of Australian junior high school students for Holland's personality type (*realistic, investigative, artistic*, etc.) and Kuder's interest areas (*outdoor, mechanical, scientific*, etc.). He found that 82% ($n = 368$) preferred the Kuder classification and that 86% thought it made more sense. When the Holland types were converted to work task dimensions (*practical, scientific, artistic, social enterprising*, and *clerical*), still 63% ($n = 366$) preferred the Kuder classification, and 68% thought it made more sense. It is not evident whether these results would hold up with an older population in the USA, but they do support the viability of the VIE scales.

TABLE 2.7
Top-ranking VIEs for Occupational and College Major Scales

Female Occupations		*Top-ranking VIEs*	
Acct. Cert. Public	Computational	Persuasive	Outdoor
Architect	Artistic	Mechanical	Outdoor
Audiol/Speech Pathologist	Social	Artistic	Science
Bank Clerk	Clerical	Computational	Persuasive
Banker	Computational	Clerical	Persuasive
Beautician	Persuasive	Clerical	Mechanical
Bookkeeper	Computational	Clerical	Persuasive
Bookstore Manager	Literary	Persuasive	Artistic
Computer Programmer	Computational	Musical	Mechanical
Counselor, High School	Persuasive	Social	Literary
Dean of Women	Literary	Musical	Social
Dental Assistant	Science	Musical	Clerical
Dentist	Science	Outdoor	Mechanical
Dept. Store - Sales	Persuasive	Musical	Clerical
Dietician	Science	Computational	Musical
Engineer	Mechanical	Computational	Science
Film/TV Prod/Dir	Persuasive	Literary	Artistic
Florist	Persuasive	Artistic	Clerical
Extension Agent	Mechanical	Persuasive	Outdoor
Insurance Agent	Persuasive	Computational	Clerical
Interior Decorator	Artistic	Persuasive	Mechanical
Journalist	Literary	Persuasive	Outdoor
Lawyer	Literary	Persuasive	Computational
Librarian	Literary	Clerical	Artistic
Math Teacher, High School	Computational	Clerical	Science
Nurse	Musical	Social	Mechanical
Nutritionist	Musical	Science	Outdoor
Occupational Therapist	Mechanical	Artistic	Social
Office Clerk	Clerical	Computational	Musical
Physical Therapist	Mechanical	Outdoor	Social
Physician	Outdoor	Science	Musical
Elementary School Teacher	Clerical	Social	Artistic
Psychologist	Literary	Science	Artistic
Religious Ed. Director	Musical	Social	Persuasive
Science Teacher, High School	Science	Outdoor	Literary
Secretary	Clerical	Persuasive	Computational
Social Worker	Social	Literary	Artistic
Veterinarian	Outdoor	Science	Literary
X-ray Technician	Musical	Science	Mechanical

Female College Majors		*Top-ranking VIEs*	
Art and Art Education	Artistic	Mechanical	Persuasive
Biological Science	Outdoor	Science	Artistic
Business Education	Persuasive	Computational	Clerical

(*continued*)

TABLE 2.7
(Continued)

Female College Majors	Top-ranking VIEs		
Drama	Persuasive	Artistic	Literary
Elementary Education	Social	Artistic	Computational
English	Literary	Persuasive	Artistic
Foreign Language	Literary	Artistic	Social
Health Professions	Science	Social	Outdoor
History	Artistic	Persuasive	Social
Home Econ. Education	Mechanical	Persuasive	Social
Mathematics	Computational	Science	Mechanical
Music & Music Education	Musical	Social	Artistic
Nursing	Musical	Social	Mechanical
Physical Education	Mechanical	Social	Artistic
Political Science	Persuasive	Artistic	Social
Psychology	Persuasive	Science	Literary
Sociology	Social	Persuasive	Artistic

Male Occupations	Top-ranking VIEs		
Acct. Cert. Public	Computational	Persuasive	Literary
Architect	Artistic	Musical	Mechanical
Audio/Speech Pathology	Social	Literary	Science
Auto Mechanic	Mechanical	Clerical	Outdoor
Auto Salesperson	Persuasive	Artistic	Musical
Banker	Computational	Clerical	Outdoor
Bookkeeper	Computational	Clerical	Musical
Bookstore Manager	Literary	Clerical	Persuasive
Bricklayer	Mechanical	Clerical	Musical
Building Contractor	Mechanical	Clerical	Outdoor
Buyer	Computational	Persuasive	Clerical
Carpenter	Mechanical	Clerical	Outdoor
Chemist	Science	Musical	Outdoor
Clothier, Retail	Persuasive	Computational	Clerical
Computer Programmer	Computational	Science	Literary
Counselor, High School	Social	Literary	Science
Extension Agent	Outdoor	Clerical	Literary
Dentist	Science	Social	Musical
Electrician	Mechanical	Clerical	Computational
Elementary School Teacher	Social	Artistic	Outdoor
Engineer	Mechanical	Science	Computational
Farmer	Outdoor	Clerical	Computational
Film/TV Prod/Dir	Musical	Artistic	Literary
Florist	Persuasive	Outdoor	Artistic
Forester	Outdoor	Clerical	Literary
Insurance Agent	Persuasive	Computational	Clerical
Interior Decorator	Artistic	Musical	Persuasive
Journalist	Literary	Clerical	Artistic

TABLE 2.7
(*Continued*)

Male Occupations	Top-ranking VIEs		
Lawyer	Literary	Artistic	Outdoor
Librarian	Literary	Clerical	Musical
Machinist	Mechanical	Clerical	Computational
Mathematician	Musical	Computational	Literary
Math Teacher, High School	Computational	Clerical	Science
Meterologist	Science	Outdoor	Musical
Minister	Social	Musical	Literary
Nurse	Social	Outdoor	Science
Plant Nursery Worker	Outdoor	Persuasive	Clerical
Optometrist	Science	Social	Musical
Painter, House	Mechanical	Artistic	Clerical
Personnel Manager	Persuasive	Social	Literary
Pharmaceutical Sales	Persuasive	Science	Musical
Pharmacist	Science	Persuasive	Computational
Photographer	Artistic	Persuasive	Mechanical
Physical Therapist	Social	Science	Mechanical
Physician	Science	Social	Musical
Plumber	Mechanical	Clerical	Outdoor
Plumbing Contractor	Mechanical	Clerical	Persuasive
Podiatrist	Science	Social	Musical
Police Officer	Clerical	Mechanical	Social
Postal Clerk	Clerical	Computational	Musical
Printer	Clerical	Mechanical	Persuasive
Psychologist	Literary	Social	Science
Radio Station Manager	Persuasive	Musical	Literary
Real Estate Agent	Persuasive	Clerical	Computational
Science Teacher, High School	Science	Outdoor	Computational
School Superintendent	Outdoor	Clerical	Computational
Social Worker	Social	Musical	Literary
Statistician	Computational	Literary	Musical
Supervisor, Industrial	Clerical	Mechanical	Musical
Travel Agent	Persuasive	Artistic	Clerical
Truck Driver	Clerical	Mechanical	Social
TV Repairer	Mechanical	Persuasive	Clerical
Veterinarian	Outdoor	Science	Clerical
Welder	Mechanical	Clerical	Outdoor
X-ray Technician	Musical	Science	Social

Male College Majors	Top-ranking VIEs		
Agriculture	Outdoor	Science	Clerical
Animal Science	Outdoor	Persuasive	Science
Architecture	Artistic	Mechanical	Musical
Art and Art Education	Artistic	Literary	Mechanical
Biological Science	Science	Social	Outdoor

(*continued*)

TABLE 2.7
(Continued)

Male Occupations	Top-ranking VIEs		
Business Administration	Computational	Persuasive	Artistic
Economics	Computational	Persuasive	Literary
Elementary Education	Social	Artistic	Outdoor
Engineering	Science	Computational	Mechanical
English	Literary	Artistic	Social
Foreign Language	Literary	Artistic	Social
Forestry	Outdoor	Science	Musical
History	Literary	Musical	Artistic
Mathematics	Computational	Science	Musical
Music & Music Education	Musical	Artistic	Literary
Physical Education	Social	Persuasive	Science
Physical Science	Science	Musical	Artistic
Political Science	Literary	Social	Persuasive
Premed/Phar/Dent	Science	Social	Computational
Psychology	Science	Literary	Social
Sociology	Social	Literary	Persuasive
Military Cadet	Science	Persuasive	Computational

PERSON-MATCHING

As detailed in the opening of this chapter, it is axiomatic that criterion-group interest measurement requires a high degree of homogeneity of interests in the occupational or college major group to make a scale. If, for instance, architects did not respond similarly to a significant portion of the items of an inventory, it would not be possible to assess the degree to which any inventory taker responds as they do.

TABLE 2.8
Conversion of VIE Percentiles to Holland Code

VIE Percentile	Holland Code
Outdoor + Mechanical ÷ 2	R
Scientific	I
Artistic + Music + Literary ÷ 3	A
Social Service	S
Persuasive	E
Computational + Clerical ÷ 2	C

Homogeneity in an interest inventory is an intricate matter. Depending on how closely one examines the occupation it may or may not appear homogeneous. Like a panel of orange in a reproduction of a Mondrian painting, it appears orange to the unaided eye, but with a 10-power lens it is seen to consist of a combination of red and yellow dots. Interest measurement has necessarily taken a position that uncovers the homogeneity of an occupation and overlooks the heterogeneity. From the perspective of an interest inventory, architects have in common a liking for drawing and sketching, for solving mechanical puzzles, and mathematics; they also share a number of dislikes. But when one looks at the occupational roles of architects, one sees great diversity. This one is employed by a large firm, and does mostly customer contact work, but others specialize in design, supervision of construction, or the business operation of the firm. Another is self-employed in a one-person office, and yet another specializes in restorations. Here is one who teaches full time, and there is one who has gone into architectural photography. Finally, this deli with the continental flair and an associated wine cellar is owned and operated by an architect who long since ceased to practice.

Dolliver and Nelson (1975) agree, saying that there are differences between groups of occupations, but that the differences within them have been disregarded. They add that the notion of homogeneity, although reflecting an element of truth, may be overused and overextended.

Is there evidence to support the idea that there is heterogeneity in occupations that is overlooked? There are a number of studies from which it might be inferred. Dunnette, Wernimont, and Abrams (1964), Erez and Shneorson (1980), Mossholder, Dewhist, and Arvey (1981), and Smalheiser (1977) have all applied a magnifying lens to occupational groups and found reliably identifiable subgroups.

Studies showing the degree to which members of an occupational group score highest on their own occupational scale (discriminant validity) reflect the homogeneity of the group relative to other occupations. Several studies using Holland's inventories (Holland & Holland, 1977; Mount & Muchinsky, 1978; Salamone & Slaney, 1978) show widely varying proportions of employed people scoring highest on the personality type congruent with their occupations. At best, the figure seems to be around 65% to 70%; at its poorest, it ranges to 25%. The KOIS correctly classifies between 40% and 90% of a sample of individuals on 30 of its scales (Kuder & Diamond, 1979).

Zytowski and Hay (1984) tested the following question directly: If interest inventories were collected from persons in occupations from each of Holland's types, to what extent could the occupational groups be recaptured by a procedure such as cluster analysis? Using Kuder's (1977) direct measure of homogeneity, two samples, each of 40 women, were selected from *physicians, architects, audiologists/speech pathologists, insurance agents,* and *CPAs.* Seven clusters emerged in the analysis of the two samples, and the five-cluster solution, on average, only recovered 18 or 19 subjects in their original occupational group.

It might be reasonable, then, as Kuder has suggested (1977, 1980) to match a person to another person, or to many persons, individually. Each person-as-a-criterion would not be treated as representative of some occupation, but only of himself or herself, with all the uniqueness of the way in which each goes about his or her occupation and career.

All that would be needed is a set of characteristics, such as those represented in interest inventory items, that tap the domain of possible interests, and a series of individuals (criterion persons) who sample the spectrum of occupational life. Instead of delivering to the inventory taker a profile of similarity scores with various groups, let the information be in the form of personal career sketches written by the persons who make the closest matches. Such a procedure would not be different than the well-used method (see Hoppock, 1977) of asking a career-seeker to interview someone who is working in the occupation under consideration.

A broad, diverse pool of items exists in the 300 activity preferences contained in the KOIS. Kuder and Hornaday (personal communication, March 1979) have developed a scoring system which weights differentially the six levels of agreement between any two answer patterns to a triad item. To date, two criterion person "pools" have been developed. One consists of 100 upper level students representing majors available at Iowa State University. The other, still in development at this writing, consists of men and women, approximately 300 each, employed in the occupations listed in the U.S. Department of Labor's *Occupational Outlook Handbook* (1984). Other special criterion pools representing various situations could be assembled; middle managers considering promotion opportunities, spinal-cord injured persons established in new occupations, graduates of liberal arts curricula, and the like.

Person-Match has been demonstrated to be feasible. Seling (1979) has shown with a criterion pool of individuals selected from the present KOIS scales that college students obtain unique profiles, none identical, each reflecting similarities with different persons not all engaged in the same occupations. Median profile stability of .88 ($n = 176$) was obtained in this study, also.

Another investigation (Laing, 1979) has shown that college student respondents matched with a criterion pool of liberal arts majors obtain more like-gendered matches (4–5 of seven) than other-gendered, with the phenomenon more pronounced for females. This study also inquired whether Person-Match, the standard KOIS profile, or both together was preferred. Sixteen percent preferred Person-Match alone, 41% the KOIS, and 43% both together. Those who preferred the KOIS appeared to be at a higher level of certainty about their choice.

A third study (Zytowski, 1981) elaborated on the preference for Person-Match compared to the regular criterion group scoring of the KOIS. Of 54 college students who sought the results of an interest inventory on a self-selected basis,

26% preferred Person-Match and 57% the regular KOIS. Seventeen percent reported that neither was satisfactory to their needs.

In Laing's (1979) and Zytowski's (1981) study, respondents were asked the reasons for their preferences. In the latter study, most frequent was some variation of "It fit with what I thought about myself." This is reminiscent of Takai and Holland's (1978) "reassurance" reason for taking an interest inventory. Twenty-three respondents offered this, only two of whom had preferred Person-Match. Nine respondents thought the career sketches superior in value to the profile information of the KOIS. For instance, one said, "It put me closer to real people." One liked the fact that Person-Match gave a greater variety of possibilities, not unlike Takai and Holland's "increase alternatives." Seven reported that they found both forms either confusing or unhelpful, although one said that the most valuable part of the experience was the stimulation afforded by the opportunity to consider one's preferences for so wide a variety of activities, not unlike Holland's (1977) concept that the Self-Directed Search affords a "rehearsal of possibilities."

The indications that the KOIS profile was more satisfying because it was relatively close to self-concepts suggests that those preferring it might be at a higher level of decidedness, as Laing (1977) found, and only seeking to confirm their plans. Conversely, Person-Match might be more useful to those who are able to tolerate ambiguity, or who wish to develop for themselves a more personalized, unique career plan.

These results might be consistent with the theorizing of Knefelkamp and Slepitza (1978). Drawing from the work of Perry (1970) on cognitive development, they constructed a process model of how people think about occupations. They identified a number of cognitive dimensions, such as locus of control, ability to analyze and synthesize into new complexities, openness to alternatives, and ability to take risky new roles. They then applied these to create a nine-position description of the movement a person makes from a simplistic, fixed, external view of career, decision making, and counseling, to a complex pluralistic, relativistic, integrated, and personally responsible view.

Viewed from the early stage of thinking of Knefelkamp and Sleptiza's model, the KOIS, which might appear to give concrete and relatively sure answers to career questions, would be preferred. However, the late-stage thinking of "commitment within relativism" allows highly individualistic career choices integrated with a clear knowledge of one's values, purposes, and identity. It would be for people at this stage of cognitive career development that Person-Match might be most helpful and accepted.

All in all, it seems reasonable to conclude from these preliminary studies that Person-Match, capitalizing on the individual differences within occupations, and the uniqueness of persons, shows promise as a new approach in career planning and counseling.

SUMMARY

Although the KOIS seems to have retained its popularity (Zytowski & Warman, 1982), it has not seen the pace of development that marked the earlier years of Kuder's inventories. Nevertheless, this chapter recounts several significant recent developments that might reasonably be called advances:

• Lambda scoring has made possible elimination of general reference groups in constructing scales, has permitted direct measurement of homogeneity of a group, improved discriminant validity, and has made male and female normed criterion group scales directly comparable.
• The report form for the KOIS has been modernized to allow inventory takers more independence in understanding and making use of their results.
• Short vocational interest estimates have been developed for socring on the KOIS, aiding in understanding the relative importance of these interests in the inventory taker and in the criterion groups for which the KOIS is scored.
• A new, barely-tested application of the KOIS, Person-Match, has been shown to be feasible and helpful to a segment of the user population.

After nearly half a century, it appears that there is still growth and development in interest measurement and in Kuder's interest inventories.

REFERENCES

Athanasou, J. A. (1982). *High school students preference for and sense of understanding of the Holland vocational interest categories.* New South Wales Department of Industrial Relations and Technology. (ERIC Document Reproduction Service No. ED 222 539).

Campbell, D. P. (1971). *Handbook for the Strong Vocational Interest Blank.* Stanford, CA: Stanford University Press.

Campbell, D. P. (1977). *Manual for the SVIB–SCII.* Stanford, CA: Stanford University Press.

Campbell, D. P., & Hansen, J. C. (1982). *Manual for the SVIB–SCII.* Stanford, CA: Stanford University Press.

Clemans, W. V. (1958). An index of item-criterion relationship. *Educational and Psychological Measurement, 18,* 167–172.

Dolliver, R. H., & Nelson, R. E. (1975). Assumptions regarding vocational counseling. *Vocational Guidance Quarterly, 24,* 12–19.

Dunnette, M., Wernimont, P., & Abrams, N. (1964). Further research and vocational interest differences among several types of engineers. *Personnel and Guidance Journal, 42,* 484–493.

Erez, M., & Shneorson, Z. (1980). Personality types and motivational characteristics of academics versus professionals in the same occupational discipline. *Journal of Vocational Behavior, 17,* 95–105.

Fryer, D. (1931). *The measurement of interests.* New York: Henry Holt.

Gottfredson, G. D., Holland, J. L., & Ogawa, D. K. (1982). *Dictionary of Holland Occupational Codes.* Palo Alto, CA: Consulting Psychologists.

Hansen, J. C., & Swanson, J. L. (1983). Stability of interests and the predictive and concurrent validity of the 1981 SCII for college majors. *Journal of Counseling Psychology, 30,* 194–201.

Holland, J. L. (1970). *Manual: Vocational Preference Inventory* (Table M). Palo Alto, CA: Consulting Psychologists.

Holland, J. L. (1977). *The Occupations Finder.* Palo Alto, CA: Consulting Psychologists.

Holland, J. L. (1979). *Vocational Preference Inventory Manual.* Palo Alto, CA: Consulting Psychologists.

Holland, J. L., & Holland, J. E. (1977). Distributions of personalities within occupations and fields of study. *Vocational Guidance Quarterly, 25,* 226–231.

Hoppock, R. (1977). *Occupational information* (4th ed.). New York: McGraw–Hill.

Jackson, D. N. (1977). *Jackson Vocational Interest Survey.* Port Huron, MI: Research Psychologists.

Knefelkamp, L., & Slepitza, R. (1978). A cognitive-developmental model of career development— An adaption of the Perry scheme. In J. Whiteley & A. Resnikoff (Eds.), *Career Counseling* (pp. 232–245). Monterey, CA: Brooks/Cole.

Kuder, F. (1948). *Kuder Preference Record—Form C (Vocational).* Chicago: Science Research.

Kuder, F. (1956). *Occupational Interest Inventory.* Chicago: Science Research.

Kuder, F. (1964). *General Interest Survey: Manual.* Chicago: Science Research.

Kuder, F. (1966). *Kuder Occupational Interest Survey, General Manual.* Chicago: Science Research.

Kuder, F. (1977). *Activity interests and occupational choice.* Chicago: Science Research.

Kuder, F. (1980). Person-matching. *Educational and Psychological Measurement, 40,* 1–8.

Kuder, F., & Diamond, E. E. (1979). *Manual for the Kuder Occupational Interest Survey.* Chicago: Science Research.

Laing, J. (1979). Person to person matching with the Kuder Occupational Interest Inventory. *Dissertation Abstracts International, 40,* 3467B. (University Microfilms No. 80–001,48).

Mossholder, K. W., Dewhist, H. D., & Arvey, R. D. (1981). Vocational interest and personality differences between development and research personnel: A field study. *Journal of Vocational Behavior, 19,* 233–242.

Mount, M., & Muchinsky, P. (1978). Person-environment congruence and employee job satisfaction: A test of Holland's theory. *Journal of Vocational Behavior, 13,* 84–100.

Perry, W. (1970). *Intellectual and ethical development in the college years.* New York: Holt, Rinehart & Winston.

Salamone, P., & Slaney, R. (1978). The applicability of Holland's theory to nonprofessional workers. *Journal of Vocational Behavior, 13,* 63–74.

Seling, M. (1979). Syncrisis: Investigation of a new assessment device. *Dissertation Abstracts International, 41,* 2346B. (University Microfilms No. 80–28,638).

Smalheiser, I. (1977). The survey of work interests: Evaluating vocational interests in terms of diagnostic pattern. *JSAS Catalogue of Selected Documents in Psychology, 7,* Ms. No. 1609.

Strong, E. K. (1966). *Strong Vocational Interest Blank, Form T399.* Stanford, CA: Stanford Press.

Takai, R., & Holland, J. L. (1978). Comparison of the Vocational Card Sort, the SCS and the Vocational Exploration and Insight Kit. *Vocational Guidance Quarterly, 27,* 312–318.

Tittle, C. K. (1979, April). *Exploration validity in interest measurement.* Paper presented at the annual meeting of the American Educational Research Association, San Francisco.

U.S. Department of Labor. (1984–85). *Occupational Outlook Handbook.* Washington, DC: U.S. Government Printing Office.

Zytowski, D. G. (1981, December). *Person-Matching: A new application of the KOIS.* Paper presented at the International Roundtable for the Advancement of Counseling, Cambridge, England.

Zytowski, D., & Hay, R. (1984). Do birds of a feather flock together? A test of the similarities within and differences between five occupations. *Journal of Vocational Behavior, 24,* 242–248.

Zytowski, D. G., & Warman, R. E. (1982). The changing use of tests in counseling. *Measurement and Evaluation in Guidance, 15,* 147–152.

3 The Self-Directed Search

John L. Holland
Johns Hopkins University

Jack R. Rayman
Pennsylvania State University

This chapter reports the origin and development of the Self-Directed Search (SDS; Holland, 1985b), its application to career counseling and other forms of career assistance, and an account of future research and development possibilities. Our goal was to provide a more complete account of why and how the SDS was developed, evaluated and revised, and how it may be revised in the future. In doing so we have written a more comprehensive history than test manuals or journal articles permit. Such reports typically provide an incomplete and somewhat misleading account of how test development has proceeded by omitting the role of a developer's experience, judgment, and occasional irrationality, and by omitting the influence of colleagues, publishers, test-takers, opportunities, and obstacles.

In short, this chapter supplements rather than supplants the content of the SDS manual. It provides a more comprehensive and clearer understanding of the SDS and its related developments so that graduate students, practitioners, and researchers will find support and stimulation for current practice and new research.

THE SDS AS AN INNOVATION

This section reminds the reader about the essential characteristics of the SDS and makes the case for its value as an innovative vocational device.

Distinctive Characteristics

The SDS is a self-administered, self-scored, and self-interpreted vocational counseling tool. It includes two booklets: an assessment booklet and an occupational classification booklet.

To use the SDS, a person fills out the assessment booklet and obtains a three-letter occupational code. The code is then used to locate suitable occupations in the occupational classification booklet, the Occupations Finder. In short, the SDS provides a vocational counseling experience by simulating what a person and a counselor might do together in several interviews. Table 3.1 summarizes how a person uses the SDS.

The SDS was developed for two main purposes: to multiply the number of people a counselor can serve and to provide a vocational counseling experience for people who do not have, or do not wish to have, access to vocational counselors.

The SDS multiplies counselor services by eliminating or reducing the time needed to proctor, mail, score, and interpret. It also eliminates unnecessary individual counseling. Consequently, counselors have more time for people who need individual counseling, and for program planning and evaluation.

TABLE 3.1
Steps in Using the SDS

Step 1
Using the Self-Assessment Booklet, a person:
-lists occupational aspirations
-indicates preferred activities in the six areas
-reports competencies in the six areas
-indicates occupational preferences in the six areas
-rates abilities in the six areas
-scores the responses he/she has given and
  calculates six summary scores
-obtains a three-letter code from the three
  highest summary scores

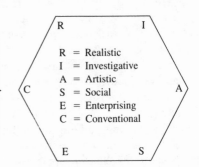

R = Realistic
I = Investigative
A = Artistic
S = Social
E = Enterprising
C = Conventional

Step 2
Using the "Occupations Finder", a person:
-locates among 1,156 occupations those with
  codes that resemble his/her summary
  code

Step 3
The person compares the code for his/her current
vocational aspiration with the summary code to
determine the degree of agreement.

Step 4
The person is encouraged to take some "Next
Steps" to enhance the quality of his/her voca-
tional decision-making.

Use of the SDS and the research about its actual influence on the client indicate that the SDS has the following desirable characteristics:

Effects. Traditionally, interest inventories have been evaluated only in terms of their reliability and validity—especially their predictive validity. These psychometric characteristics are important, but the impact of taking an interest inventory is equally important, because an inventory is both an assessment of vocational potential and a vocational treatment. Experimental studies (Holland, 1979) show that the SDS increases self-understanding, number of vocational alternatives considered, satisfaction with current vocational aspirations, and knowledge of the Holland typology.

Self-Direction. Because the use of the SDS is controlled by its user, it stimulates initiative and learning. The SDS can be used in private, when and where a person wishes to use it. In a sense, the SDS is similar to a programmed learning experience. Giving more control to the client also helps to demystify the vocational counseling process.

Simplicity. The SDS eliminates the need for separate answer sheets, proctors, special testing dates, mailing delays, scoring-service costs, scoring stencils, and elaborate and complex score reports. Norms are incorporated in the three-letter occupational codes. Everything needed to obtain and use SDS scores is included in a pair of booklets.

Comprehensive Exploration. The SDS provides an exploration of the entire range of occupational possibilities. The relations between personal characteristics and the 1,156 occupations in the Occupations Finder are easily understood, because they are grouped by the same code letters used to summarize a person's characteristics. The 1,156 occupations include more than 99% of all workers.

Safeguards. The SDS contains five major safeguards to prevent errors or harmful outcomes:

1. A person's resemblance to each of the six types of the personal assessment is determined five different ways, not one way.
2. The personal assessment is used in a conservative fashion: a person is instructed to search for all permutations of the three-letter summary code, not just one permutation.
3. A person compares the summary code with the codes of his or her occupational daydreams, and is instructed to seek help if the summary code and daydream codes conflict.

4. The user is referred to a counselor if more information or other kinds of help are desired.

5. The character of the exercise itself communicates the approximate, or imprecise, nature of interest measurement.

Innovative Characteristics

The SDS is an advance in interest assessment as well as an advance in vocational treatment for several reasons.

First, it provides a bare-bones simulation of perhaps the most common vocational counseling experience: A person's vocational aspirations, interests, competencies, and self-rated abilities are organized according to a particular theory and then related to a comprehensive occupational classification that uses the same theory.

Second, the SDS can be used with or without counselor assistance, because it can be self-administered, self-scored, and self-interpreted.

Third, the SDS is an interest inventory as well as a personality inventory, a values inventory, and a competency inventory. The research about the SDS (Holland, 1985b), the Vocational Preference Inventory (VPI; Holland, 1985c), and the theory that led to the SDS (Holland, 1985a) support these assumptions.

Fourth, the SDS meets some of the criteria for an ideal innovation. It is an inexpensive assessment-intervention that requires little special training to use and is not labor-intensive; It is compatible with many existing career materials rather than displacing them.

Fifth, the theoretical base of the SDS provides long term research and development support that ensures continued and constructive revisions.

Sixth, the evaluations of the effects of the SDS on test-takers indicate that it has several desirable effects. Three of four studies suggest that the SDS is rated as highly as PhD counselors (Holland, 1985b).

Seventh, the SDS is an "open" inventory. The transparency of the scale scoring communicates an important message to the test-taker—the tentative nature of measured interests. The undisguised grouping of items on the same scale also communicates the structure of vocational interests so that the test-taker learns a systematic way of thinking about work and personal characteristics. This advantage is not available in inventories with disguised self- or computer-scoring systems.

Finally, the SDS and its related theory represent a technological–theoretical advance, because they form an elegant solution to several complex, difficult, and expensive problems in test construction and in the practice of career counseling. Together, the SDS and its theory provide an organization for mapping and understanding the massive information about people and occupations and the relation of one to the other. The need for expensive occupation-by-occupation empirical keying, which has produced less than 100 occupational keys in 40 years, has been eliminated. The SDS and its interpretive theory have served as a model for the development of similar inventories. Nearly all of the SDS innovative characteristics, reviewed earlier, flow from its related theory. For example, the theory implied a relatively simple form of test construction and arrangement that was especially amenable to self-scoring and self-interpretation.

ORIGIN AND DEVELOPMENT

The SDS was stimulated and shaped by Holland's pragmatism, theory, and experience and by the development of the VPI (Holland, 1985c). In addition, the SDS was stimulated and shaped by practitioners, researchers, test-takers, and publishers. This section is a brief account of how these diverse influences led to the SDS and its revisions. A recent interview (Weinrach, 1980) and the current revision of Holland's (1985a) theory provide more detail.

Holland's Theory

The SDS is a good illustration of the value of useful theory. Without a useful theory, the SDS would not have been possible, because its development required both a typology of persons and a classification of occupations that used parallel constructs: in this case, the six personality types—*realistic, investigative, artistic, social, enterprising,* and *conventional* and the six occupational classes with the same names. The use of the typology in renovating the Strong–Campbell Interest Inventory (SCII; Campbell & Hansen, 1981), in creating imitations of the SDS, and in organizing occupational information, are other illustrations of the theory's usefulness.

Like the theory, the SDS evolved over a long period, and its development was interwoven with that of the theory and the VPI (Holland, 1985c). The VPI came first and demonstrated that short scales—scored all *yes*—would work, and that such an inventory was easy to score by hand, if the scales were of equal length and arranged in cyclical order. It took from 1953 to 1958 to go from scales of unequal length with randomly arranged items to these simple, but effective, solutions.

Personality Types.   The rationale for the first six VPI scales formed a primitive account of what became the six personality types. The first formulations for interpreting the VPI scales were obtained by classifying and reviewing the 30 or more handscoring keys for the occupational scales of the old Strong Vocational Interest Blank (SVIB; Strong, 1943) and by writing brief interpretations that Holland had learned to make by reading an obscure article by Forer (1948). Forer gave lessons in how to make inferences about personality from a person's favorite activities and interests. Later, this initial training was sharpened by supportive clinicians (Harold Geidt, Richard Sanders, Bart Stone) in a VA psychiatric hospital who tutored Holland in a wide range of diagnostic activities.

The Classification. The classificatory ideas came from the author's experience and that of fellow counselors who found it difficult to relate SVIB or Kuder profiles to the occupations in the *Dictionary of Occupational Titles* (U.S. Department of Labor, 1977). In short, we thought, "Wouldn't it be useful if interest inventories were accompanied by parallel occupational classification systems?" That question was pursued from 1959 to the present time and culminated in 1982 as *The Dictionary of Holland Occupational Codes* (Gottfredson, Holland, & Ogawa, 1982).

The classification was initiated with the assumption that all occupations could be organized into six groups that paralleled the six types (Holland, 1959). This idea came from looking at correlation matrices and factor analyses of interest and personality inventories (French, 1953; Guilford, Christensen, Bond, & Sutton, 1954; Holland, Krause, Nixon, & Trembath, 1953; Strong, 1943; Vernon, 1949). These early analyses suggested that occupations could be categorized in five to ten groups. Although there was no consensus on how many groups might be optimal, it was clear that classifications like the DOT grossly exaggerate the differences among occupations by capitalizing on small differences to create categories.

The first a priori classification used the occupations in the first six VPI scales to categorize occupations. Later, mean VPI profiles for occupations and fields of training were used to create three-letter occupational codes (Holland, 1966a). And still later, a wide range of other techniques were employed to extend the classification to nearly all occupations (Holland, 1985a).

The Hexagonal Model. The arrangement of the classification according to a hexagonal model was stimulated by a desire to have occupational categories in an order that was consistent with occupational data. To this end, Strong (1943) struggled with the classification of occupations in the old SVIB profile and performed some factor analyses to map occupations. That map (Strong, 1943, Figs. 5 and 6, p. 146) anticipated the hexagonal model. Holland also believed that the correlation matrices for the VPI (1953–1969) implied an ordering of vocational interests. In search of this implied order, Whitney and Holland were daydreaming one day that the VPI correlation matrices for college men and women (Holland, Whitney, Cole, & Richards, 1969) might contain the data for arranging the classification in a rational way. The following explains how Whitney and Holland discovered the hexagonal model:

> We began by starting with the Realistic scale, because it was the first VPI scale and because we had to start somewhere. Then we scanned the matrix for the scale with the highest correlation with R, it was I. Then we looked for the highest correlation with I, it was A. Then A was followed by S; S by E, and last C by R.

We both saw that these simple correlations created a circle of RIASEC. At this point, we were surprised and pleased but unaware of the value of these relationships, so we made a diagram with the correlations around the perimeter and filled in all the intermediate values. Then we noticed that the values around the perimeter were, on the average, the largest correlations, that the intermediate distances were associated with smaller correlations and the greatest distances (opposed scales on the circle) had the smallest correlations. Whitney noticed that we had a circular diagram; Holland said that Roe (1956) had a claim on the circle, but we could have a hexagon. (Geometry was the only mathematical subject in which Holland excelled).

Several simple but important events then flowed from the discovery of the hexagonal model. Occupations were first organized into six main categories (*R-I-A-S-E-C*); then it was assumed that subcategories could be created by following the hexagonal model in clockwise order: *RI, RA, RS, RE, RC;* then *RIA, RIS, RIE, RIC;* then *RAS, RAE, RAC, RAI;* and so on. Next, it was assumed, and later noticed, that this procedure organized occupations according to their psychological relatedness; closely related occupations were adjacent to one another. Subsequent studies of work histories and aspirational recollections support this assumption (Holland, 1985a). Somewhat later Viernstein (1973) performed a field force analysis, using the hexagon, to map occupations. Other analyses by Cole, Whitney, and Holland (1971) and by Prediger (1982) provide similar maps.

When the hexagon was discovered (1969), Holland was working on a revision of the theory and saw that the hexagonal model might be a vehicle for defining and integrating the main concepts in the theory. For example, the a priori notions of consistency (Holland, 1966b) could be redefined according to three, rather than two, levels and the definitions created by the hexagonal model were very similar to those stimulated earlier by clinical observation and rational analysis. Likewise, the hexagonal model implied some graduated levels of congruence rather than the a priori all or none definitions proposed earlier. Still later, Zener and Schnuelle (1976) developed a 7-step index for assessing congruence in a more precise way. And most recently, Iachan (1984) has developed a 28-step agreement index that provides a more precise technique for the assessment of person-environment congruence or the degree of agreement between any two three-letter codes. Fortunately, the Iachan and Zener–Schnuelle indices are highly correlated.

Parenthetically, Holland learned much later how fortuitous it was to have had in hand a large, diverse sample of 2-year college students from 65 colleges (Holland et al., 1969). No sample since then has fitted the model so well. We assume this is so because most researchers use small samples that have a very uneven distribution of types and that tend to be homogeneous on many demographic and psychological variables.

Aspirations and Intentions

The Daydreams section (SDS) also has a fortuitous origin. In an early 4-year longitudinal study Holland (1963) discovered that six SVIB scales, selected to represent the personality types, did not predict the category of a person's vocational aspiration any better than the category of a person's aspiration 4 years earlier. This theoretical study would not have been done if someone had not collected the necessary data for another project and if the data had not been the most accessible data at the time.

This early monograph led to both depression and excitement. If a revered interest inventory could not predict future aspiration any better than an earlier aspiration, "What good is an interest inventory?"

The first response was to incorporate vocational aspirations in the SDS to provide a simple check on the validity of the summary code.

Later coded aspirations were used in *combination* with SDS codes to attain more efficient predictions. For example, interest inventories that use a six-variable structure have concurrent or predictive validity hit rates of 39–55%. In contrast, when a person's vocational aspiration and interest profile share the same category (person aspires to teacher, and his or her social or educational score is the high point of the profile) predictions of correct identification of future aspiration or occupation range 60–85% for intervals of 1–11 years for the SDS, SVIB, or VPI (Bartling & Hood, 1981; Borgen & Seling, 1978; Dolliver, 1969; Holland & Gottfredson, 1975; Holland & Lutz, 1968; Touchton & Magoon, 1977).

The last step, now in progress, is the exploration of the relation of vocational identity (Holland, Daiger, & Power, 1980) to the agreement between a person's current aspiration and SDS code. Earlier research had shown that the degree of congruence between SDS code and aspiration was positively correlated with an identity measure (Holland, Gottfredson, & Nafziger, 1975). Other research indicates that vocational identity is negatively correlated with the number and variety of a person's vocational aspirations (Power, Holland, Daiger, & Takai, 1979). Likewise, identity is positively correlated with student and adult ratings of the SDS (Pallas, Dahmann, Gucer, & Holland, 1983; Power et al., 1979). We hope to establish soon that a person's history of vocational aspirations is a useful unobtrusive measure of identity that can be used to understand career and personal development.

Content, Format, and Self-Scoring

The content and format of the SDS were anticipated in many respects by two earlier assessment devices: The Personal Survey (Holland, 1966b, Appendix B) and the American College Testing Program (ACT) Guidance Profile (Holland, 1968). The Personal Survey—a collection of the most discriminating items among the personality types—was published, but rarely used, because of its unwieldy scoring problems. The ACT Guidance Profile was a more coherent but asymmetrical collection of items and scales (the entire VPI, sets of self-rating activity and competency scales, and so on). Both inventories were the outcome of multiple National Merit Student Surveys developed by Astin (1963), Holland (1963), and others in the period 1956–1963.

The ACT Guidance Profile was printed on a single piece of paper (42 in long) and was scored by an electronic machine, but the different kinds of scales— activity, competency, occupational, and so on, were not always comparable from one part to the next. In 1967 Charles Elton stimulated the next step toward the SDS when he said: "If you could make it possible for a person to score their own profile, you would have something really useful." Holland regarded that task as impossible and turned to easier tasks.

About 3 years later (1970) Thomas Magoon told Holland that his counselors voted to use a career guidance tool during freshmen orientation and asked if Holland had anything they could use. Holland had been working slowly on an inventory called "I Think I Know What I Want to Do: a Self Guidance Experience for Educational and Vocational Planning" a horrible title according to Magoon and everyone else. At that time, it was decided to develop an assessment in which scales of different domains would follow the theory explicitly: six scales in each domain (activities, competencies, self-ratings, and occupations), arranged in $R-I-A-S-E-C$ order, and of equal length within each domain. This task was accomplished by reviewing multiple item analyses and theoretical studies for the period 1959–1969. This turned out to be the easiest task. Self-scoring required numerous revisions from 1970 to 1977. The last revision in 1977 was stimulated by a neighbor—a nurse who suggested that all the subscores should be assembled and added together on a single page to reduce errors. Her solution reduced errors and made self-scoring so easy that even most fourth graders could accomplish this task without help. Informal experience suggests that some college students and workers have more difficulty because they do not read or pay careful attention to the directions. The end of attempts to eliminate scoring errors is probably at hand.

Research Colleagues

The development of the SDS and theory has been directly influenced by a host of researchers. Astin stimulated the classification work by developing and testing the Environmental Assessment Technique (EAT; Astin, 1963; Astin & Holland, 1961; Astin & Panos, 1969). Richards and his colleagues extended, revised, and tested the EAT in multiple studies of college environments (Richards, Rand, & Rand, 1966; Richards, Seligman, & Jones, 1970). Tom Magoon shepherded the SDS through its formative stages and got many students to perform evaluations and validity studies. Many other colleagues (Charles Elton, Gary Gottfredson,

Linda Gottfredson, Harriet Rose, Keith Taylor, Joseph Johnston, Bruce Walsh, Paul Muchinsky, Mary Viernstein, David Campbell, Jack Rayman, James Wiggins, and others) either performed research or gave advice. The SDS was a large scale effort loosely coordinated by its author.

Interests, Personality, and Values

The comprehensive use of Holland's theory has led to a career simulation that integrates a person's vocational aspirations, vocational interests (Activities and Occupations sections), competencies (reports of aptitudes and skills), self-estimates of abilities (indirect and incomplete measures of self-concept and abilities) as well as a parallel classification system. In addition, the SDS research indicates that the SDS can be interpreted as a useful inventory of personality and values.

For example, the relation of the SDS to the Neuroticism–Extroversion–Openness Inventory (NEO; Costa & McCrae, 1980) indicates that the SDS measures selected personality variables. The NEO inventory was developed to measure the major dimensions of personality. Two NEO scales parallel Eysenck's (1960) Neuroticism and Extroversion dimensions, and a new measure—Openness to Experience in the areas of fantasy, aesthetics, feelings, actions, ideas, and values—has been added.

The patterns of correlations in Table 3.2 are generally consistent with earlier evidence and interpretations of the SDS scales (Holland, 1979). Extroversion is positively correlated with the *social* and *enterprising* scales; and Openness is positively correlated with the *investigative* and *artistic* scales. Note that this pattern of moderately positive correlations holds for each of the subscales for each type (activities, competencies, occupations, and abilities). In addition, these results are very similar for men and women in this adult sample ranging in age from 21 to 89.

Several other observations are important. The SDS scales have only insignificant or very small correlations with the *neuroticism* scale or with age. In contrast, the SDS has small to strong correlations with gender that replicate the common finding that men's and women's interests remain different in some areas. Finally, some correlations are about as high as the reliabilities of the scales involved would permit—many correlations in the range .50–.65. These correlational patterns still hold, although the correlations are lower, when spouses' ratings of the NEO variables are correlated with the SDS scales (Costa, McCrae, & Holland, 1984).

There is also substantial evidence that the SDS scales measure a person's values. The analyses of the relation of the SDS to the study of values (Allport, Vernon, & Lindsey, 1951; Laudeman & Griffeth, 1978; Williams, 1972) indicate that the types are usually associated with expected values. See Holland (1985a, p. 69) for a summary. Gordon's (1975) Survey of Interpersonal Values (SIV) yields a values typology that usually corresponds to the types. For exam-

TABLE 3.2
Correlations of Self-Reported Neuroticism, Extraversion, and Openness Scores with Self-Directed Search (SDS) Scales for Men and Women

SDS Scales	Men (N = 217)			Women (N = 144)			Total (N = 394)	
	N	E	O	N	E	O	Age	Sex
Realistic								
Activities	−08	13	17*	12	00	11	−12	−45**
Competencies	−03	10	12	10	00	19*	−02	−60**
Occupations	−06	12	03	11	06	17*	−08	−47**
Abilities	−11	12	09	00	09	08	−07	−38**
Total	−08	14*	12	09	05	17*	−08	−55**
Investigative								
Activities	−14*	−05	26**	−03	06	30**	00	−27**
Competencies	−17*	08	22*	−03	15	40**	−03	−45**
Occupations	−04	−01	37**	02	07	32**	01	−19**
Abilities	−12	−01	21*	−15	20*	28**	−04	−43**
Total	−13*	00	33**	−05	14	40**	−01	−38**
Artistic								
Activities	11	16*	50**	03	20*	50**	−24*	28**
Competencies	−03	18*	30**	11	24*	49**	−14*	15*
Occupations	23**	11	41**	−01	31**	39**	−20*	15*
Abilities	14*	15*	36**	00	30**	38**	−19*	20**
Total	16*	18*	49**	03	33**	53**	−24*	24**
Social								
Activities	−05	44**	07	−05	35**	14	−03	23**
Competencies	−10	52**	12	−26*	43**	24*	−12*	23**
Occupations	02	23**	14*	−06	25*	25*	−03	07
Abilities	−19*	42**	18*	−19*	40**	23*	−07	08
Total	−09	50**	17*	−17*	43**	28**	−08	18**
Enterprising								
Activities	−06	54**	16*	−04	41**	28**	−15*	−14*
Competencies	−22*	57**	16*	−17*	51**	20*	−03	−22**
Occupations	09	45**	11	05	30**	10	−19*	−19**
Abilities	02	54**	07	−09	42**	16	−16*	−13*
Total	−04	65**	16*	−08	51**	23*	−17*	−21**
Conventional								
Activities	−05	07	−04	08	−23*	−24*	00	15*
Competencies	07	21*	13	07	−05	−04	−22*	11*
Occupations	04	12	00	01	−03	−07	−05	−08
Abilities	10	08	−07	−07	−02	−12	−07	21**
Total	05	15*	00	02	−10	−15	−10*	12*

Note: Decimal points omitted.
*p < .05.
**p < .001.

ple, the Enterprising type is a clear counterpart of Control of Others (CO); The Social type is "equivalent to Service to Others (SO);" the Investigative type "corresponds to Self-Determination (SD);" the Conventional and Realistic types "are similar to Institutional Restraint (IR);" and the Artistic type "corresponds to Self-Expression (SE)."

Gordon tested the generality of his values model by performing Q–factor analyses of the Allport Study of Values (ASV; Allport, Vernon & Lindzey, 1951) and the Edwards Personal Preference Schedule (EPPS; Edwards, 1953). Table 3.3 taken from Gordon (1975, Table 6.3, p. 84) compares the typologies extracted from two values inventories and one personality inventory by Q–factor analyses and the relation of these types to Holland types. The resemblances across these diverse inventories suggests a strong convergence between interests, personality, and values.

REVISIONS, ADAPTATIONS, AND ACCESSORY MATERIALS

The use of the SDS in career work has led to numerous revisions, foreign adaptations, and to some helpful accessory materials. Many of these were stimulated by counselors, test takers, and social critics.

For example, every form of the SDS has resulted in a more comprehensive Occupations Finder (500 titles in 1978), but some users still called for more. The Dictionary of Holland Occupational Codes (DHOC; Gottfredson, Holland, & Ogawa, 1982), which organizes the DOT into an extensive Occupations Finder with 12,099 titles and an alphabetized index, was a response to this thirst for more titles. Now counselors occasionally complain that there are too many low status occupations or that they prefer alternate titles to the defined DOT titles.

The SDS has been revised so that women's aspirations will be broadened and not narrowed (Gottfredson, Holland, & Holland, 1978), but there is no persuasive evidence that these revisions have had a substantial impact. The research on the effects of inventories reviewed later appears to be a more promising strategy for fostering the career development of women and all other groups.

The interpretive booklet, *Understanding Yourself and Your Career* (Holland, 1977), grew out of complaints that the SDS was not as self-interpreting as the author claimed and that the light grey, interpretive material on the back of the SCII profile sheet was hard to read. At that time (about 1975–1976) Holland's vision was decreasing, and he was sensitive to the needs of the visually impaired—so, why not create a readable booklet that would permit the SDS user to understand the SDS via the essentials of the theory, rather than just supplying a description of the types? Two booklets were developed (long and short) and evaluated by students in terms of readability and helpfulness. The short form was favored by the publisher and by students. The major criticism came from Hol-

TABLE 3.3
A Comparison of Types Obtained in Four Different Factor Analyses

Pole	GSIV[a]	AVL[b]	EPPS[c]	Holland types
Positive	Control of Others	Economic-Political	Dominant Striving	Enterprising
Negative	Reciprocal Support	Warm-Supportive	None	None
Positive	Service to Others	Social	Friendly Interest	Social
Negative	(Negative)	(Negative)	None	None
	Service to Others	Social		
Positive	Self-Determination	Theoretical	Adolescent Revolt	Investigative
Negative	Institutional Service	None	None	None
Positive	Institutional Restraint	Christian Conservative	Docility	Conventional Realistic
Negative	(Self-Expression)	(Aesthetic)	None	Artistic

[a]Gordon Survey of Interpersonal Values. [b]Allport–Vernon-Lindsay Study of Values. [c]Edwards Personal Preference Schedule.

land's older brother who said the booklet "read as if a psychologist wrote it." The current SDS interpretive booklet is called *You and Your Career* (Holland, 1985d).

The SDS has also been revised for poor readers (Form Easy). That revision was initiated by Katherine Davies (1971) as a master's paper under Tom Magoon's supervision. She modified the SDS so fourth, fifth, and sixth graders could take it but could not score it; a task left for Holland to accomplish. Her paper had several interesting outcomes. The SDS profiles of these children were about as well-defined as those of high school students, and they yielded the same pattern of sex differences. Their vocational aspirations were also coherent rather than chaotic.

Somewhat later, and after a simplified scoring procedure had been worked out, Form E was administered to a fourth grade class of children with average academic talent. They filled out and scored the SDS with no more difficulty than high school students have with the regular form.

The SDS has been translated or adapted for use in Australia, New Zealand, Canada, Japan, the Netherlands, Switzerland, Italy, Nigeria, and Guyana. It has also been translated into French, Vietnamese, and Spanish. (See Holland, 1985a, for more detail.) In every country where the relevant research was done, the construct validity and reliability results are similar to that obtained in the United States. The transportability of the SDS and the resultant research data provide strong evidence for its validity.

The incorporation of the SDS in computer-assisted career systems was stimulated by guidance systems that needed a tested career assessment and exploration system (Rayman & Harris-Bowlsbey, 1977). In many systems, the SDS or a similar instrument form the chief asset.

APPLICATIONS AND UNEXPECTED OUTCOMES

The publication and evaluation of the SDS has led to both expected and unexpected outcomes. Initially, the goal was only to create a self-scored inventory so that the unavoidable problems associated with electronically scored inventories would be eliminated. No one anticipated the multiple fringe benefits that emanated from the use of a self-scored test: test-taker excitement and satisfaction, self-understanding spurred by the obvious scoring structure, multiplication of counselor ability to reach more clients, and the challenging of one-to-one career services.

Influence Experiments

The first experimental evaluation of the SDS was initiated by Thelma Zener and Leslie Schnuelle (1976), who compared the effects of the SDS, the VPI, and no treatment. High school students taking the SDS or the VPI evaluated the inventories as moderately positive, reported feeling more satisfied with their current occupational choice, and were considering more occupational alternatives than the control group both the day after the experiment and three weeks later. Students taking the SDS selected occupations that were more consistent with their personality traits and reported less need to see a counselor immediately.

Subsequently, more than 20 experiments have followed the general design suggested by Zener and Schnuelle (1976) and have used many of the same outcome measures. The most common findings are that the SDS: (a) increases the number of vocational options a person is considering; (b) increases satisfaction with a vocational aspiration; and (c) increases self-understanding.

The most recent large scale evaluation (Pallas et al., 1983), using samples of high school and college students as well as workers, resulted in similar findings. Like the Zener and Schnuelle (1976) study, the effects of the SDS were positive and not related to race or sex. These and other studies (Collins & Sedlacek, 1972; Croft, 1976; Kimball, Sedlacek, & Brooks, 1973; Lewis & Sedlacek, 1972) have indicated that the *effects* of the SDS do not depend on a test-taker's age, gender, race, social class, education, or intelligence. The SDS manual (Holland, 1985b) provides a more complete account of the first 20 evaluations as well as a discussion of the influence of age, sex, social class, and intelligence on SDS scores.

Vocational Exploration and Insight Kit

The early evaluations led to several other outcomes. The Vocational Exploration and Insight Kit (Holland, Birk, Dolliver, Dewey, & Tyler, 1979), which included a card sort, the SDS, the interpretive booklet (*Understanding Yourself and Your Career;* Holland, 1977), and an action plan, was developed to increase the impact of the SDS. However, experimental evaluations of high school (Takai & Holland, 1979) and college women (Talbot & Birk, 1979) failed to show that this three-module intervention had more beneficial influence than the SDS alone.

Career Courses

The next stage in career treatment was to assemble a collection of interventions (interest inventories, vocational exercises, interviewing occupational representatives, etc.) and create a career course or seminar in an attempt to have a greater impact. The My Vocational Situation (MVS; Holland, Daiger, & Power, 1980) and similar scales have then been used to assess influence in pre–post or related designs. A large scale study (Rayman, Bernard, Holland, & Barnett, 1983) illustrates this kind of intervention and its evaluation. In this evaluation a career course, implemented in 22 sections by 11 instructors, had substantial effects according to pre–post MVS scores, but no interactions were observed for instructor or student characteristics. At the same time, it is clear that this and similar courses have more influence than the SDS or similar inventories alone.

Unexpected Events and Lessons

The development, introduction, and use of the SDS with a wide range of groups in the United States and foreign countries (high school and college students, workers, and retirees) and with a wide range of professionals and nonprofessionals (counselors, personnel workers, and psychologists) has produced many surprises. In retrospect, many should have been anticipated, but other events still appear unpredictable.

Introduction.   The SDS was introduced to professionals through the publisher's catalogue and Holland's talks and workshops (four or five a year). Most people were receptive, but many were not. One prominent counseling psychologist said that "the SDS borders on the unethical," because it was self-scored. A graduate student at the University of Maryland called Holland, because many of his clients disappeared once they had the SDS in hand. Holland suggested that the counselor locate his clients and find out what had happened. Later, the counselor reported that most of his "no-shows" had obtained what they sought from the SDS (apparently reassurance) and saw no need to return. Holland noticed the same phenomena with an occasional student and with faculty members who stopped by his office for an SDS—ostensibly for their children or wives, but not always. One college administrator called late at night to report that he had obtained the code for college administrator. Holland refrained from telling him that this occurrence—having his three-letter SDS code match the three-letter code of his current occupation—has only a modest probability of occurrence. These experiences implied that there was much unmet need for vocational exploration and reassurance, and that it may be helpful to think of vocational assistance according to levels of complexity, need, and cost rather than to push all clients through complex, labor-intensive, expensive treatments.

As the SDS became popular, neither the author nor the publisher could keep up with the correspondence from professionals. The author naively believed that more data and more comprehensive manuals would solve the problem. Three manuals were prepared in 13 years (Holland, 1972, 1979, 1985b); each one was more complex, comprehensive, and expensive than its predecessor. Eventually, correspondence and phone calls did fade, but considerable anecdotal evidence suggests that very few professionals ever read or studied the SDS manuals. Like many test takers, professionals believed that the SDS was so obviously simple that there was no need for more information.

Several examples suggest how few people have read any SDS manual. The second manual (Holland, 1972) contained an error in the Counselor Self-Test (p. 32), but no one ever reported it. On the other hand, someone did complain about the ratio of high status females and males on the cover design. The next cover became so abstract that it was difficult to discern whether the workers were even human. The error in the self-test was corrected, but only to satisfy the author.

Some other examples: At an SDS workshop, a high school counselor's question indicated that he didn't know that there was a manual. Likewise, some involved professionals do not read manuals. For instance, a friend, who had been given the most recent manual, reported several years later that he had just read the manual, because he had to prepare a book chapter in which the SDS was a topic. Presumably, he would never have read the manual if the writing commitment had not come along.

At this point, test manuals appear to be unread status symbols that attest to an inventory's scientific status and whose chief usage may be as a merchandising vehicle. In the near future, manuals will also serve, in conjunction with the forthcoming test standards (American Psychological Association, 1984), as a legal document that lawyers, plaintiffs, and publishers will read pro and con. It is too bad that the APA test standards do not require all professionals to read—at least once every 6 years—the test manuals for those devices they use daily. This is a standard that is explicit, needed, and does not require lengthy calculations. At a later date, the APA could require a simple achievement test where 50% correct could be a passing score.

Test Development.   The development of the SDS was dominated by the author's concern for an assessment that would be especially practical, that is, easily scored and interpretable. Consequently, it was necessary to ignore much conventional wisdom: (a) "build lengthy scales" (Current total scales are 38 items each.); (b) "scale length should mainly be concerned with validity and reliability considerations" (Instead scales were made the same length to facilitate booklet format and ease of scoring.); (c) "control for acquiescence set" (All items are scored *yes, like,* or *positively* to facilitate scoring and interpretation.); and (d) "items should be randomized to minimize contextual effects and to disguise scale meanings" (All items are arranged scale-by-scale in transparent fashion to facilitate scoring and interpretation.). Depending on one's interpretation of the relevant literature, the SDS exemplifies a practical solution to a complex problem—a psychometric achievement—or a large collection of methodological and psychometric faux pas.

The evidence suggests an achievement. The validity (construct, predictive, content, concurrent) studies appear to be as positive and clear as that for similar inventories (Holland, 1979, 1985b). Not only did Rorer (1965) lay acquiescence response set to rest for the MMPI, studies of the SDS indicate that the SDS scales have only negligible correlations ($-.09$ to $.15$) with the Crowne–Marlowe Social Desirability index (Aranya, Barak, & Amernic, 1981). In addition, the tendency to respond *yes* should affect each of the SDS scales in similar ways, because each scale has 38 items scored *yes* so that whatever acquiescence is present is controlled; the shape of the profile is what counts.

The evidence pro and con for the use of transparent scales (items belonging to each scale are arranged in a single block or location) is largely indirect: (a) the validity studies imply as much validity for the SDS scales as for those in other interest inventories; (b) the effects on the test taker for the regular SDS and a randomized SDS, using the same items, were not significantly different in an experimental evaluation (Holland, Takai, Gottfredson, & Hanau, 1978); and (c) earlier research (Halpern, 1967) has demonstrated that the item arrangement of interest inventory items had no effect on item responses.

In a related experiment, Lyman (1949) demonstrated that use of scrambled or blocked items in a multi-scale school attitude inventory resulted in no consistent differences in scale means, standard deviations, reliabilities, or validities.

Usage and Evaluation.   Both the author and the publisher were surprised and pleased by the rapid rate at which the SDS was embraced by professionals and the general public. On the other hand, they were not thrilled by the imitation of the SDS by other publishers. It has also been surprising to find that the SDS had as much predictive and concurrent validity as every interest inventory with which it can be compared (Dolliver, 1975; Gottfredson & Holland, 1985; Hanson, Noeth, & Prediger, 1977; Holland & Gottfredson, 1975; Hughes, 1972; O'Neil, Magoon, & Tracey, 1978; Touchton & Magoon, 1977; Wiggins & Weslander, 1977). Indeed many professionals find it hard to believe that a relatively brief assessment could have as much validity as inventories developed through the use of complex methods and lengthy scales.

In this regard, it was reassuring to read that Meehl's (1972) long-term attempt to build a better MMPI led him to conclude that ideal scales are brief (15–20 items), homogeneous, and easily interpreted by both clients and theorists. In addition, ideal scales should function effectively "in subpopulations [which are] homogeneous with regard to age, sex, education, IQ, race, social class" (p. 173). Burisch (1984) has recently come to a closely related point of view: "Comparative studies revealed no consistent superiority of any strategy (test construction) in terms of validity or predictive effectiveness. But deductive scales normally communicate information more directly. . . . Self-rating scales narrowly but consistently outdo questionnaire scales in terms of validity and are clearly superior in terms of communicability. . . . The more commonsensical approaches to personality measurement have a lot to offer" (p. 214).

FUTURE RESEARCH, DEVELOPMENT, AND THEORY

Future test revisions will continue to be shaped by experimental evaluations of the impact of the SDS on test takers, by evaluations of the accuracy of SDS materials, and by the testing of Holland's theory and its extension to new topics. Future revisions will also be guided by the author, his advisors, and the publisher. Finally, the course of revisions will probably be deflected by social, technological, and theoretical events that cannot be anticipated or controlled. The following sections summarize what has been accomplished in the areas of research, development, and theory, and they outline what should be done in the next 10 years. More explicitly, new work would include: (a) making the SDS more understandable to the test taker; (b) increasing validity; (c) increasing the likelihood that the test taker will complete the SDS and explore all potential options; (d) increasing counselor and clinician knowledge; (e) increasing the number of occupational titles in the Occupations Finder; (f) using the evaluations of the SDS and career courses to make appropriate revisions; (g) evaluating and revising the SDS according to the new APA test standards; and (h) evaluating the use and revision of the SDS in computer-assisted systems and in foreign adaptations or foreign languages. Some goals are ambiguous and unobtainable; others are attainable and explicit. The following summaries focus on the more attainable and explicit goals.

Research

It is helpful to begin with a summary of what has been learned from the SDS research from 1970 to 1984 and then to outline a strategy for new work.

Experimental Evaluations.   The experimental evaluations (1972–1984) indicate that the SDS increases the number of vocational options a person is considering, increases satisfaction with a vocational aspiration, and increases self-understanding. These studies indicate that the beneficial effects do not depend on a test-taker's age, gender, race, or social class. On the other hand, two studies (Pallas et al., 1983; Power et al., 1979) found that a test-taker's vocational identity (Holland et al., 1980) was positively associated with positive ratings of the SDS. In short, people with a clear sense of vocational identity liked the SDS experience, found it reassuring, and would recommend it to a friend. Finally, although the size of these effects are usually small, the effects of the SDS equaled that provided by professional counselors in three of four experiments (Holland, 1985b).

Many other studies have used specific criteria that no other investigator has tried to replicate or found effects that were not replicated. For instance, Zener and Schnuelle (1976) found that the SDS failed to stimulate vocational exploration according to a behavioral criterion, but Redmond (1973) found positive results with a different sample of high school students. Zener and Schnuelle (1976) also found that high school students who took the SDS had an increased understanding of Holland's typology according to a simple achievement test, but this examination test of acquired typological knowledge was never replicated.

New work should entail a more comprehensive attempt to assess what test takers learn or remember from the assessment experience. Such studies should focus revisions. For instance, the booklet, *Understanding Yourself and Your Career* (Holland, 1977), underwent two evaluations by undergraduate authors; two more evaluations than most accessory materials receive, but hardly sufficient. Similar evaluations need to be made of computer interpretations. We also need to know how long correct and incorrect interpretations are retained by the test taker and what the test taker acts upon. This kind of research is as important as any psychometric research. Predictive information—no matter how valid—is of little value if it cannot be clearly communicated and retained.

The evaluations of career courses (Rayman et al., 1983; Rayman, Lucas, & Hay, 1984), in which the SDS is only a single component, clearly suggest that the impact of the course is greater than the SDS or any other course component. New work should include an attempt to define an optimal mix of interventions or to identify the most useful or compatible set of interventions. The SDS and other assessment devices are, after all, only part of a larger treatment plan.

Diagnostic Studies.   The search for diagnostic systems for people with vocational problems has rarely been very successful, although the need is apparent to everyone, and the proposed schemes have always appeared plausible. See Crites (1969) for a review of earlier schemes. More recently, the diagnostic schemes proposed by Holland et al. (1980) and Osipow, Carney, Winer, Yanico, & Roschir (1976) appear to have promise. And Fretz (1981) has recommended some methodological remedies for finding client-intervention interactions and thus a clearer knowledge of what treatments will be optimal for what kinds of problems.

The Holland et al. (1980) proposal for a diagnostic scheme led to *My Vocational Situation*, a two-page form containing three scales: the Vocational Identity Scale, the Need for Information Scale, and the Barriers Scale. Initially, it was expected that these scales would yield significant client-treatment interactions in evaluation experiments. No replicated interactions occurred. In general, only weak and unreplicated interactions have been reported for any client-treatment interaction in the career counseling literature (Krumboltz, 1979; Rayman et al., 1983). Only one experiment (Kivlighan, Hageseth, Tipton, & McGovern, 1981) is a clear exception to this generalization.

Now a more useful strategy may be to use the diagnostic scheme implied by the MVS as a first attempt at learning who needs long-term, intense help, and who needs short term and relatively superficial assistance. The MVS can also be used at the beginning of a course or treatment to identify those who will need special attention. Rayman et al. (1984) carried this strategy one step further by interviewing students early in a career course to learn who was not making satisfactory progress, or who was gaining little from a standard set of interventions. In doing so, the investigators achieved substantial course effects.

This experience implies an educational model of intervention that resembles criterion-referenced testing. Why not concentrate on bringing everyone up to the criterion by the early identification of "no progress" after receiving some standard treatments and by the selection of supplemental treatments? The chief treatment goal would be to maximize effects by having no treatment failures. This goal would be attained by polishing the effective main treatments according to regular evaluations and by occasionally aborting the main treatments when other methods appear more helpful for specific individuals.

The research evaluations would focus on a set of influential treatments and the revision or development of influential treatments that would be helpful to the majority. In contrast, the search for client-treatment interactions would be given a lower priority for several reasons. The search for such interactions presents a long-term search for a formidable number of complex interactions using very small samples. The participants who do not respond to standard treatments are collectively a minority, so research investigations will have tiny samples of participants with particular needs or problems. In addition, the search for interactions has a poor track record. They rarely occur; they are rarely replicated; and the size of the effects are often too small to guide practice.

A more promising strategy would be to cumulate standard data for all treatment failures until the N's are large enough to warrant analysis. In addition, such analyses might focus on what kinds of participants required different amounts and lengthy treatments rather than an attempt to create unassailable diagnostic formulations. The track record for diagnostic formulations in the career field is worse than that for client-treatment interactions. Finally, it may be helpful to continue the search for signs of special needs or forms of vocational assistance, for there is some evidence (Taylor, Kelso, Longthorp, & Pattison, 1980) that some concepts (i.e., identity, indecision, differentiation) can provide useful information. At the same time, the validation of these ideas appears less promising than the criterion-reference strategy.

Validation Studies. The studies of concurrent and predictive validity need to be extended in several ways. Although the first SDS predictive studies yielded positive results, large scale longitudinal studies using three-letter rather than only one-letter codes are needed to test the validity of the SDS in more detail with criteria such as: occupation held (but also special roles played), job satisfaction, level of achievement, character of achievement, interpersonal relations, and so on. Of special importance, the study of vocational daydreams, current job, work history, and MVS variables in conjunction with SDS variables remains incomplete despite some very successful studies (Borgen & Seling, 1978; Gottfredson & Holland, 1975; Holland & Gottfredson, 1975; O'Neil, Magoon, & Tracey, 1978; Touchton & Magoon, 1977). Nearly all earlier studies could be surpassed by the use of larger samples, more comprehensive use of SDS variables, and multiple socially relevant criteria.

The different sections of the SDS could be explored following the Gottfredson and Holland (1975) example. In particular the competency scales should be compared with conventional aptitude variables for their predictive validity—both success on the job and the relation of the competency scales to field of work. The Kelso, Holland, and Gottfredson (1977) study of the relation of the SDS to the Armed Services Vocational Aptitude Battery (ASVAB; Armed Forces Testing Group, 1973) scales was a small beginning, but a large scale study of predictive relations would be more helpful.

Psychometric Analyses.   The old and new psychometric analyses of the SDS scales imply several simple strategies, such as increasing scale independence, for increasing concurrent and predictive validity. On the other hand, any psychometric strategy appears weak when it is compared with the use and study of SDS scales in combination with vocational aspirations. The new test standards should be complied with as much as possible, but the wave of the future may lie in more analytical studies of interest scales and aspirations guided by career theory.

Incidentally, a few of the revisions made to increase women's responses to the Realistic scales have backfired, so a few items no longer work for men. Attempts should be made to find better items without trivializing the Realistic scales by using items such as "I can watch for forest fires." This kind of item eliminates the visually disabled, but no one else, and reduces content validity.

Development

The main goal of any new developments or revisions should be to make the SDS more useful to the test taker. This means to increase: validity and reliability, if possible; the scoring accuracy; the ease and validity of the interpretive process; the ability of the test taker to interpret the results accurately; and the beneficial effects on the test taker. Revisions should also stimulate professionals (via a revised manual) and incorporate the relevant research and experience of researchers and practitioners.

Assessment and Classification Booklets.   An attempt should be made to increase the independence of SDS scales within each section: activities, competencies, occupations, and self-ratings. If this goal is achieved, the validity of the SDS may be increased slightly. About 15 of the 228 SDS items appear weak by one or more criteria in recent item analyses using adults aged 20 to 88. No revisions in format or scoring appear warranted. Perhaps it may be helpful to emphasize rescoring by a friend, teacher, or counselor.

The Occupations Finder could be extended from 500 to 750 or 1000 occupational titles. Such a revision to stimulate exploration of more options or to give reassurance about a particular option could be tested in some simple experiments. It is possible that more options will simply lengthen testing time without increasing exploration or satisfaction.

The construct validity of the Occupations Finder should be reexamined by comparisons of current occupational codes with the codes in the *Dictionary of Holland Occupational Codes* (Gottfredson et al., 1982) and with the codes obtained from new interest assessments or job analyses. The classification should also be reviewed for weak areas that require interest testing.

Accessory Materials.   All accessory materials should be reevaluated for their strengths and weaknesses: *Understanding Yourself and Your Career* (Holland, 1977, 1985d), the *DHOC* (Gottfredson et al., 1982), and the *Professional Manual* (Holland, 1985b). New materials might include a computer-scored and interpreted SDS. Likewise, the forms of the SDS (Holland, 1985b) for special populations could be reviewed and revised: Form E for poor readers, the SDS for the visually disabled, and the SDS for the mentally retarded. The SDS adaptations for some foreign languages may be abandoned, because the new test standards may make adaptations and translations inordinately expensive, if an author and publisher are required to repeat the validity, reliability, and other development tasks.

Theoretical Work

The experimental evaluations of the SDS and other interest inventories along with the evaluations of career courses and seminars is leading to a theory of career instruction in which the SDS and other interventions are part of a special chain of treatments. Holland (1985a) has outlined a cognitive-emotional theory of career assistance. In this formulation, the SDS and its theory provide a comprehensive structure for understanding self and occupations and the relation of self to occupation. Career courses and career counseling perform a similar function with more elaborate interventions over a longer time interval. As this theory becomes more explicit and useful, it may be possible to revise the SDS for greater impact.

Another source of revision lies in the application of Holland's theory, via the SDS or VPI to problems in recreation, retirement, psychotherapy, and interpersonal relations (see Holland, 1985a). The beginning work in these areas is promising and may provide practitioners with ideas for more useful service.

Lingering Problems

There remain several problems in SDS usage that appear intractable. Some are unique to the SDS; others appear to be afflictions of most inventories and tests. For instance, test takers (Pallas et al., 1983) cannot always report their SDS code, do not search the Occupations Finder for all code permutations, or do not read the interpretive booklet. The importance of completing these simple tasks has been documented; the extent of treatment is significantly related to positive ratings of the SDS (Pallas et al., 1983). This problem can be dealt with in group treatments by the gentle use of limits, but when test takers work on their own, there are usually no influential monitors.

As we indicated earlier, professionals are also reluctant to read or study manuals. It is true that these documents are not exciting reading, but they are the most economical way to communicate extensive information to a large audience. Workshops are a poor substitute; workshop experience often confirms how little reading has taken place. We have often been confronted with participants who range from nonreaders to skilled and well-informed professionals who could lead the same workshop. Such experience makes clear the wide gap that exists between what a publisher prints and what the average practitioner comprehends and applies in daily work. A creative solution is needed. It appears likely that the new test standards will only contribute to the reading difficulty level of revised manuals.

ACKNOWLEDGMENT

We are indebted to Gary D. Gottfredson, Linda S. Gottfredson, and John J. Horan for their critical review of an earlier draft of this chapter.

REFERENCES

Allport, G. W., Vernon, P. E., & Lindsey, G. (1951). *A study of values.* Boston: Houghton Mifflin.
American Psychological Association. (1984). *Joint technical standards for educational and psychological testing.* (Fourth draft). Washington, DC: Author.
Aranya, N., Barak, A., & Amernic, J. (1981). A test of Holland's theory in a population of accountants. *Journal of Vocational Behavior, 19,* 15–24.
Armed Forces Vocational Testing Group. (1973). *Counselor's Manual. Vol. 1.* Department of Defense 1304.12X. Randolph Air Force Base, TX: Author.
Astin, A. W. (1963). Further validation of the environmental assessment technique. *Journal of Educational Psychology, 54,* 217–226.
Astin, A. W., & Holland, J. L. (1961). The environmental assessment technique: A way to measure college environments. *Journal of Educational Psychology, 52,* 308–316.
Astin, A. W., & Panos, R. J. (1969). *The educational and vocational development of American college students.* Washington, DC: American Council on Education.
Bartling, H. C., & Hood, A. B. (1981). An 11–year follow-up of measured interest and vocational choice. *Journal of Counseling Psychology, 28,* 27–35.
Borgen, F. H., & Seling, M. J. (1978). Expressed and inventoried interests revisited: Perspicacity in the person. *Journal of Counseling Psychology, 25,* 536–543.
Burisch, M. (1984). Approaches to personality inventory construction: A comparison of merits. *American Psychologist, 39,* 214–227.
Campbell, D. P., & Hansen, J. C. (1981). *Manual for the SVIB–SCII.* Stanford, CA: Stanford University Press.
Cole, N. S., Whitney, D. R., & Holland, J. L. (1971). A spatial configuration of occupations. *Journal of Vocational Behavior, 1,* 1–9.
Collins, A. M., & Sedlacek, W. E. (1972). Comparison of satisfied and dissatisfied users of Holland's Self-Directed Search. *Journal of Counseling Psychology, 19,* 393–398.

Costa, Jr., P. T., & McCrae, R. R. (1980). Still stable after all these years: Personality as a key to some issues in adulthood and old age. In P. Baltes & O. Brim (Eds.), *Life-span development and behavior* (Vol. 3, pp. 65–102). New York: Academic.

Costa, P. T., Jr., McCrae, R. R., & Holland, J. L. (1984). Personality and vocational interests in adulthood. *Journal of Applied Psychology, 69,* 390–400.

Crites, J. O. (1969). *Vocational psychology.* New York: McGraw–Hill.

Croft, D. B. (1976). *Predictors of success in college for low prior educational attainment multicultural students.* (Grant No. OEG–0–74–1912) Educational Research Center, Las Cruces: New Mexico State University.

Davies, K. F. (1971). *A comparative and normative study of Holland's Self-Directed Search Modified for elementary school students.* Unpublished paper required for masters degree, University of Maryland, College Park.

Dolliver, R. H. (1969). Strong Vocational Interest Blank versus expressed occupational interests: A review. *Psychological Bulletin, 72,* 94–107.

Dolliver, R. H. (1975). Concurrent prediction from the Strong Vocational Interest Blank. *Journal of Counseling Psychology, 22,* 199–203.

Edwards, A. L. (1953). *Manual for the Edwards Personal Preference Schedule.* New York: Psychological.

Eysenck, H. J. (1960). *The structure of human personality.* London: Methuen.

Forer, B. R. (1948). A diagnostic interest blank. *Rorschach Research Exchange and Journal of Projective Techniques, 12,* 1–11.

French, J. W. (1953). *The description of personality measurements in terms of rotated factors.* Princeton, NJ: Educational Testing Service. (Multilith, 287 pages).

Fretz, B. R. (1981). Evaluating the effectiveness of career interventions. (Monograph) *Journal of Counseling Psychology, 28,* 77–90.

Gordon, L. V. (1975). *The measurement of interpersonal values.* Chicago: Science Research.

Gottfredson, G. D., & Holland, J. L. (1975). Vocational choices of men and women: A comparison of predictors from the Self-Directed Search. *Journal of Counseling Psychology, 22,* 28–34.

Gottfredson, G. D., Holland, J. L., & Holland, J. E. (1978). The Seventh revision of the Vocational Preference Inventory. *Psychological Documents, 8,* 98. (Ms. 1783).

Gottfredson, G. D., Holland, J. L., & Ogawa, D. K. (1982). *Dictionary of Holland Occupational Codes.* Palo Alto, CA: Consulting Psychologists.

Guilford, J. P., Christensen, P. R., Bond, N. A., Jr., & Sutton, M. A. (1954). A factor analysis study of human interests. *Psychological Monographs, 68,* (4, Whole No. 375).

Halpern, G. (1967). *Item arrangement and bias in an interest test.* (Research Bulletin 67–39). Princeton, NJ: Educational Testing Service.

Hanson, G. R., Noeth, R. J., & Prediger, D. J. (1977). The validity of diverse procedures for reporting interest scores: An analysis of longitudinal data. *Journal of Counseling Psychology, 24,* 487–493.

Holland, J. L. (1959). A theory of vocational choice. *Journal of Counseling Psychology, 6,* 33–45.

Holland, J. L. (1963). Explorations of a theory of vocational choice and achievement: II. A four-year prediction study. *Psychological Reports, 12,* 537–594.

Holland, J. L. (1966a). A psychological classification scheme for vocations and major fields. *Journal of Counseling Psychology, 13,* 278–288.

Holland, J. L. (1966b). *The Psychology of Vocational Choice.* Waltham, MA: Blaisdell.

Holland, J. L. (1968). *Manual for the ACT Guidance Profile-Two-year College Edition.* Iowa City: American College Testing Program.

Holland, J. L. (1972). *Professional Manual for the Self-Directed Search.* Palo Alto, CA: Consulting Psychologists Press.

Holland, J. L. (1977). *Understanding yourself and your career.* Palo Alto, CA: Consulting Psychologists Press.

Holland, J. L. (1985a). *Making vocational choices: A theory of vocational personalities and work environments*. Englewood Cliffs, NJ: Prentice–Hall.

Holland, J. L. (1985b). *Professional manual for the Self-Directed Search*. Odessa, FL: Psychological Assessment Resources.

Holland, J. L. (1985c). *Manual for the Vocational Preference Inventory*. Odessa, FL: Psychological Assessment Resources.

Holland, J. L. (1985d). *You and your career*. Odessa, FL: Psychological Assessment Resources.

Holland, J. L., Birk, Dolliver, Dewey, & Tyler. (1979). *Manual for the Vocational Exploration and Insight Kit*. Palo Alto, CA: Consulting Psychologists.

Holland, J. L., Daiger, D. C., & Power, P. G. (1980). Some diagnostic scales for research in decision-making and personality: Identity, Information and Barriers. *Journal of Personality and Social Psychology, 39,* 1191–1200.

Holland, J. L., & Gottfredson, G. D. (1975). Predictive value and psychological meaning of vocational aspirations. *Journal of Vocational Behavior, 6,* 349–363.

Holland, J. L., Gottfredson, G. D., & Nafziger, D. H. (1975). Testing the validity of some theoretical signs of vocational decision-making ability. *Journal of Counseling Psychology, 22,* 411–422.

Holland, J. L., Krause, A. H., Nixon, M. E., & Trembath, M. F. (1953). The classification of occupations by means of Kuder interest profiles. *Journal of Applied Psychology, 37,* 263–269.

Holland, J. L., & Lutz, S. W. (1968). The predictive value of a student's choice of vocation. *Personnel and Guidance Journal, 46,* 428–436.

Holland, J. L., Takai, R., Gottfredson, G. D., & Hanau, C. A. (1978). Multivariate analysis of the effects of the Self-Directed Search on high school girls. *Journal of Counseling Psychology, 25,* 384–389.

Holland, J. L., Whitney, D. R., Cole, N. S., & Richards, J. M., Jr. (1969). *An empirical occupational classification derived from a theory of personality and intended for practice and research.* (ACT Research Report No. 29) Iowa City: The American College Testing Program.

Hughes, H. M., Jr. (1972). Vocational choice, level, and consistency: An investigation of Holland's theory in an employed sample. *Journal of Vocational Behavior, 2,* 377–388.

Iachan, R. (1984). A measure of agreement for use with the Holland classification system. *Journal of Vocational Behavior, 24,* 133–141.

Kelso, G. I., Holland, J. L., & Gottfredson, G. D. (1977). The relation of self-reported competencies to aptitude test scores. *Journal of Vocational Behavior, 10,* 99–103.

Kimball, R. L., Sedlacek, W. E., & Brooks, G. C., Jr. (1973). Black and white vocational interests in Holland's Self-Directed Search (SDS). *Journal of Negro Education, 42,* 1–4.

Kivlighan, Jr., D. M., Hageseth, J. A., Tipton, R. M., & McGovern, T. V. (1981). Effects of matching treatment approaches and personality types in group vocational counseling. *Journal of Counseling Psychology, 28,* 315–320.

Krumboltz, J. D. (1979). *The effect of alternative career decision-making strategies on the quality of resulting decision.* (Final report. U.S. Office of Education Grant No. GOO7605241); Stanford CA: School of Education, Stanford University.

Laudeman, K. A., & Griffeth, P. (1978). Holland's theory of vocational choice and postulated value dimensions. *Educational and Psychological Measurement, 38,* 1165–1175.

Lewis, A. H., & Sedlacek, W. E. (1972). Socioeconomic level differences on Holland's Self-Directed Search (SDS). *Proceedings, 80th Annual Convention of the American Psychological Association,* 587–588.

Lyman, H. B. (1949). A comparison of the use of scrambled and blocked items in a multi-scale school attitude inventory. *Journal of Educational Research, December,* 287–292.

Meehl, P. E. (1972). Reactions, reflections, projections. In J. N. Butcher (Ed.), *Objective personality assessment* (pp. 131–189). New York: Academic.

O'Neil, J. M., Magoon, T. M., & Tracey, T. J. (1978). Status of Holland's investigative personality types and their consistency levels seven years later. *Journal of Counseling Psychology, 25,* 530–535.

Osipow, S. H., Carney, C. G., Winer, J., Yanico, B., & Koschir, M. (1976). *The Career Decision Scale.* Columbus, OH: Marathon Consulting & Press.

Pallas, A. M., Dahmann, J. S., Gucer, P. W., & Holland, J. L. (1983). Test-taker evaluations of the Self-Directed Search and other psychological tests. *Psychological Documents, 13,* 11 (Ms. No. 2550).

Power, P. G., Holland, J. L., Daiger, D. C., & Takai, R. T. (1979). The relation of student characteristics to the influence of the Self-Directed Search. *Measurement and Evaluation in Guidance, 12,* 98–107.

Prediger, D. J. (1982). Dimensions underlying Holland's hexagon: Missing link between interests and occupations? *Journal of Vocational Behavior, 21,* 259–287.

Rayman, J. R., Bernard, C. B., Holland, J. L., & Barnett, D. C. (1983). The effects of a career course and some other popular treatments. *Journal of Vocational Behavior, 23,* 346–355.

Rayman, J. R., & Harris-Bowlsbey, J. (1977): Discover: A Model for a systematic career guidance program. *Vocational Guidance Quarterly, 26,* 3–12.

Rayman, J. R., Lucas, M. S., & Hay, R. G. (1984). *The effects of three career courses and selected career treatments.* Unpublished manuscript. University Park: Pennsylvania State University, Career Development and Placement Center.

Redmond, R. E. (1973). Increasing vocational information-seeking behaviors of high school students (Doctoral dissertation, University of Maryland, College Park, 1972). *Dissertation Abstracts International, 34,* 2311A–2312A. (University Microfilms No. 73–17, 046).

Richards, J. M., Jr., Rand, L. P., & Rand, L. M. (1966). Description of junior colleges. *Journal of Educational Psychology, 57,* 207–214.

Richards, J. M., Jr., Seligman, R., & Jones, P. K. (1970). Faculty and curriculum as measures of college environment. *Journal of Educational Psychology, 61,* 324–332.

Roe, A. (1956). *The Psychology of Occupations.* New York: Wiley.

Rorer, L. G. (1965). The great response style myth. *Psychological Bulletin, 63,* 129–156.

Strong, E. K., Jr. (1943). *Vocational Interests of Men and Women.* Stanford, CA: Stanford University Press.

Takai, R., & Holland, J. L. (1979). Comparative influence of the Vocational Card Sort, the Self-Directed Search, and the Vocational Exploration and Insight Kit. *Vocational Guidance Quarterly, 27,* 312–318.

Talbot, D., & Birk, J. M. (1979). Impact of three career exploration treatments on the vocational exploration behavior of women. *Journal of Counseling Psychology, 26,* 359–362.

Taylor, K. F., Kelso, G. I., Longthorp, N. E., & Pattison, P. E. (1980). Differentiation as a construct in vocational theory and a diagnostic sign in practice. *Melbourne Psychology Reports, 68.*

Touchton, J. G., & Magoon, T. M. (1977). Occupational daydreams as predictors of vocational plans of college women. *Journal of Vocational Behavior, 10,* 156–166.

U.S. Department of Labor. (1977). *Dictionary of Occupational Titles* (4th ed.). Washington, DC: U.S. Government Printing Office.

Vernon, P. E. (1949). Classifying high grade occupational interests. *Journal of Abnormal and Social Psychology, 44,* 85–96.

Viernstein, M. C. (1973). *A field force analysis of Holland's occupational classification.* Unpublished manuscript.

Weinrach, S. G. (1980). Have hexagon will travel: An interview with John Holland. *Personnel and Guidance Journal, 58,* 406–414.

Wiggins, J. D., & Weslander, D. (1977). Expressed vocational choices and later employment compared with Vocational Preference Inventory and Kuder Preference Record-Vocational scores. *Journal of Vocational Behavior, 11,* 158–165.

Williams, C. M. (1972). Occupational choice of male graduate students as related to values and personality: A test of Holland's theory. *Journal of Vocational Behavior, 2,* 39–46.

Zener, T. B., & Schnuelle, L. (1976). Effects of the Self-Directed Search on high school students. *Journal of Counseling Psychology, 23,* 353–359.

4 New Approaches to the Assessment of Interests

Fred H. Borgen
Iowa State University

> *Every discovery is made more than once and none is made all at once.*
>
> —Sigmund Freud (1920/1977, p. 257)

INTRODUCTION

The focus of this chapter is innovation in interest measurement. A brief historical sketch is provided of landmark innovations in the major inventories covered in the preceding chapters. Separate chapters have preceded on each of the "Big Three" interest inventories—those generated by the work of Strong (1927), Kuder (1966), and Holland (1958, 1977, 1979). In this chapter specific attention is directed to newer interest inventories and how they have built upon—or gone beyond—the Big Three inventories. The focus is on conceptual and psychometric change and the implications of such change for counseling use. This is not intended to be an explicit critique of instruments as one might find in Buros' (1978, p. xxxv) "frankly critical" reviews, or invidious comparisons of instruments. The focus is more on the state of the art in interest measurement, its evolution, and underlying theoretical, psychometric, and counseling issues. My concerns are with the way different inventories have handled issues in interest measurement, and with the way some of the newer inventories reflect innovative approaches or a continuation of established traditions.

From one perspective, the history of interest measurement shows a remarkably sustained continuity. The benchmark methods of today have roots directly to Strong's (1927) early work, showing that the interests of people in different

83

occupations could be empirically differentiated by scales. This was the first application of the contrasted-groups method of constructing empirical scales, a method that was later to be adapted in the Minnesota Multiphasic Personality Inventory (MMPI). Today such kinds of scales continue a vigorous tradition in the Strong–Campbell Interest Inventory (SCII; Campbell & Hansen, 1981) and the Career Assessment Inventory (CAI; Johansson, 1982), and also the Kuder Occupational Interest Survey (KOIS; Kuder, 1966; Zytowski, 1985), with its somewhat different approach to occupational scale construction.

The State of the Art: Circa 1965

After nearly 40 years of interest measurement research, dominated by the giants Strong and Kuder, there were in the mid 1960s two visible and prototypic approaches to interest measurement. From the beginning, Strong had pioneered the empirical keying approach using contrasted groups of an occupation and Men-in-General. Kuder's early work had focused quite differently on measuring dimensions of interests in homogeneous scales, and visible in the pin-prick answer sheet of the Kuder Preference Record. In the background was Clark's Minnesota Vocational Interest Inventory (MVII), a highly sophisticated approach (Clark, 1961), but one with a muted public and practitioner impact. (Clark's perceptive book remains required reading for someone thinking about building an inventory.) Much of Holland's pioneering work was completed, but it had not yet burst into the forefront of vocational counseling.

The rate of innovation in interest measurement has accelerated since 1965. A watershed was crossed when Kuder (1966) introduced occupational scales in the KOIS. Then the Strong and the Kuder inventories became more directly competitive, with each offering the possibility of comparing one's interests with those of people in a variety of occupations. (In the KOIS, Kuder also innovated with empirical college major scales.) There were important practical and commercial implications for these Big Two. It was very expensive to conduct the research for such empirical scales, because each new occupational scale required collecting data for at least 200 people, often more, in that occupation. Scoring of such scales was tedious and complex and became a task for computers. Thus self-scoring of these inventories became nonexistent as the item weights became nonpublic, proprietary information and scoring could be obtained only by computerized scoring services designated by the copyright holders.

Interest assessment, as exemplified by the psychometric sophistication of Strong and Kuder, has a venerable and remarkably successful tradition, extending over 50 years. An innovator choosing to stray from that tradition must be bold indeed. Holland's work represents a successful divergence from that psychometric tradition. He did try it by introducing simplicity:

• Self-scoring.

- Simple, nonempirical scales.
- Simple occupational classifications.

Beginning in 1950, Holland was quietly, but resolutely, going in the opposite direction from the actuarial, high-tech approach of the Strong and Kuder inventories. His Vocational Preference Inventory (VPI), consisting merely of 160 occupational titles, evolved through seven revisions. Most importantly for our perspective here, his bent was conceptual, theoretical, and practical rather than psychometric. An avid student of Strong's and others' data, he proceeded to conceptualize and simplify. Holland could never be accused of psychometric folderol. In fact, many academics were slow to accept his inventories because of their obvious simplicity. A current view suggests that in many ways Holland's approach was the right one. Burisch (1984), for example, amasses a convincing case that simple methods of personality scale construction are often preferable. Likewise, the introduction of homogeneous scales (first Basic Interest Scales by Campbell, Borgen, Eastes, Johansson, and Peterson in 1968 and then the Holland General Occupational Theme scales by Campbell and Holland in 1972) into the Strong inventories reflected a growing recognition of scales simpler than the traditional empirical occupational scales. This topic of scale simplicity is considered more later in the chapter in the section on simplicity.

Holland succeeded in capturing a core of occupational interest variance in his hexagon and six $R-I-A-S-E-C$ dimensions. There followed a merger of paradigms that can be considered the most significant of all the innovation we have seen thus far. Holland's scales, and thus his theory, were incorporated into the Strong. Campbell and Holland (1972) arranged the marriage of "Strong's data" and "Holland's theory." This may be the most important of the several major revisions the Strong inventories have undergone. This merger is especially remarkable because the Strong tradition had been so firmly atheoretical, a prototype of dustbowl empiricism.

The Big Three of Interest Assessment: 1972 to the Present

With the incorporation of the six Holland dimensions in the Strong inventory, we have clear evidence that Holland's work had arrived commercially and practically. Thus, by 1972 the Big Three in interest inventories had become those begun by Strong, Kuder, and Holland. Holland's specific products were evident in the Vocational Preference Inventory (VPI; 1958, 1977) and the Self-Directed Search (SDS; 1970, 1979).

Two recent studies documented the most frequently used tests in counseling. Engen, Lamb, and Prediger (1982) surveyed test use at the secondary school level, and Zytowski and Warman (1982) assayed the use of tests in private practice, colleges and universities. High on both lists were the SCII, KOIS, and SDS.

The Matching Model: "Birds of a Feather . . ."

Rarely has vocational psychology seen its implicit propositions stated as explicitly as they were by Parsons (1909). The core Parsonian assumption of matching people and jobs (although no longer by "true reasoning") is central to many prominent vocational assessment tools, and especially interest measurement as seen in the long tradition underlying the Big Three inventories. Zytowski and Borgen (1983) sketched the assumptions of this model:

> This *congruence* assumption is that occupational outcome results from the fit between characteristics of people and the characteristics of jobs. It approaches the stature of a paradigm (Kuhn, 1970) in a very large segment of our tradition of measuring people and jobs. It is a central tenet of Paterson and Darley's (1936) *Men, Women, and Jobs* and it is equally central today in the work of Darley's student: John Holland's (1973) *Making Vocational Choices: A Theory of Careers.* It is the typical approach taken when psychology's traditional approach to individual differences has been applied to vocational behavior. . . . Here we see the roots of modern interest measurement, especially in empirically-based occupational scales (Strong and Kuder). . . . Recent theorists have given conceptual shape to the vast data base emerging from that early period. Holland is the most influential of these conceptualizers . . .Some of the central assumptions of the *congruence* model can be spelled out . . . :
>
> • The well-adapted individuals within an occupation share certain psychological characteristics. In aphorisms of the congruence model: "Birds of a feather flock together;" "Similarity breeds contentment."
> • There are measurable and practical significant differences in people and in occupations.
> • Individual differences interact differentially with occupational differences. In other words, outcome is a function of individual–environment fit (cf. Pervin, 1968); and there is benefit to be achieved by person–job matching.
> • Person and job characteristics show sufficient temporal and situational consistency to justify prediction of outcome over the longer term. (pp. 8–9)

From these general assumptions the dominant congruence model in interest assessment translates as follows: Interests can be reliably measured, and they show substantial stability over time for adults. Occupations tend to differ in the interests of their members: occupations tend to be composed of people with similar interests. A person in an occupation with others with congruent interests is likely to be more satisfied and also to remain in that occupation. With one exception, there is much literature supporting all of these assumptions with data that are convincing by usual psychometric standards. The sole exception may be the most important for our career counseling clients, namely that having congruent interests with others in one's occupation will lead to greater job satisfaction. Research on this crucial validity outcome is sparse, and the results of the few studies that have been conducted have usually been considered disappointing. The topic is considered separately in a later section on interests and job satisfaction.

Although this congruence model is pivotal historically and currently in interest assessment, it is not without critics. Katz and Shatkin (1983), for example, present a stimulating and provocative comparison of alternative models of vocational counseling. Their comparison of traditional interest measurement and the career decision-making model of their computer-based career guidance system highlights contrasts between the congruence and developmental models of such counseling. Stated alternatively, these are the matching model, with links to Parsons, and the change model, with links perhaps most directly to Super (1957).

Is the Matching Model in Transition?   Many of the controversial issues of the last 15 years are related to efforts to push the limits or expand the capacities of the matching model. The congruence and developmental models in vocational psychology persist with an uneasy coexistence—like a behaviorist and an analyst sharing the same office corridor. In the formal literature they reside as opposed alternatives (Osipow, 1983), yet a counselor might in one session readily mix an interest inventory (matching model) with a career development inventory (change model). Each has research traditions relatively independent from the other. Thus, for example, the new volume edited by Gysbers (1984) on *Designing Careers* presents a developmental subtext, with the index showing 52 entries for Super, and one for E. K. Strong, albeit unrelated to interest measurement. In the Gysbers book there is no index entry for "interests." Assessment is represented by Crites' (1984) chapter on career development inventories; without mentioning interest measurement, Dawis (1984) writes an otherwise comprehensive review of job satisfaction, presumed in the matching model to be a goal of interest inventories.

The matching model has probably generated more research than any other in vocational psychology. It accounts for most of the aptitude research, all the early Minnesota Employment Stabilization Research Institute studies (Paterson & Darley, 1936), nearly all the research in the tradition of vocational interest measurement, and the research stimulated by the congruence theories of Roe and Holland. So in sheer numbers the matching model has had a large impact. Substantively, there is an enduring knowledge base, best exemplified by the prolific research associated with the theoretical positions of Holland (1985) and Dawis and Lofquist (1984).

Choice Versus Change: Mixing Our Models.   In a comprehensive chapter on Diagnosis and Treatment of Vocational Problems, Rounds and Tinsley (1984) argue that vocational counseling should be seen as a subset of psychotherapy. We need, they say, better methods of classification of presenting problems, so that we can take advantage of emerging sophisticated designs for psychotherapy research, and thus, better understand counseling efficacy and the specifics of the change process. Their position is important for much of vocational counseling, but has an important omission for the traditional matching model often central to interest assessment. Career counseling, especially for career choice, does not necessarily involve a *change process* in the sense that term conveys. The person–job matching model implies that the person, *if properly placed* in a compatible environment will be better off, will have more favorable outcomes such as job satisfaction. There is nothing that says the individual must somehow change personal attributes in the sense that is usually implied for psychotherapeutic contexts. All that needs to change in the trait model is the individual's choice of environment in order to maximize outcomes. The individual's characteristics can be taken as a given. It is an allocation problem, rather than a change problem. It is not unlike dining in a restaurant with a diverse menu. The diner is not asked to change to have a satisfying meal—merely select the meal that will be satisfying.

Impacts of Innovation in Interest Assessment

This volume reflects the innovative vigor by developers of interest inventories in the last 15 years. Perhaps, as Gottfredson (this volume) documents, the greatest amount of effort has been directed to the sex bias and sex fairness of interest inventories (see also AMEG Commission on Sex Bias in Measurement, 1977; Borgen & Bernard, 1982; Diamond, 1975; Schlossberg & Goodman, 1972; Tittle & Zytowski, 1978; Zytowski & Borgen, 1983). No field of measurement, including the measurement of personality and ability, has undergone such extensive revision of widely used instruments (Campbell, 1972). For example, the venerable MMPI, which was modeled technically after Strong's (1927) successful creation of contrasted-groups occupational scales, continues in practical use to have the essential format that it began with in 1939. (The MMPI is currently undergoing revision, but there are no indications the revisions will be as extensive as those occuring in the Strong inventory since 1968.)

What have been the payoffs to the extensive technical revisions that have occurred in the last 15 years of interest measurement? It is useful to ask this question alternatively from several perspectives: commercial, beneficial counseling use—to use Gottfredson's (this volume) apt phrase—and scientific advances in vocational behavior.

My observations about payoffs are these:

Innovation has had commercial payoffs. Changes in the dominant inventories, namely the SCII and KOIS, have led to their continued commercial durability. Other inventories have been introduced incorporating the newest trends and carved successful niches. Several of these inventories are described in this chapter. They tend to include efforts to attain sex fairness, a variety of scale types, and use of occupational classifications. On the other hand, the scale of revision in Holland's VPI and SDS has been minor, especially with respect to differential sex norms, and yet his counseling tools continue to be widely used.

It is difficult to document empirically the beneficial effects of these innovations on clients. The apparent counselor acceptance of many of the changes can be taken as some indication that clients likewise are benefitting. On the other hand, the evidence Gottfredson cites in this volume about the lack of differential effects reported by clients taking different inventories is dismaying. It suggests that the impacts may be so minor on clients that they are not detectable. Perhaps we have not studied the issue adequately.

The scientific payoffs from all the efforts of the past 15 years are disappointing. It is hard to see clearly how all the recent research and development has led to a visible consensus that we understand vocational interests better than we did in 1970. With the singular exception of Holland's work, there are not conceptually based approaches to interests with research programs that have substantially influenced others in obvious ways.

Why Holland's Work Has Been So Influential. It is significant that Holland's measurement approaches have always been the simplest. This has permitted him to also look at interests theoretically. He has transcended the measurement problems and gone to the central conceptual issues (Burisch, 1984). The amount of research generated by Holland's approach is unequaled in vocational behavior in the past 15 years (Holland, 1979, 1985). This is due to the simplicity and elegance of his propositions, their focus on core conceptual issues, and the fact that they have permitted disconfirmation.

TIMELINES OF INNOVATION: THE BIG THREE AND BEYOND

Innovation Within the Big Three

Over the history of interest measurement, major sources of innovation have flowed from three nodes represented by the Big Three inventories—those of Strong, Kuder, and Holland. Development of the Strong inventory has been continued first by Campbell, and more recently by Hansen. Zytowski is now the major developer of the Kuder inventory. Table 4.1 presents a historical timeline of events I consider truly innovative in interest measurement. (For a chronology of the Strong inventories see Campbell, 1968.) It is evident in Table 4.1 that the Big Three have played a major and often pioneering role in introducing conceptual and technical advances in interest measurement. Many of these changes have been discussed earlier in this chapter, and also earlier in greater detail (Borgen &

TABLE 4.1
Interest Innovations Within the Big Three: A Timeline

Date	Originator	Contribution
1909	Frank Parsons	Matching people and jobs
1927	E. K. Strong	Strong Vocational Interest Blank (SVIB). Empirical, contrasted groups scoring of occupational scales Choice of separate approaches for men & women
1933	E. K. Strong	Women's SVIB
1946	Elmer Hankes	Creates first automatic scoring machine for SVIB
1948	Frederic Kuder	Kuder Preference Record Homogeneous scales, internal consistency
1956	Anne Roe	Developmental theory Occupational classification
1958–	John Holland	Vocational Preference Inventory Self-Directed Search Self-scoring Simplicity Theory Occupational Classification
1961	Kenneth Clark	Minnesota Vocational Interest Inventory Noncollege occupational scales
1962	National Computer Systems	Constructs first SVIB scoring machine using the digital computer
1966	Frederic Kuder	Kuder Occupational Interest Survey Clemans' lambda: occupational scales without a general reference group College major scales
1968	David Campbell	Basic Interest Scales added to SVIB Beyond occupational scales
1972	David Campbell John Holland	A merger of the Strong and Holland's classification
1981	David Campbell Jo-Ida Hansen	Strong–Campbell Interest Inventory A major revision combined for males & females

Bernard, 1982; Zytowski & Borgen, 1983). As noted previously in this chapter, my nominee for the clearest innovation is the 1972 merger by Campbell and Holland, with the addition of Holland's system and scales to the Strong Campbell Interest Inventory; Campbell has termed this a merger of Holland's theory and Strong's data.

Innovations Beyond the Big Three

Table 4.2 presents some nominations of innovative work outside the orbits of the Big Three. These advances, all since 1974, have been grouped as: (a) addressing

TABLE 4.2
Interest Innovations Beyond the Big Three: A Timeline

Date	Originator	Contribution
Addressing Sex Differences		
1975	NIE, AMEG	Guidelines for reducing sex bias in interest inventories
1976	Jack Rayman	Sex and the single interest inventory
1977	ACT	UNIACT: Unisex Edition of the ACT Interest Inventory
		Selection of items to reduce sex differences
1970s	Frederic Kuder	Kuder Occupational Interest Survey—other sex scoring
1977	Patricia Lunneborg	Vocational Interest Inventory
		Selection of items to reduce sex differences
1981	David Campbell	Strong–Campbell Interest Inventory
	Jo-Ida Hansen	
Classifications		
Roe		
1974	Lila Knapp	California Occuaptional Preference System Interest
	Robert Knapp	Inventory
1977	Patricia Lunneborg	Vocational Interest Inventory
Holland		
1958–	John Holland	Vocational Preference Inventory, Self-Directed Search
1972	David Campbell	Strong–Campbell Interest Inventory
	John Holland	
1974	ACT	ACT Assessment Program
1975	Charles Johansson	Career Assessment Inventory
Other		
1977	Douglas Jackson	Jackson Vocational Interest Inventory
Broader Coverage		
1975,	Charles Johansson	Career Assessment Inventory
1982		Occupational scales for noncollege occupations
Bootstrapping: The Power of Regression		
1977	Douglas Jackson	Jackson Vocational Interest Survey
		Accessing the Strong data archives through Jackson's
		homogeneous dimensions.
1982	Gary Gottfredson,	*Dictionary of Holland Occupational Codes*
	John Holland,	RIASEC codes for 12,000 DOT occupations
	Deborah Ogawa	
People-Matching		
1977	Frederic Kuder	People-matching: individuals as templates for career
	Donald Zytowski	exploration.

Note: NIE = National Institute of Education; AMEG = Association for Measurement and Evaluation in Guidance; ACT = American College Testing Program.

sex differences; (b) applying occupational classifications; (c) broadening the coverage of occupations; (d) bootstrapping through the power of regression; and (e) people-matching. Even here, the influence of the Big Three is often evident. The following section elaborates on many of the developments in Table 4.2.

NEWER INTEREST INVENTORIES: BEYOND THE BIG THREE

Here attention is given to some representative inventories that have been developed since 1965. Four inventories are selected that represent innovative directions and also appear to be having impact with users. Each inventory is briefly sketched to show its basic features, as well as those that are distinctive and innovative. Some of the inventories are discussed at greater length, because of the several ways in which they exemplify leading edges or controversies in interest assessment.

Career Assessment Inventory

In its technical features, The Career Assessment Inventory (CAI) is a near clone of the SCII. It differs only in its target audience, people wishing to consider "nonprofessional" occupations, that is, those not requiring postgraduate education. Created by Charles Johansson (1975, 1982) at National Computer Systems (NCS), the CAI has a direct lineage to the Strong inventories. Throughout his undergraduate and graduate work, Johansson was Campbell's key assistant for computer work. He was a central participant in the major revisions occurring in the SVIB from 1961 to 1970.

Although E. K. Strong had reservations about the feasibility of developing occupational scales for nonprofessional occupations, Clark's (1961) Minnesota Vocational Interest Inventory (MVII) demonstrated that it could be done. The MVII, however, has very few scales, and it has not continued to have major use. Later the KOIS (Kuder, 1966) was introduced with a mix of occupational scales for people with or without college training. With 91 occupational scales, the 1982 edition of the CAI is the most complete inventory for careers requiring college or lesser education.

Like the SCII, the CAI has three tiers of scales: occupational scales, Basic Interest Area Scales, and Holland-type General Theme scales. It is wholly computer-scored, and available with an extended narrative interpretive report. Its psychometric properties are as good as those for the SCII, and reviewers have viewed it favorably (Lohnes, 1982). Lohnes praises the manual but does lament, however, that "A serious problem is posed by the total absence of information about predictive validities" (p. 55). No other inventory has such a range and number of occupational scales focused on noncollege graduates, so it has been widely used, especially in nonuniversity settings. It continues the successful tradition of the Strong inventory, both its classic features and the major changes brought to the Strong in the 1970s by Campbell and Hansen (Borgen & Bernard, 1982).

Jackson Vocational Interest Survey

Jackson has long been a leader in personality research and psychometrics. The Jackson Personality Inventory (Jackson, 1976) is a model of application of state-of-the-art psychometrics, especially the use of forced-choice formats and complex item selection techniques to control for a variety of response biases. In the 1970s he turned his attention to building a wholly new interest inventory, publishing the Jackson Vocational Interest Survey (JVIS) in 1977. The JVIS incorporates many of the best features in extant technology as well as introducing several less common, or wholly new features that show a distinctive Jackson touch.

Adaptation of Mainstream Features. Like the SCII, and others, the JVIS incorporates a mix of scale types, ranging from broad bandwidth Holland-type scales, to basic homogeneous scales, to specific measures of occupational similarity. Like the KOIS, it yields scores showing similarity to college majors. Also like the KOIS, it uses a forced-choice item format. Like the SCII and Holland's system, it uses an occupational taxonomy. It is computer-scored, producing several score profiles and narrative interpretations linked to additional occupational classifications and information. In sum, it has incorporated many of the attractive features of the Big Three inventories, and in fact has more such features than any single one of them. As is discussed later, some statistical leapfrogging was required to produce some of these features, and these moves will not be satisfactory to all users.

Distinctive Features. The most unusual features of the JVIS are threefold: (a) emphasis on work styles rather than interests; (b) explicit intent to build an inventory well suited for research; and (c) the use of sophisticated multivariate techniques to build scales and occupational classifications. Each of these features merits specific discussion.

Work Styles. The JVIS begins with 34 Basic Scales derived from items about preferences for work activities. Many of these are traditional interest dimensions, but Jackson calls them work roles: creative arts, mathematics, skilled trades, social work, office work, and sales. Other basic scales refer to what Jackson (1977) introduces as *work styles:* "preferences for situations requiring a certain mode of behavior, such as characterized by the Planfulness scale" (p. 15). He further elaborates:

> The interpretation of scales reflecting work styles is a bit more complicated. Work style scales . . . include Dominant Leadership, Job Security, Stamina, Accountability, Academic Achievement, Independence, Planfulness, and Interpersonal Confidence. The immediate tendency is to treat these as personality characteristics, and to interpret the score as indicating the degree to which the respondent possesses the trait indicated by the scale name. A better interpretation within the context of vocational interests is to consider these as interests in working in environments placing a premium upon or requiring the behavior implied by the scale. (p. 17)

This is similar to the environmental press concepts that are central to job needs theories such as the Minnesota Work Adjustment Project (Dawis & Lofquist, 1984). Some of the Basic Scales also seem to be measures of personality (e.g., his *interpersonal confidence* seems to be related to generic *introversion–extraversion*), but Jackson is explicit in saying the work styles are "not personality dimensions as such" (p. 19). Other Basic Scales, such as *dominant leadership* and *stamina,* seem to be clearly some mix of personality measures and job needs. These issues, of course, should be resolvable by future research.

Research and Scientific Goals.   The Jackson inventory is notable for his intentions for it as a tool for theorizing and conceptualizing interests as constructs. Jackson (1977) states that the JVIS is designed not only for career counseling, "but also as a means of contributing to the understanding of the nature of vocational interests and to the psychology of vocational decision making. . . .the emphasis upon Basic Interest scales is consistent with Loevinger's (1957) conceptualization of psychological tests as instruments of psychological theory . . . emphasis on Basic Scales has the advantage that the constructs underlying interest in work may be better understood" (p. 79).

Because the Basic Scales are numerous and relatively independent, they are well suited to research work. Jackson's work with the JVIS is the best exemplar of contruct validation intentions for an inventory. Lunneborg's (1979, 1981) work, and its tie to Roe's (1956) theory, can be seen as a close second.

High Tech Statistics.   The JVIS is a psychometric tour de force. Advanced item selection techniques are used to construct the scales. Factor analysis is used to reduce the 34 Basic Scales down to 10 General Occupational Themes, more than the usual Holland 6 that seem so well entrenched in use. Two of the factors tap clear work styles. Cluster analysis is used to form a taxonomy of occupations, with 32 occupational clusters (Jackson, 1977; Jackson & Williams, 1975). Recent work has clustered college majors to form 17 clusters (Jackson, Holden, Locklin, & Marks, 1984). Jackson's classification work adds to both conceptual systems and ways of counseling. There is a related strategic issue about complexity. Holland has gotten mileage from a simple system, with six types. Will the complexity of Jackson's system catch on?

Reverse Engineering. For observers of innovation, by far the most remarkable aspect of the JVIS is the use of a creative statistical maneuver to bring the SVIB Occupational Scales into the JVIS. Jackson used a sample of 538 Pennsylvania State University males to bootstrap the linkage between the JVIS and SVIB, and eventually the SVIB Occupational Groups in the SVIB Handbook (Campbell, 1971). After the sample had responded to both the JVIS and SVIB, the homogeneous basic scales of each were scored, and a regression approach was used to predict SVIB Basic Scales from JVIS Basic Scales. Because the SVIB handbook gives mean Basic Scales for each occupational group, Jackson similarly was able to predict SVIB Occupational Scales from his JVIS Basic Scales. Thus, the JVIS incorporates, through modest data collection, the occupational scales that were originally developed through data collection and analysis from more than 50,000 subjects. (Some reviewers, such as Covington, 1982, misread what actually took place and conclude that Jackson collected data from 50,000 people.)

Multivariate Viewpoints. Interest measurement is inherently multivariate. The interests of people are multivariately structured, and the occupational world is multivariately structured. Some examples of work that have applied multivariate techniques such as discriminant function analysis and cluster analysis in this domain are Cooley and Lohnes (1968), Borgen (1972), the American College Testing Program (ACT; see following section), and perhaps most visibly Jackson. Although people such as Jackson have advocated a sophisticated multivariate approach to interests, Holland's famed R–I–A–S–E–C typology has set in motion a grassroots approach to the structure of vocational interests, albeit in a two-dimensional space.

Unisex Edition of the ACT Interest Inventory

Research Milieu. The Unisex Edition of the ACT Interest Inventory (UNIACT) emerged out of the most visibly active program of research and advocacy in interest assessment in the 1970s. Therefore, given this chapter's focus on innovation, it is apt to begin a discussion of the UNIACT with a look at the milieu in which it was developed. The other new inventories discussed here are, of course, products of substantial research programs. But those programs have not involved as many researchers nor as many large-scale national studies directed to such a range of issues.

Following an 11–year program of research, the UNIACT was released (Lamb & Prediger, 1981) by ACT. The UNIACT is the fourth edition of the evolving ACT Interest Inventory. Lamb and Prediger (1981, pp. 63–64) list the 30 ACT-generated research papers leading to the UNIACT. The list of participants is long: Nancy Cole, Gary Hanson, Joan Laing, Richard Lamb, Rick Noeth, Dale Prediger, Jack Rayman, John Roth, and Robert Schussel. Significant foci of their developmental work have included: (a) the definition and determination of sex bias; (b) utility of alternative methods of reporting interest scores and for determining their validity; (c) the basic dimensions of interests associated with occupations and people; (d) the relationships of interests to educational and occupational criteria; and (e) the determination of the effects of interest inventories on students.

The ACT research on interests is important because of the breadth of basic issues that have been addressed, often with fresh perspectives. The product does not mimic predecessors, except for adopting as its core the popular six dimensions articulated by John Holland. That too is an ACT product, in a sense, in that Holland was the first Vice President for Research at ACT (1963), and it was at ACT that Holland and his colleagues "discovered" the hexagonal model of interests (Holland, Whitney, Cole, & Richards, 1969).

The current impact of the UNIACT is large. As a core component of the ACT Assessment Program (the "ACT") and four career planning services, the UNIACT is administered annually to 1.5 million high school students, college students, and adults. Thus, it is presented as a career guidance tool to a sizable segment of the nation's youth.

Core Features of the UNIACT.   The UNIACT consists of 90 items equally distributed across six Holland-type BIS. Items describe work-related activities (e.g., "make creative photographs," "use a computer") that are responded to in a Likert format (*dislike, indifferent,* or *like*). Lamb and Prediger (1981) provide an overview of the goals of the UNIACT:

> The UNIACT is intended for use by persons (junior high school students through adults) who are in the early stages of career planning or replanning. The primary purpose of UNIACT is to stimulate and facilitate self/career exploration; that is, the exploration of self in relation to careers. UNIACT's major function is to help individuals identify personality relevant educational and vocational (career) options . . . UNIACT was constructed with the goal that the career options suggested to males and females would be similar. (p. 1)

The ACT approach has been to forgo traditional empirical occupational scales in favor of simple homogeneous scales that are then used in a multivariate predictive model to estimate similarity to career groups. Their strategy, thus, is similar to Lunneborg's (1979, 1981) with the VII and Jackson's (1977) with the JVIS. The similarities to Lunneborg's work are especially marked because the UNIACT and the VII are the key exemplars of efforts to eliminate sex differences in interest inventories by selecting items with minimal sex differences.

Unisex Inventories. Led by Prediger, ACT researchers have vigorously advocated that, to enhance validity, interest inventories should be designed to minimize sex differences (see Lamb & Prediger, 1981). In addition to controlling for sex differences at the item level, they have argued for norming methods to minimize differences. This led to a lively controversy in the literature focused on Holland's use of raw scores in his SDS and VPI.

Interpreting Interests with a Two-dimensional Model. The UNIACT begins with the six Holland dimensions, which are then further reduced to the two bipolar summary scales—*data/ideas* and *things/people*. These dimensions are thought to underly the Holland (1985) and Roe (1956) typologies based on ACT research (ACT, 1974; Hanson, 1974; Prediger, 1976, 1981, 1982). Figure 4.1

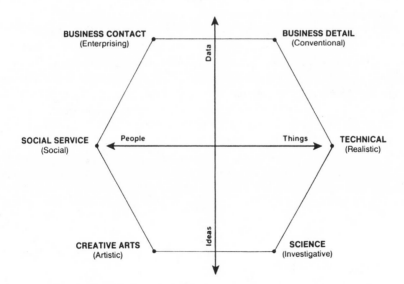

FIG. 4.1. Relationship between UNIACT scales and the data/ideas and things/people work task dimensions (Holland types corresponding to UNIACT scales are shown in parantheses.) Reproduced from Lamb and Prediger (1981, p. 2) by permission of ACT. Copyright 1981 by The American College Testing Program.

shows how the dimensions fit the Holland hexagon. With perhaps the ultimate in simplicity in interest assessment, this schema has several payoffs. It accounts for a major portion of variance in the mean interests of several hundred career groups on the VPI, ACT Interest Inventory, and SVIB/CAI (Prediger, 1982). It matches the dimensions of the world of work, long proposed by the U.S. Department of Labor (1977) in its *Dictionary of Occupational Titles* (DOT). Thus, ACT is able to match the test-taker's results with the full range of occupations in the DOT.

DOT occupations are grouped by ACT in job families (25 originally, 23 currently) with relatively homogeneous involvement with data/ideas and things/people work tasks. The respondent's scores on Data/Ideas and Things/People are then used to plot the person's similarity to job families on the World of Work Map (Fig. 4.2). If the plotting is done by hand, the two scores are each obtained from a different subset of 30 UNIACT items. If plotting is done by computer, the full multivariate information is derived from a linear composite of the six BIS. In addition, a similar strategy is used to show the person's similarity to students majoring in different college curricula. Figure 4.3 illustrates the Map of College Majors, which contains 34 four-year college majors and 18 vocational/technical programs at two-year colleges. Like Lunneborg's (1981) work, the college majors map follows a longitudinal, prospective design that compares the person's interests with those of precollege students who later majored in various college curricula. Lamb and Prediger (1981) summarize the research building the data base for the college majors map.

ACT's simple two-dimensional system makes the interpretive maps work. Results can be simply plotted in a readily communicated format. It remains an open question how great are the trade-offs to this ultimate simplicity. The two-dimensional map does a quite adequate job of summarizing the variance in the six Holland dimensions. When interests are defined more broadly than these six dimensions, a two-space may leave important variance unrepresented. As discussed in the following section on Lunneborg's Vocational Interest Inventory (VII), there is evidence (e.g., Jackson, 1977; Lunneborg & Lunneborg, 1975, 1978) that at least three and possibly considerably more dimensions may be necessary to adequately account for the full potential variance in vocational interests.

Vocational Interest Inventory

In 1968 Lunneborg began a research program leading to the current version of the VII (Lunneborg, 1979, 1981). Innovation in the VII is evident in four relatively distinctive features: (a) from the outset, it has been organized by Roe's (1956) occupational classification; (b) like the UNIACT, it is one of the few inventories designed to minimize sex differences at the *item level,* and it is also the first such effort (Lunneborg, 1980; Mitchell, Lunneborg, & Lunneborg, 1971); (c) it uses a prospective predictive design that permits high school stu-

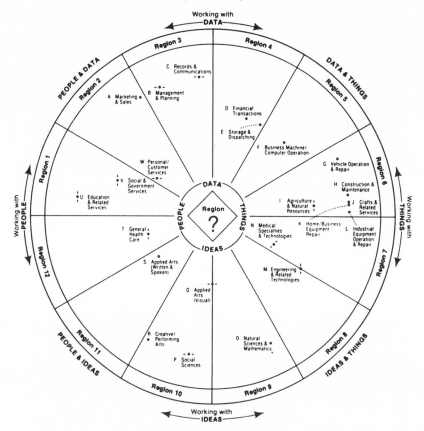

WORLD-OF-WORK MAP
(2nd Edition)

About the World-of-Work Map

The location of a Job Family on the map shows how much it involves working with DATA, IDEAS, PEOPLE, and THINGS. Arrows by a Job Family show that work tasks often heavily involve both PEOPLE and THINGS (◄─►) or DATA and IDEAS (↕). Although each Job Family is shown as a single point, the jobs in a family vary in their locations. Most jobs, however, are located near the point shown for the Job Family.

FIG. 4.2.   The ACT World-of-Work Map. Reproduced from The American College Testing Program (1984, p. 7) by permission of ACT. Copyright 1984 by The American College Testing Program.

MAP OF COLLEGE MAJORS

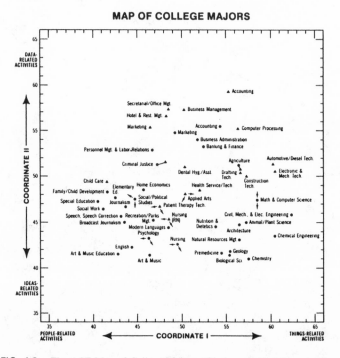

FIG. 4.3.   The ACT Map of College Majors. (Circles represent 4-year college majors, triangles represent 2-year college majors.) Reproduced from Lamb and Prediger (1981, p. 6) by permission of ACT. Copyright 1981 by The American College Testing Program.

dents to compare themselves with students of like age who later went on to specific career fields in college; and (d) like the JVIS and UNIACT, much of the developmental and validation work has been conducted from an explicit multivariate perspective.

Targeted at the high school group of career planners, especially those planning for college, the VII consists of 112 forced-choice statements intended to minimize troublesome "flat profiles." Eight homogeneous scales, representing the Roe groups, are computer-scored, with item content reserved as proprietary information. The VII is scored by Western Psychological Services, which provides a set of profiles and a narrative report intended for the student. Norms are based on a mixed-sex group of some 25,000 high school juniors and seniors participating in the Washington Pre-College Testing Program. The materials encourage exploration in historically nontraditional areas for the student's sex.

Roe's Occupational Classification.   Although Roe's eight-group classification has been influential, the six-group Holland schema has been most frequently adapted in interest inventories (e.g., SDS, VPI, SCII, CAI, UNIACT). Lunneborg's VII and the California Occupational Preference System Interest Inventory (COPS; Knapp & Knapp, 1974) are two examples of application of the Roe system. The earliest developmental work with the VII was directed to validating the use of the Roe system (Mitchell, Lunneborg, & Lunneborg, 1971).

Minimizing Sex Differences. Perhaps the most distinctive feature of the VII is the extensive effort to create an inventory with minimal sex restrictiveness. In constructing and revising the test, this has entailed an intensive effort to exclude items with sex differences. Lunneborg was forced to include some items with up to about 15% sex differences in response rates; these small differences cumulated at the scale level, as also occurred in the similar effort with the UNIACT, so some of the ubiquitous sex differences in interests remain at the scale level. In scoring and presenting the results, special emphasis is given to encouraging exploration in occupations nontraditional for one's sex. In part, this is accomplished by reporting nontraditional high scores "in the 50th to 75th percentile range for the six scales that still show these small sex differences" (Lunneborg, 1981, p. 48).

Prospective Design. From the beginning imprint of Strong's (1927) successful occupational scales, the predictive approach in mainstream interest assessment has uniformly had a specific character. To my knowledge, this approach has never been given a name, but for my purposes I call it the *retrospective* approach. Typically adults in a given occupation have been identified. Their responses have become the template against which testees, even very young adults or adolescents, have been measured in the occupational scale or another prediction equation. Like most retrospective approaches, the research design is cross-sectional, that is, all of the data can be collected for people in the target criterion groups at one point in time. The potential flaw in this design is that it does not account for developmental change in youthful, developing cohorts of potential test takers. Moreover, it may build in predictive noise in the template for specific interests that are due to the fact that the person is now an incumbent in the occupation. To my knowledge, it has never been well documented how much validity is vitiated by these potential problems of the dominant retrospective design. Indirect evidence that it is a nonproblem is often presented by showing the strong stability of interests *after young adulthood on the average* (Campbell, 1971; Hansen, 1984a). It is plausible, however, that this may be a serious problem for high school and younger age groups. It may also be a causal factor in the flat profiles seen frequently even in post-high school age groups. (The KOIS implicitly addresses this with its special scales reflecting the youthfulness of the test taker.)

The *prospective* design, in contrast, involves longitudinal data collection, collecting inventory responses from the age-mates cohort of potential test takers and then following the members of the cohort until they branch into career fields. Lunneborg followed this strategy for the VII by inventorying large samples of high school juniors and seniors through the Washington Pre-college Testing Program and then following them as they branched into major fields and graduation from college. As a result, high school students end up comparing their interests with the scores of graduating college students when the graduates were high school juniors. As Lunneborg (1981, p. 26) phrases it, the high school student can ask: "To which successful graduating group am I most similar?" For those of us so accustomed to the traditional approach, this may take some getting used to, but it has the promise of removing sources of invalidity present in the retrospective approach, and is actually closer to the true predictive purpose for using inventories.

Multivariate Perspective.   Like Jackson and the ACT researchers, Lunneborg has been at the forefront of research viewing interest assessment and prediction as a multivariate problem. The first general problem is determining the efficient multivariate space to represent the structure of individual differences in interests. Lunneborg and Lunneborg (1975, 1978) have addressed this question through factor analysis. Their conclusion is that four dimensions are necessary to account adequately for the variance, and the two-space models that are common (Roe's, Holland's, and the UNIACT's) may under represent the important variance.

The second general problem is the dimensionality of the predictive variance. Lunneborg and Lunneborg have addressed this issue with discriminant analysis (1977, 1978) and concluded that for the eight Roe groups, three discriminant dimensions are appropriate. Thus, they raise the issue of the completeness of the ACT Map of College Majors that is necessarily in a two-space. While recognizing the distinct communication advantages of the simpler models, they have suggested useful ways multidimensional information might be communicated (Lunneborg & Lunneborg, 1977, 1978). They have also (1978) shown how the discriminant functions might be rotated to enhance their communication value.

Overall, the Lunneborg's multivariate work illustrates several issues on the leading edge of interest assessment technology. They suggest that scores of interest dimensions, as in the occupational scales of several instruments, are psychometrically excessive and redundant, while the elegant, but two-space models such as Holland's hexagon and the ACT map of the world of work are *too* simple to represent all the variance. The simpler models have clearly earned a place in both theory and practice, but these lessons of greater complexity of multivariate structure should also be applied where it is feasible. Those who develop or revise interest inventories and prediction schemes will profit from maintaining these multivariate perspectives. The Lunneborg's results are constrained by the simplicity of the VII, which has only eight core dimensions. Thus the complexity of the *potential* interest space is even greater than suggested by their results. For example, Jackson's (1977) work with the JVIS shows his 34 scales can be reduced to 10 factors. His results, however, may be too complex to represent the usual interest space because the JVIS has scales also tapping work styles and (presumably) personality. As another example with traditional measures, Borgen's (1972, p. 206) predictive work with the SVIB suggested a minimum of four significant discriminant dimensions.

The advantages of the computer should routinely be applied to exploiting our emerging multivariate knowledge. If the computer is doing the predictive work, *all* the relevant dimensions should be part of the equation. This is evident, for example, in the VII (Lunneborg, 1981) and JVIS (Jackson, 1977) predictions to college majors. (It is also implicitly the case in an occupational scale on the SCII, CAI, and KOIS, for example.)

The multivariate perspective will be very useful when we activate the power of interactive computing. Then it will be possible graphically to display results in three dimensions, or to display results successively in alternate dimensions. Additionally, the test taker can query the computer about similarity in specific occupations and the computer can calculate a response. Or the computer can first collect information about the relevant interest dimensions by administering a tailored set of items. At least, this latter flexibility is a possibility if we fully pursue the potentials in a multivariate approach to interest assessment.

ISSUES IN INTEREST ASSESSMENT

Attention is now given to several issues that remain to be resolved in our theoretical and practical use of interest inventories. The focus is on problems that continue to be nettlesome. Often these are issues that are not adequately addressed in the literature or by test authors. There are many other noncontroversial themes in interest measurement, such as test reliability and concurrent differences between occupations, that are well treated elsewhere and therefore deemphasized here. Most test manuals address these issues, and the evidence and implications are clear. Good general reviews are readily available (Campbell, 1971; Hansen, 1984a, 1984b; Holland, 1979, 1985; Walsh & Betz, 1985). In contrast, the issues that follow need more attention if we are to continue to see scientific and counseling advances in interest assessment.

Simplicity

Kuder (1970) gave this summation of how an interest inventory should be constructed: "A person who follows these principles should not be surprised if he produces a deceptively simple questionnaire which looks like something a junior high school student might have thrown together on a rainy Saturday afternoon. That's the way it *should* look!" (p. 255).

"Keep it simple" is also the recent admonition of Burisch (1984), who reviewed the payoffs from using personality scales of varying degrees of complexity. For interest measurement these results imply that the long tradition of psychometric sophistication may not be necessary. The article by Burisch should be at the top of the reading list for anyone considering building an interest inventory. Burisch contrasts three types of approaches to scale construction. In interest measurement the externalist builds the empirical, contrasted-groups occupational scale; the inductivist produces the homogeneous scale; and the deductivist uses the informed armchair approach, akin to Campbell and Holland's (1972) construction of the SCII General Occupational Theme Scales. Burisch concluded that the comparative studies he reviewed:

> revealed no consistent superiority of any strategy in terms of validity or predictive effectiveness. But deductive scales normally communicate information more directly to an assessor, and they are definitely more economical to build and administer. Thus, wherever there is a genuine choice, the simple deductive approach is recommended. Furthermore, self-rating scales narrowly but consistently outdo questionnaire scales in terms of validity and are clearly superior in terms of communicability and economy. There may not be many situations in which the widespread preference for questionnaires is justified. It is concluded that the more commonsensical approaches to personality measurement have a lot to offer. (p. 214)

In 1925 it was true that no one really knew how engineers and actors differed in their responses to inventory items. Today we do. It is intriguing to consider what an informed deductivist could do to construct an interest inventory. Do we really need to collect new data for each occupation? We have a quite satisfactory map of the occupational world and we know how, within general dimensions, to place an individual in that map. What we could really use is a technology for taking a new occupation and placing that occupation in the occupational space without extensive new collection of data. (It is possible that we already have it. Prediger, 1981, for example, can use Department of Labor job analysis data or the three-letter codes in Gottfredson, Holland, and Ogawa's, 1982 *Dictionary of Occupational Codes* to map any of the 12,099 unique occupations in the 4th Edition DOT; U.S. Department of Labor, 1977.)

Mapping the Occupational Space.   Measuring interests is a template problem. We match an individual's interests with the interests of groups of people in occupations. Fifty years ago there were few data about the specific pattern of interests within an occupation. So for each new occupation, it was necessary to build a new scale by collecting data from a new reference group. Today we have a vast amount of information about the interests of people in occupations. We have extensive maps about the occupational space. Now we can and should be asking whether every occupational prediction should start afresh with new data collection. Why not use our knowledge base to build templates of the occupational space? Approaches such as the ACT World of Work Map (Lamb & Prediger, 1981) and the Gottfredson et al. (1982) *Dictionary of Holland Occupational Codes* move us in this direction.

Are Occupational Scales Necessary?   Burisch (1984) highlighted three distinctive approaches to inventory construction; the long tradition of interest measurement has now produced several data sets where all three kinds of data coexist. Some common inventories having external, internal, *and* deductive scales are the SCII, CAI, and JVIS. They have a finite dimensionality, and there is clearly overlapping variance between the kinds of scales.

As this stage, it is illuminating to address the question of whether occupational scales are necessary. Historically, occupational scales, especially as pioneered in the SVIB and KOIS, have been the bedrock of interest measurement technology. Thus, it is now heresy to consider that we (counselors and theorists alike) might get along fine, with added benefits, if we set aside occupational scales.

The approach by Strong first, and Kuder later in the KOIS (1966), was to measure the similarity of a test taker to a particular occupational scale. Inherent in this approach are the common dimensions of similarity, say sales, as well as some *unique dimensions for that particular occupation*. This uniqueness came to be called *item subtlety* when transferred to the MMPI context (Meehl, 1945). In 1971 Jackson argued persuasively that item subtlety carries a much smaller measurement load than previously believed. This argument has rarely been explicitly addressed in the interest measurement literature, but it is just as relevant here.

Beginning in 1968 with the addition of Basic Interest Scales to the SVIB (Campbell, Borgen, Eastes, Johansson, & Peterson, 1968), and then in 1972 (Campbell & Holland), with the addition of Holland's General Occupational Theme scores, it has been easy to compare whether different types of scales tap different interest variance. The sequence of studies conducted suggests that a major of the variance in most of the occupational scales can be explained by using the homogeneous scales (Borgen, 1972; Reilly & Echternacht, 1979). This is evidence that for at least some occupational scales, there is no important unique variance.

Occupational Scales Can be Bootstrapped.   Jackson's (1977) bootstrapping of SCII-type occupational scales from his homogeneous basic scales demonstrates that it is quite possible to measure the occupational space with simple, communicable scales. Burisch (1984) most forcefully makes the case for simplicity, though he cites only Borgen (1972) as evidence in interest measurement. Surely, the success of Holland's approach is another general piece of evidence.

We need broad bandwidth measuring devices in counseling. If unique variance in occupations is at work, it is probably minor, and thus not of practical significance.

Instruments with a diversity of scale types have been commercially successful and appealing to counselors. They have an appealing face validity suggesting multiple utilities. In contrast, the scientific perspective suggests these diverse scale types are merely different ways of slicing the same pie, and can suggest a false sophistication. Look at all the enterprises that have been successful without empirical scales. Holland is the best example. He was able to be successful theoretically, because he was not conceptually dependent on the occupational scales.

Construct Validity: Bringing Theory to Interests

The history of interest measurement is notable for its practical potency and success, and yet virtual emptiness of psychological conceptualization. This is a history of the actuarial method, with its dustbowl empiricism and general avoidance of conceptualizing. Yet in many ways it has been clearly successful, first in the SVIB, and later in the MMPI. That tradition continues in two of the most popularly used inventories—the SCII and the KOIS. In contrast, Holland's theoretical and empirical work stands as a successful counterpoint to this tradition (Holland, 1985).

There's Much More to Know. Paradoxically, there is a vast literature of interest measurement, yet there is a much larger domain of what we do not know about interests. Part of this is because the model is actuarial, driven by a blind empiricism. Thus, much of what we have are a lot of facts. These facts have the form of "real estate sales people like sales activities and dislike science." Explanations for these facts are few. There is no theory of vocational interests. The empiricism is blind. At what age do realtors develop their patterns of interests? Most realtors dislike science. Is it necessary to dislike science in order to be a successful realtor?

Blind is Not Dumb. Blind empiricism is not dumb. It just does not focus on the total picture. As Meehl (1954) demonstrated in his classic monograph, actuarial methods set an achievement standard when the objective is prediction. It is quite possible to have an actuarial method that predicts well, and yet not understand fully why or how it works, what developmental process underlies it, and what psychological processes mediate its effects. Thus, interest inventories have enjoyed wide commercial success and counseling application, with lesser contributions to scientific knowledge as constructs.

Are Interests and Personality Linked? Are interests phenomena unto themselves, or are they linked to other psychological variables? It is my hunch that interests have important conceptual and empirical linkages to other domains in psychology (Holland, 1985, pp. 7–11). It is unfortunate that the vigor in the large literature of interest measurement has not extended to linking interest measurement to other domains such as personality, emotion, and motivation (Zajonc, 1980, 1984). An adequate effort has not been made to establish the extent of these linkages.

One gets a curious mix of signals in examining various writers' views of the relationship of vocational interests and personality measures. On the one hand, reviewers such as Hansen (1984a), have concluded that the relationship is minimal. Super's (1957) earlier conclusion was similar: "Personality traits seem to have no clear-cut and practical significant differential relation to vocational preference" (pp. 240–241). On the other hand, Holland's (1985) popular theory elevates interests to precisely a measure of personality, and his chapter 5 presents considerable evidence for his position. Given the centrality of Holland's position in current interest assessment and conceptualizing, the field is in big trouble if there is no demonstrable link between interests and personality.

Whereas Hansen (1984a) concluded from her review that "for the most part, correlational studies between interest scores and personality scores have been extremely disappointing" (p. 117), Costa, McCrae, and Holland (1984) concluded from their study that "personality dispositions show strong consistent associations with vocational interests" (p. 390). It is enlightening to examine how such disparate evaluations could appear in the same year. Such an examination reveals that the disparate opinions are based on similar empirical findings, which, in turn, are given quite different conceptual interpretations.

Hansen (1984a) did not have the benefit of the Costa et al. (1984) study in conducting her review. The Costa study is the best research to date on the linkage of interests and personality, and provides persuasive evidence on how interests and personality *are* and *are not* related. Closer scrutiny shows consistent results with the historical work reviewed by Hansen, but suggests a more optimistic cast to the work she has reviewed.

The results of the Costa et al. (1984) study deserve serious attention because their work is clearly the best study addressed to the relationships of personality and interests. Special strengths of their study were:

1. Use of a personality measure tapping the full range of major dimensions within a normal population.
2. Use of a personality inventory without explicit vocational interest items.
3. Use of a moderately large adult sample with a full age range.
4. Separate analyses for males and females.
5. Use of homogeneous interest dimensions rather than heterogeneous occupational scales.

6. A 6–month interval between administration of the personality inventory and the interest inventory, thus ensuring a conservative estimate of the relationship between interests and personality.

7. Supplementary assessment of personality with spouse ratings.

Costa et al's results.   Table 4.3 displays a summary of some of the Costa et al. (1984) results (recalculated from their Table 1); their correlation results for total SDS scales were averaged for males and females using the Fisher *z* transformation. Costa et al. have used major dimensions of interests and personality and identified major common variance across these domains. In addition, they have shown certain dimensions in each domain that are not linked to a counterpart in the other domain. Figure 4.4 portrays their results by representing a slice from the six-dimensional interest domain and a slice from the three-dimensional personality domain. The vertical lines in the figure depict the linkages. Corners of slices without vertical lines represent dimensions in their study without links across the two domains. Personality and vocational psychologists have sliced up the world of individual differences with their unique concepts, but they are often looking at the same world.

The lack of linkage of Neuroticism with interests explains why Hansen's review (1984a) concludes that previously research has often been disappointing. Much of the early work was based on traditional instruments where predominant variance taps primarily psychoticism and neuroticism. Costa et al. replicate this result. But they do find strong links for Extraversion and Openness to Experience, as does Hansen (1984a, pp. 117–118) in reviewing earlier work. She characterizes these results as limited, but I would agree with Costa et al.'s (1984)

TABLE 4.3
A Summation of the Costa et al. Results

Interest Scales	Personality Scales								
	Neuroticism			*Extraversion*			*Openness*		
	M	*F*	*Total*	*M*	*F*	*Total*	*M*	*F*	*Total*
Realistic									
Investigative							.33	.40	.36
Artistic							.49	.53	.51
Social				.50	.43	.46			
Enterprising				.65	.51	.58			
Conventional									

Note: Data adapted from Costa et al. (1984), Table 1, p. 395, by permission of Paul T. Costa, Jr. Copyright 1984 by the American Psychological Association. Significant correlations are shown for Self-Directed Search combined scales. Total correlations are averaged for males and females using the Fisher *z* transformation.

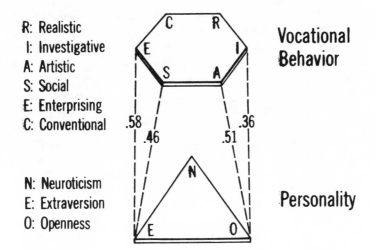

R: Realistic
I: Investigative
A: Artistic
S: Social
E: Enterprising
C: Conventional

Vocational
Behavior

N: Neuroticism
E: Extraversion
O: Openness

Personality

FIG. 4.4. Relationships between vocational behavior and personality as shown in Costa et al. (1984).

arguments that these are major dimensions of normal personality. Thus, I side with Costa et al.'s (1984) conclusion that "personality dispositions show strong consistent associations with vocational interests" (p. 390).

Predictive Validity of Interests: Are "Birds of a Feather" More Satisfied?

It is certainly an anomaly that interest inventories are so widely used, and yet as visible a figure in vocational psychology as Crites (1984) can speak so pessimistically about their value:

> In the past, measures of aptitudes and interests have been largely used to predict educational and vocational behaviors. The focus has been on estimating how well individuals can be expected to achieve academically or occupationally (scholastic and vocational aptitudes) and how long and how well satisfied they would be in different occupations interests). Unfortunately, the initial promise of these traditional instruments for prediction has been dimmed by their subsequent mediocre validity. As a consequence of their disappointing predictive validity, and with the advent of career development inventories, which focus more on career choice process than on content, there has been a marked shift in the use of tests and inventories from *prediction* to *description* (Zytowski, 1982). (p. 268)

How is it possible that Crites can be correct, and yet interest inventories are by far the most widely used inventories in career counseling (Engen et al., 1982; Zytowski & Warman, 1982), taken by an estimated 3.5 million people each year

(Tittle & Zytowski, 1978, p. xv)? Many people obviously believe interest inventories are useful. Interests seem to be an area with high face validity. Apparently, it is obvious to many counselors and clients that personal compatibility with one's job has something to do with happiness on the job. It must seem obvious to many that if you are interested in your job, you will be happier doing it. Thus, clear data showing predictive validity may have seemed almost superfluous. This section reexamines this core assumption of interest assessment, namely whether similarity of interests leads to job satisfaction.

This discussion of predictive validity is not intended to be comprehensive, but it touches on topics with heuristic potential. It reports on two important recent studies on interests and job satisfaction that are not published: a doctoral dissertation by Rounds (1981) and a convention paper by Gottfredson (1981). In each case they found significant predictive validity coefficients, but expressed a lack of enthusiasm about the magnitude of the effects. I suggest, for various methodological reasons, that these results should be counted as validation of the congruence assumption, certainly at the theoretical level, and perhaps also at the practical counseling level.

Gottfredson (1981).   Gottfredson studied the relationship of measured interests to job satisfaction of bank clerks hired by one firm. He seems generally to find the results disappointing. The actual data do not look as bad to me as his text suggests. Congruence correlated significantly with overall satisfaction (.28) and with the Job Descriptive Index (JDI; Smith, Kendall, & Hulin, 1969) work component (.27) but not the other JDI components. Moreover, the *conventional* scale correlated with overall job satisfaction (.32), whereas the *social* and *artistic* scales correlated negatively (−.21 and −.29) with satisfaction.

The pattern of the results seems to generally support the hypothesis, even though the size of the results is potentially disappointing for practical prediction for individuals. For example, the results for the JDI and overall satisfaction measures make sense, as does the lack of relationships with satisfaction with many of the demographic and miscellaneous predictors.

His "interesting" results for Expected Satisfaction—the highest correlations found with overall satisfaction (.55)—could be interpreted in terms of Watson and Clark's (1984) "negative affectivity." These results suggest a strong individual differences component in reporting positively, either prospectively or after time on the job. This component to job satisfaction may be a larger component of job satisfaction than previously realized. It suggests theoretical tests of job satisfaction should be prepared to control for individual differences in this often pervasive personality disposition.

Rounds (1981).   Rounds' dissertation is unusually complex, running to 346 pages, but addressed to the core issues of vocational psychology. His carefully designed study examined the relations between interests and needs (Dawis &

Lofquist, 1984) and the extent to which each separately was successful in predicting job satisfaction for a diverse group of vocational counseling clients. He found some validation for both, with correlations between SCII occupational scales and job satisfaction of .15 for males and .48 for females. For the SCII General Occupational Theme scales the correlations with job satisfaction were .28 for males and .27 for females (p. 199).

The Limits of Our Methods.   Rounds' (1981) and Gottfredson's (1981) studies demonstrate that it is extraordinarily difficult to do high quality research to address adequately the central questions of interest measurement. Specifically, they are testing whether person–job congruence leads to satisfaction. For several reasons this is a very demanding research paradigm:

1. It demands the meshing of three sets of variables: personal characteristics, job characteristics, and job satisfaction.
2. All of these areas have potential problems in conceptualization, appropriateness, and measurement.
3. The measurement of the match between personal characteristics and job characteristics is not simple or obvious. Witness the extensive research conducted by Dawis and Lofquist (1984) and their associates. It is conceivable that portions of the sets are more important to the matching template than others, and it is a continuing challenge to identify them. For example, perhaps it is essential for satisfaction of salespeople that they match the environment on liking sales, but unessential whether they match on interests in science (which happens to be a distinctive feature of salespeople).
4. All of the problems in validation of job measures are at work here (e.g., selection, restriction of range).
5. As is evident in Dawis' (1984) review, much about job satisfaction is not well understood. This is especially true at the conceptual, theoretical level, even though there are considerable descriptive data.

How High Do We Want Our Validity Coefficients to Be?   Gottfredson (1981) and Rounds (1981) conducted important and ambitious studies directed to the core question of the ability of interest measures to predict job satisfaction. While finding significant relationships, each expressed disappointment with the magnitude of the effects, implying that considerably larger correlations are desirable.

Their papers stimulated my thinking about what really would be the level of correlation one would expect. I have concluded that significant correlations of the order they have obtained (around .30) do not constitute a failure at all of the model theoretically, although they may cause some problems for the counseling use of instruments. Is it realistic, or even desirable, to expect validity coefficients of .60 and higher when testing the validity of interests for predicting satisfaction?

There are several reasons to expect modest empirical relationships between interests and job satisfaction (Lamb & Prediger, 1981; Spokane & Derby, 1979; Swaney & Prediger, 1985; Wallace, 1978; Wiener & Klein, 1978). By the laws of psychometrics, the reliabilities of the individual measures set a limit on the validity coefficients. High validity coefficients, around the limit permitted by the reliabilities of the measures, say .70, would mean that *all* the predictable variance in job satisfaction can be explained by interest–job congruence. Such a state of affairs would be an embarrassment (and a surprise) to theoretician and counselor alike. Such a result would say none of the behavioral variance needs a situational or sociological (Gottfredson, this volume) explanation. Aware modern theorists know that person–variables, such as interests, need explanatory help from situational variables. Moreover, problems with the criterion limit the size of validity coefficients that can be obtained. Finally, many people in career counseling are interested in the vocational change process and the process of exploration. If validity coefficients are too high, there is no variance left in the system to permit the change paradigm to operate.

Demonstrated relationships on the order of .30 for the congruence assumption should not discourage our theoretical efforts. For our counseling, they suggest appropriate caution about using interest results in isolation. For researchers, they point to one source for predicting career behavior, ultimately to be merged with other contributing sources.

Measured Interests and Expressed Choice

Recent work in personality assessment suggests considerable utility for self-assessments (Burisch, 1984; Shrauger & Osberg, 1981). In interest assessment there is a long history of assuming the superiority of measured interests over expressed choices. The wide use of interest inventories implies they provide some special information beyond asking the person, "What are you interested in as a career?" Early research showed that persons' answers to this question were inconsistent with their inventory results, so the evident "unreliability" of expressed choice led to the conclusion that measured interests had superior validity (Darley & Hagenah, 1955, p. 180). Then the seminal Dolliver (1969) and Holland and Lutz (1968) papers began a critical examination of the evidence for the common dogma of the superiority of measured interests. Subsequently, their evidence, and the questions they raised, have led to some 20 studies that give a new credence to the predictive value of expressed choice. This work is touched on in the following and in more detail elsewhere (Borgen & Seling, 1978; Holland, Magoon, & Spokane, 1981; Laing, Swaney, & Prediger, 1984; Slaney, 1984; Zytowski & Borgen, 1983).

The robust conclusion from the quite varied studies contrasting the validity of the two approaches is that expressed interests are at least as predictive of future career behavior as inventory results. This simple net box score might have been taken as evidence for abandoning interest inventories. Fortunately, more complex questions have subsequently been addressed beyond the net validities of each approach. These further inquiries have been productive in expanding both the counseling and theoretical frontiers of interest assessment.

Combined Validities of Expressed and Measured Interests.   Going beyond the comparative validity box score, studies examined inventories and expressed choices jointly as predictors (Bartling & Hood, 1981; Borgen & Seling, 1978; Cairo, 1982; Dolliver & Will, 1977; Holland & Gottfredson, 1975; Holland & Lutz, 1968; Laing et al., 1984; Touchton & Magoon, 1977). These studies are inspired by the pragmatic counseling question of what to trust—person or test—when they disagree. The results showed that when the two sources disagreed, expressed choices often had superior predictive or concurrent validity to measured interests. When they agreed, predictive validity was even better. For example, Borgen and Seling's (1978) results illustrate how dramatically the predictive payoff is enhanced by this joint use of the two kinds of information: If expressed and measured interests disagreed, hit rates in predicting career were 41% for expressed interests, but just 22% for measured (SVIB) interests; when both sources agreed, hit rate jumped to 70%.

Others have continued to study the interaction of expressed and measured interests with greater precision. Laing et al. (1984) moved beyond the dichotomous measure of congruence between expressed and measured interests. Using four distinct levels of congruence, they found, "The likelihood of persisting in an expressed choice increases systematically as congruence between measured interests and that choice increases" (pp. 309, 313).

Continued Pursuit.   The emerging evidence for the interactive effects of measured and expressed interests has spawned additional questions with theoretical and counseling import. For example, Slaney has established himself as the leader in the study of expressed interests. Through a series of studies he has successively examined crucial issues central to the counseling implications of expressed vocational interests. Slaney and Russell (1981) found that undergraduate women with low measured–expressed congruence were more undecided about their career choices than those with higher congruence. Following this clue of a relationship between changes in expressed choices and career indecision, Slaney (1983, 1984) demonstrated that changers were more likely to be initially career indecisive. With Slaney's and others' work, we now have the beginning of a nomological net spelling out some of the developmental processes in expressed career choice. Illustrating a quite different spinoff is the approach by Malett, Spokane, and Vance (1978), who developed a counseling intervention to increase the agreement between expressed and measured interests.

Implications and Applications.   There is continued promise from such new ways of looking at measured and expressed interests. They may enlarge our theoretical understanding of the very concept of vocational interests as well as guide the counseling process when the client's self-appraisals disagree with test results. Some immediate implications for counseling are suggested. The degree of match between the client's expressed and measured interests should determine the interpretive weight given to each source of information. When the client's expressed and measured interests agree, counselor and client can accept the interest results as confirmation of choices and increase their forecasting confidence. When expressed and measured interests disagree, counseling should move with caution, looking for alternative sources of information, or alternative counseling actions, such as exploration.

In summary, for theorists, there is an emerging picture of meaningful relationships among these various concepts. For counselors, there is information about how career indecision, expressed choices, and inventories might be *combined* to enhance understanding and prediction. For computer specialists and test developers, there is now an opportunity to combine these multiple sources of information in a more explicit and comprehensive prediction system. For theorists and researchers, there is a suggestion that the predictive validity of inventories will be enhanced if these moderator relationships are added. For example, the previous section discussed the Rounds (1981) and Gottfredson (1981) studies predicting job satisfaction from interests. Their work merits scrutiny from the perspective that interest inventories, in isolation, give an incomplete predictive picture, which can be significantly enhanced by adding expressed choices. In the main, the studies comparing expressed and inventoried interests predicted to occupational membership; the single exception is the study by Reeves and Booth (1979) predicting occupational *success*. Apparently, no study has yet been done predicting job satisfaction from the joint use of expressed and measured interests. It now seems plausible that the inclusion of expressed choices in such research will enhance the prediction, and thus lead to stronger confirmation of the link between interests and job satisfaction.

COMPUTERS AND THE FUTURE
OF INTEREST ASSESSMENT

There is no question that computers, especially micros, will have some dramatic impact on interest assessment in the 1990s, if not long before. What is not apparent is the shape of that influence. We can note some of the revolution now in process and view its immediate and near-term impacts. We can view the leading edges of these developments in recent books (Schwartz, 1984) or in journals such as *Computers in Psychiatry/Psychology*. We can also suggest some of the possible applications for hardware that is increasingly inexpensive, high-powered, and ubiquitous.

Hardware Without Practical Limits

The days when a Strong Vocational Interest Blank, with item scoring weights of −4 to +4, required 1 hour of scoring time by a skilled clerk are long past. With current, working technology (an optical reader and a microcomputer) the scoring is completed in seconds, slowed only by the speed of the printer producing the profile. Illustrating the scope of the hardware revolution, statistician Tukey (1985) says, "It will indeed soon be cheaper to do a million arithmetic operations than pay for one second of an investigator's or statistician's time" (p. 13). Wozniak, the engineering genius behind the first Apple computer, tells us ("What's Next," 1985) that the next revolutionary wave will be spawned by the optical laser disk:

> Ordinary video is a very interesting way to present information, (but) it's not interactive. It can quiz you and you answer yes or no, but it hasn't combined yet the full graphics of video with the interaction of the computer. The optical disk will be useful in that sort of education. After a few years it will just explode, and it will be a standard device on every personal computer because you can store such huge amounts of data. One little optical disk can store 400 megabytes of data on one side. Now we have to think, "What 400 megabytes would we want?" I did a calculation once for a full-size optical laser disk, and I found I could store 300 copies of the Encyclopaedia Britannica on it. With graphics and everything, I could only store one copy. (p. 2B)

Harris-Bowlsbey (1983), the developer of the Discover computerized guidance system, exalts the prospects for this technology: "The videodisc offers the potential to make 104,000 pictures available as an additional (and until this time totally unavailable) data file to the user as he or she decides about occupations or educational institutions" (p. 13).

The Commercial Paradigm

Most of the major inventories have entered the big-business world of exclusively computerized scoring. Single tests now generate millions of dollars for scoring services, authors, and copyright holders. Disruptions of these valuable relationships create major rumbles and echoes. Lawyers and managers have as much to say about the future of a test as do psychologists. Although the content often is no more public than hushed conversations at conventions, there has recently been—in salient public view—a wrenching transition with the Strong–Campbell Interest Inventory. The fallout has reached the courts, but the issue has not been resolved.

No less visible a journal than *Science* has chronicled Campbell's recent odyssey in seeking legal redress from his publisher (Holden, 1984, 1985). Without consulting Campbell, the SCII publisher, Stanford University Press, moved to terminate all previous scoring arrangements. The Press assigned all management and scoring responsibilities, including research and development, to Consulting Psychologists Press (CPP). Campbell sued Stanford University Press (Holden, 1984), hoping to halt the transfer to CPP. Dispositions abounded, even from researchers peripherally involved. In December, 1984, the judge dismissed Campbell's suit on the grounds that "Stanford's action did not depart from 'established practice' as Campbell alleged, and that Stanford did not transfer its 'interest' in the inventory since it still owns the copyrights" (Holden, 1985, p. 37).

The repercussions are several. National Computer Systems (NCS), previously the central scoring service for the SCII, lost a major portion of its business, with mail-in scoring of the SCII terminated after July 1, 1985. (NCS will continue to provide teleprocessing service.) Holland, whose VPI and SDS previously had been among the major tests distributed by CPP, changed publishers. The domino effects can be expected to continue.

High Tech and High Touch:
Trends of Development

Once upon a time there were pencil-and-paper tests. Counselors selected one or more (or none) as they thought appropriate. They used the test results in counseling in various ways (Goldman, 1971), most often informally. Counselors' predictions were often put together "clinically," despite the long-standing evidence (Meehl, 1954) that "using their heads" was typically inferior to "using the formula." In those low-tech days, some counselors were very skilled in using tests for their clients' benefits; alas, others were not, or just disinterested.

Now counseling assessment has gingerly entered the high-tech world, most often with the initiative and economic base of commercial entrepreneurs and creators. The economic incentives are considerable as computerized expert systems are developed to produce test interpretations as good or better than those of typical clinicians. "Cookbook" interpretations of many tests are now available at a fraction of the cost for like interpretations by an expensive clinician.

The emerging impact of the computer on vocational counseling and interest assessment can be grouped under four themes: (a) automation of conventional tests: administration and scoring; (b) computerized interpretation of conventional tests; (c) computerized guidance systems; and (d) computerized adaptive testing. The four topics are ordered by how completely the computerized potentials of each application have been realized. Automation, going back to Hankes' first scoring machine for the SVIB in 1946 (see Table 4.1 and also Klett & Pumroy, 1971), has long been with us. Most of the popular interest inventories are routinely computer-scored, and frequently accompanied by the computer's narrative interpretation and suggestions for career explorations. Total systems are now at work to guide the client in assessment and career planning. The fourth topic, adaptive testing, is yet to become a fully activated working reality for vocational interest assessment.

Computerized Guidance Systems. Computer-based systems emulating career counselors have become commonplace in counseling offices. Drier (1980) listed seven such systems. Two of the most popular are Discover and SIGI, described by their respective developers (Harris-Bowlsbey, 1983; Katz & Shatkin, 1983) in a special issue on the topic in a 1983 issue of *The Counseling Psychologist*. Other reviews are presented by Myers (1978), Sampson (1983), and Harris-Bowlsbey (1984). Evolution in these systems is continuing as their developers exploit the growing capacity of technology to store and present large amounts of occupational information.

Thus far, the extant systems are only vestigial expert systems. Although they do it very effectively, they are largely quick librarians looking up information. In the judgment of reviewers such as Cairo (1983), their capacity for interactive testing and decision making is minimal. Cairo laments, "Ironically, the computer has the capability of individualizing users' interactions on the basis of their responses to various system components, but evaluators seem to have rarely taken advantage of this capacity" (p. 58). Cairo also urges that more focus be given to evaluating, not just the popularity of the systems, but their impact on specific aspects of career development and the career decision-making process. He concludes: "The most significant finding to emerge from this review is that we still know very little about the impact that computer-assisted counseling systems have on the career development of users" (p. 57).

Thoughtware

The automation of paper-and-pencil tests has already had major practical and commercial impacts. If we now exploit the prospects for expert systems in vocational assessment and counseling, we may see qualitatively different payoffs in our science and practice.

Computers cause us to think about our models, especially if we do not use them merely to mimic traditional paper-and-pencil tests. Computers are digital, discrete, and linear. They are not naturally fuzzy, tentative, or ambiguous.

Adaptive, Tailored Testing. The computer gives us an opportunity to rethink how we do measurement. In traditional methods we tend to develop paper-and-pencil instruments to ask the same question, address the same issues, with all test takers. With the computer we have the opportunity to be selective, to tailor the assessment objectives more to the individual, even to change the issues during the course of the assessment. The whole process can become more individualized, and yet retain important nomothetic advantages.

Weiss (1983), who reminds us that Binet constructed the first adaptive test, summarizes the approach:

> Adaptive testing, also sometimes called tailored testing, involves the selection of test items during the process of administering a test so that the items administered to each individual are appropriate in difficulty for that individual. The result is a test that is "adapted" or "tailored" to each individual's ability or trait level during the process of test administration, so that the test is neither too easy or too difficult for the individual. (p. 5)

In presenting the state of the art using the latent trait model for computerized adaptive testing (CAT), Weiss' (1983) volume shows how the early work on CAT has been focused on ability measurement. One does not find a reference to personality in the Weiss book. Similarly, the special issue on Microcomputers in Educational Measurement in *Educational Measurement: Issues and Practice* (Brzezinski & Hiscox, 1984) is exclusively devoted to ability testing. The state of the art for CAT-based personality measurement is less advanced. Much of the latent trait work is concerned with a single dimension, while interest measurement is inherently a problem of classification within a multidimensioned space. This suggests that although the leading work done in CAT for ability measurement (such as evident in Weiss, 1983) may have heuristic value for interest measurement, a quite different conceptual approach may ultimately be most productive.

Adaptive assessment of interests would permit the test taker to specify the purposes of testing, and then answer an inventory tailored to that purpose. Some possible queries to such an "intelligent" interest inventory might include:

- "I want to compare myself with geologists."
- "I want to be a social worker. Do my interests say that would be a good choice?"
- "I want to explore occupations where few women have been employed."
- "I don't want to go to college. What are some possibilities for me?"

A Menu of Models.   Vocational psychology might benefit from an eclectic viewpoint. For psychotherapy, technical eclecticism has come to mean providing the client with the appropriate treatment for the client's particular circumstances. A future scenario for vocational counseling might permit the client to select (or be guided to) alternate models of career counseling. If there is evidence the client's interests are crystallized (e.g., the client has low vocational indecision, Slaney, 1984), then the matching actuarial model of interest measurement can be used. If the opposite is true, then the person would not be considered a good bet for the matching model and would shift over to a model emphasizing change, growth, development and/or exploration.

Serendipity. Research with computer-based testing and counseling should be energetically addressed, even if it turns out not to be commercially profitable. The effort, if pursued appropriately, will cause us to ask good questions and will teach us much that we do not currently know.

A NOT TOO SHORT LIST OF OPTIONS
FOR FUTURE TEST DEVELOPERS

If one were to start from scratch today to build an interest inventory, with generous resources, what issues should be addressed and how should they be resolved? Table 4.4 lists only some of the considerations that an aware developer of a contemporary interest inventory might consider. This chapter touches on many of these themes. Most of these topics have become salient in the last 20 years. Several of the choices a developer must make are of even more recent origin, generated by the impacts of high tech and big business on interest in-

TABLE 4.4
Some Decisions for Those Building an
Interest Inventory for the 1990s

Level of application: College vs. noncollege
Item types
Sex bias
   Item differences
   Norm groups
   Exploration in nontraditional occupations
Homogeneous vs. empirical scales
Retrospective vs. prospective models
Using prior tests and technologies
Simplicity vs. complexity
Multivariate models
Use of a classification system
Communication impact
User needs and acceptance
Secrecy of scoring system
Hand scoring vs. computer scoring
Microcomputer administration
Interactive assessment
Beyond interest measurement
   Work styles, values, needs
   Leisure activities
   Personality
   Career development
   Aspirations, expressed interests

ventories and their use. The list of choices facing E. K. Strong in preparing his 1927 inventory was different, and certainly shorter.

ACKNOWLEDGMENTS

I am grateful to the following colleagues who provided me with helpful comments on an earlier draft of this chapter: David Campbell, Linda Gottfredson, Jo-Ida Hansen, John Holland, Douglas Jackson, Charles Johansson, Patricia Lunneborg, Samuel Osipow, Dale Prediger, Bruce Walsh, and Donald Zytowski.

REFERENCES

AMEG Commission on Sex Bias in Measurement. (1977). A case history of change: A review of the responses to the challenge of sex bias in interest inventories. *Measurement and Evaluation in Guidance, 10,* 148–152.

The American College Testing Program. (1974). *Career planning program, grades 8–11, handbook.* Boston: Houghton Mifflin.

The American College Testing Program. (1984). *Vocational interest, experience and skill assessment user's handbook.* Iowa City: Author.

Bartling, H. C., & Hood, A. B. (1981). An 11-year follow-up of measured interest and vocational choice. *Journal of Counseling Psychology, 28,* 27–35.

Borgen, F. H. (1972). Predicting career choice of able college men from occupational and basic interest scales of the Strong Vocational Interest Blank. *Journal of Counseling Psychology, 19,* 202–211.

Borgen, F. H., & Bernard, C. B. (1982). [Review of *Strong–Campbell Interest Inventory Third Edition*]. *Measurement and Evaluation in Guidance, 14,* 208–212.

Borgen, F. H., & Seling, M. J. (1978). Expressed and inventoried interests re-visited: Perspicacity in the person. *Journal of Counseling Psychology, 25,* 536–543.

Brzezinski, E. J., & Hiscox, M. D. (Eds.). (1984). Microcomputers in educational measurement [special issue]. *Educational Measurement: Issues and Practice, 3*(2).

Burisch, M. (1984). Approaches to personality inventory construction. *American Psychologist, 39,* 214–227.

Buros, O. K. (Ed.). (1978). *The eighth mental measurements yearbook* (Vol. 1). Highland Park, NJ: Gryphon.

Cairo, P. C. (1982). Measured interests versus expressed interests as predictors of long-term occupational membership. *Journal of Vocational Behavior, 20,* 343–353.

Cairo, P. C. (1983). Evaluating the effects of computer-assisted counseling systems: A selective review. *The Counseling Psychologist, 11*(4), 55–59.

Campbell, D. P. (1968). The Strong Vocational Interest Blank: 1927–1967. In P. McReynolds (Ed.), *Advances in psychological assessment* (Vol. 1, pp. 105–131). Palo Alto, CA: Science and Behavior Books.

Campbell, D. P. (1971). *Handbook for the Strong Vocational Interest Blank.* Stanford, CA: Stanford University Press.

Campbell, D. P. (1972). The practical problems of revising an established psychological test. In J. N. Butcher (Ed.), *Objective personality assessment: Changing perspectives* (pp. 117–130). New York: Academic.

Campbell, D. P., Borgen, F. H., Eastes, S., Johansson, C. B., & Peterson, R. A. (1968). A set of Basic Interest Scales for the Strong Vocational Interest Blank for men. *Journal of Applied Psychology Monographs, 52,* (6, Pt. 2).

Campbell, D. P., & Hansen, J. C. (1981). *Manual for the SVIB–SCII* (3rd ed). Stanford, CA: Stanford University Press.

Campbell, D. P., & Holland, J. L. (1972). A merger in vocational interest research: Applying Holland's theory to Strong's data. *Journal of Vocational Behavior, 2,* 353–376.

Clark, K. E. (1961). *The vocational interests of nonprofessional men.* Minneapolis: University of Minnesota Press.

Cooley, W. W., & Lohnes, P. R. (1968). *Predicting development of young adults.* Palo Alto, CA: American Institutes for Research.

Costa, P. T., Jr., McCrae, R. R., & Holland, J. L. (1984). Personality and vocational interests in an adult sample. *Journal of Applied Psychology, 69,* 390–400.

Covington, J. E. (1982). [Review of *Jackson Vocational Interest Inventory*]. In J. T. Kapes & M. M. Mastie (Eds.), *A counselor's guide to vocational guidance instruments* (pp. 64–68). Falls Church, VA: National Vocational Guidance Association.

Crites, J. O. (1984). Instruments for assessing career development. In N. C. Gysbers (Ed.), *Designing careers* (pp. 248–274). San Francisco: Jossey–Bass.

Darley, J. G., & Hagenah, T. (1955). *Vocational interest measurement.* Minneapolis: University of Minnesota Press.

Dawis, R. V. (1984). Job satisfaction: Worker aspirations, attitudes, and behaviors. In N. C. Gysbers (Ed.), *Designing careers* (pp. 275–301). San Francisco: Jossey–Bass.

Dawis, R. V., & Lofquist, L. H. (1984). *A psychological theory of work adjustment: An individual differences model and its applications.* Minneapolis: University of Minnesota Press.

Diamond, E. E. (Ed.). (1975). *Issues of sex bias and sex fairness in career interest measurement.* Washington, DC: National Institute of Education.

Dolliver, R. H. (1969). Strong Vocational Interest Blank versus expressed occupational interests: A review. *Psychological Bulletin, 72,* 94–107.

Dolliver, R. H., & Will, J. (1977). Ten-year follow-up of the Tyler Vocational Card Sort and the Strong Vocational Interest Blank. *Journal of Counseling Psychology, 24,* 48–54.

Drier, H. N. (1980). Career information for youth in transition: The need, systems, and models. *Vocational Guidance Quarterly, 29,* 135–143.

Engen, H. B., Lamb, R. R., & Prediger, D. J. (1982). Are secondary schools still using standardized tests? *Personnel and Guidance Journal, 60,* 287–290.

Freud, S. (1977). *Introductory lectures on psychoanalysis.* New York: W. W. Norton. (Original work published 1920).

Goldman, L. (1971). *Using tests in counseling.* Englewood Cliffs, NJ: Prentice-Hall.

Gottfredson, G. D. (1981, August). *Why don't interests predict job satisfaction better than they do?* Paper presented at meeting of American Psychological Association, Los Angeles.

Gottfredson, G. D., Holland, J. L., & Ogawa, D. K. (1982). *Dictionary of Holland occupational codes.* Palo Alto, CA: Consulting Psychologists.

Gysbers, N. C. (Ed.). (1984). *Designing careers.* San Francisco: Jossey-Bass.

Hansen, J. C. (1984a). The measurement of vocational interests: Issues and future directions. In S. D. Brown & R. W. Lent (Eds.), *Handbook of counseling psychology* (pp. 99–136). New York: Wiley.

Hansen, J. C. (1984b). Interest inventories. In G. Goldstein & M. Hersen (Eds.), *Handbook of psychological assessment* (pp. 157–177). New York: Pergamon.

Hanson, G. R. (1974). *Assessing the career interests of college youth: Summary of research and applications* (ACT Research Report No. 67). Iowa City: The American College Testing Program.

Harris-Bowlsbey, J. (1983). The computer and the decider. *The Counseling Psychologist, 11*(4), 9–14.

Harris-Bowlsbey, J. (1984). The computer as a tool in career guidance programs. In N. C. Gysbers, (Ed.), *Designing careers* (pp. 362–383). San Francisco: Jossey-Bass.

Holden, C. (1984). Test-maker sues Stanford. *Science, 226,* 325.

Holden, C. (1985). Psychologist's suit dismissed. *Science, 227,* 37.

Holland, J. L. (1958). A personality inventory employing occupational titles. *Journal of Applied Psychology, 42,* 336–342.

Holland, J. L. (1970). *The Self-Directed Search: A guide to educational and vocational planning.* Palo Alto: Consulting Psychologists.

Holland, J. L. (1973). *Making vocational choices: A theory of careers.* Englewood Cliffs, NJ: Prentice-Hall.

Holland, J. L. (1977). *Manual for the Vocational Preference Inventory.* Palo Alto, CA: Consulting Psychologists.

Holland, J. L. (1979). *The Self-Directed Search: Professional manual.* Palo Alto, CA: Consulting Psychologists.

Holland, J. L. (1985). *Making vocational choices: A theory of vocational personalities & work environments* (2nd ed). Englewood Cliffs, NJ: Prentice-Hall.

Holland, J. L., & Gottfredson, G. D. (1975). Predictive value and psychological meaning of vocational aspirations. *Journal of Vocational Behavior, 6,* 349–363.

Holland, J. L., & Lutz, S. W. (1968). The predictive value of a student's choice of vocation. *Personnel and Guidance Journal, 46,* 428–436.

Holland, J. L., Magoon, T. M., & Spokane, A. R. (1981). Counseling psychology: Career interventions, research, and theory. *Annual Review of Psychology, 32,* 279–305.

Holland, J. L., Whitney, D. R., Cole, N. S., & Richards, J. M., Jr. (1969). *An empirical occupational classification derived from a theory of personality and intended for practice and research* (ACT Research Report No. 29). Iowa City: The American College Testing Program.

Jackson, D. N. (1971). The dynamics of structured personality tests: 1971. *Psychological Review, 78,* 229–248.

Jackson, D. N. (1976). *Jackson Personality Inventory manual.* Port Huron, MI: Research Psychologists.

Jackson, D. N. (1977). *Manual for the Jackson Vocational Interest Survey.* Port Huron, MI: Research Psychologists.

Jackson, D. N., Holden, R. R., Locklin, R. H., & Marks, E. (1984). Taxonomy of vocational interests of academic major areas. *Journal of Educational Measurement, 21,* 261–275.

Jackson, D. N., & Williams, D. R. (1975). Occupational classification in terms of interest patterns. *Journal of Vocational Behavior, 6,* 269–280.

Johansson, C. B. (1975). *Manual for the Career Assessment Inventory.* Minneapolis: National Computer Systems.

Johansson, C. B. (1982). *Manual for the Career Assessment Inventory* (2nd ed.). Minneapolis: National Computer Systems.

Katz, M. R., & Shatkin, L. (1983). Characteristics of computer-assisted guidance. *The Counseling Psychologist, 11*(4), 15–31.

Klett, C. J., & Pumroy, D. K. (1971). Automated procedures in psychological assessment. In P. McReynolds (Ed.), *Advances in psychological assessment* (Vol. 2, pp. 105–131). Palo Alto, CA: Science and Behavior Books.

Knapp, R. R., & Knapp, L. (1974). *California Occupational Preference System Interest Inventory.* San Diego, CA: EdITS.

Kuder, G. F. (1966). The Occupational Interest Survey. *Personnel and Guidance Journal, 45,* 72–77.

Kuder, G. F. (1970). Some principles of interest measurement. *Educational and Psychological Measurement, 30,* 205–26.

Kuder, G. F. (1977). Career matching. *Personnel Psychology, 30,* 1–4.

Kuhn, T. S. (1970). *The structure of scientific revolutions* (2nd ed.). Chicago: University of Chicago Press.

Laing, J., Swaney, K., & Prediger, D. J. (1984). Integrating vocational interest results and expressed choices. *Journal of Vocational Behavior, 25,* 304–315.

Lamb, R. R., & Prediger, D. J. (1981). *Technical report for the unisex edition of the ACT Interest Inventory (UNIACT).* Iowa City: American College Testing Program.

Loevinger, J. (1957). Objective tests as instruments of psychological theory. *Psychological Reports, 3,* 635–694.

Lohnes, P. R. (1982). [Review of *Career Assessment Inventory*]. In J. T. Kapes & M. M. Mastie (Eds.), *A counselor's guide to vocational guidance instruments* (pp. 53–57). Falls Church, VA: National Vocational Guidance Association.

Lunneborg, C. E., & Lunneborg, P. W. (1975). Factor structure of the vocational interest models of Roe and Holland. *Journal of Vocational Behavior, 7,* 313–326.

Lunneborg, C. E., & Lunneborg, P. W. (1977). Is there room for a third dimension in vocational interest differentiation? *Journal of Vocational Behavior, 11,* 120–127.

Lunneborg, C. E., & Lunneborg, P. W. (1978). Improved counseling information through rotation of discriminant functions. *Educational and Psychological Measurement, 38,* 737–754.

Lunneborg, P. W. (1979). The Vocational Interest Inventory: Development and validation. *Educational and Psychological Measurement, 39,* 445–451.

Lunneborg, P. W. (1980). Reducing sex bias in interest measurement at the item level. *Journal of Vocational Behavior, 16,* 226–234.

Lunneborg, P. W. (1981). *The Vocational Interest Inventory Manual.* Los Angeles: Western Psychological Services.

Malett, S. D., Spokane, A. R., & Vance, F. L. (1978). The effects of vocationally relevant information on the expressed and measured interests of freshmen males. *Journal of Counseling Psychology, 25,* 292–305.

Meehl, P. E. (1945). The dynamics of structured personality tests. *Journal of Clinical Psychology, 1,* 296–303.

Meehl, P. E. (1954). *Clinical versus statistical prediction: A theoretical analysis and a review of the evidence.* Minneapolis: University of Minnesota Press.

Mitchell, S. K., Lunneborg, P. W., & Lunneborg, C. E. (1971). Vocational Interest Inventory based on Roe's interest areas. *Proceedings, 79th Annual Convention of the American Psychological Association,* 569–570.

Myers, R. A. (1978). Exploration with the computer. *The Counseling Psychologist, 7*(3), 51–55.

Osipow, S. H. (1983). *Theories of career development* (3rd ed.). Englewood Cliffs, NJ: Prentice-Hall.

Parsons, F. (1909). *Choosing a vocation.* Boston: Houghton Mifflin.

Paterson, D. G., & Darley, J. G. (1936). *Men, women and jobs: A study in human engineering.* Minneapolis: University of Minnesota Press.

Pervin, L. A. (1968). Performance and satisfaction as a function of individual-environment fit. *Psychological Bulletin, 69,* 56–68.

Prediger, D. J. (1976). A world-of-work map for career exploration. *Vocational Guidance Quarterly, 24,* 198–208.

Prediger, D. J. (1981). Mapping occupations and interests: A graphic aid for vocational guidance and research. *Vocational Guidance Quarterly, 30,* 21–36.

Prediger, D. J. (1982). Dimensions underlying Holland's hexagon: Missing link between interests and occupations? *Journal of Vocational Behavior, 21,* 259–287.

Reeves, D. J., & Booth, R. F. (1979). Expressed vs inventoried interests as predictors of paramedical effectiveness. *Journal of Vocational Behavior, 15,* 155–163.

Reilly, R. R., & Echternacht, G. J. (1979). Validation and comparison of homogeneous and occupational interest scales. *Applied Psychological Measurement, 3,* 177–185.

Roe, A. (1956). *The psychology of occupations.* New York: Wiley.

Rounds, J. B., Jr. (1981). The comparative and combined utility of need and interest data in the prediction of job satisfaction (Doctoral dissertation, University of Minnesota, 1981). *Dissertation Abstracts International, 42,* 4920–B.

Rounds, J. B., Jr., & Tinsley, H. E. A. (1984). Diagnosis and treatment of vocational problems. In S. D. Brown & R. W. Lent (Eds.), *Handbook of counseling psychology* (pp. 137–177). New York: Wiley.

Sampson, J. P. (1983). An integrated approach to computer applications in counseling psychology. *The Counseling Psychologist, 11*(4), 65–74.

Schlossberg, N. K., & Goodman, J. (1972). Imperative for change: Counselor use of the Strong Vocational Interest Blanks. *Impact, 2,* 25–29.

Schwartz, M. D. (Ed.). (1984). *Using computers in clinical practice.* New York: Haworth.

Shrauger, J. S., & Osberg, T. M. (1981). The relative accuracy of self-prediction and judgments by others in psychological assessment. *Psychological Bulletin, 90,* 322–351.

Slaney, R. B. (1983). Influence of career indecision on treatments exploring the vocational interests of college women. *Journal of Counseling Psychology, 30,* 55–63.

Slaney, R. B. (1984). Relation of career indecision to changes in expressed vocational interests. *Journal of Counseling Psychology, 31,* 349–355.

Slaney, R. B., & Russell, J. E. A. (1981). An investigation of different levels of agreement between expressed and inventoried vocational interests among college women. *Journal of Counseling Psychology, 28,* 221–228.

Smith, P. C., Kendall, L. M., & Hulin, C. L. (1969). *The measurement of satisfaction in work and retirement.* Chicago: Rand McNally.

Spokane, A. R., & Derby, D. P. (1979). Congruence, personality pattern, and satisfaction in college women. *Journal of Vocational Behavior, 15,* 36–42.

Strong, E. K., Jr. (1927). Vocational interest test. *Educational Record, 8,* 107–121.

Super, D. E. (1957). *The psychology of careers: An introduction to vocational development.* New York: Harper & Brothers.

Swaney, K., & Prediger, D. J. (1985). The relationship between interest-occupation congruence and job satisfaction. *Journal of Vocational Behavior, 26,* 13–24.

Tittle, C. K., & Zytowski, D. G. (Eds.). (1978). *Sex-fair interest measurement: Research and implications.* Washington, DC: National Institute of Education.

Touchton, J. B., & Magoon, T. M. (1977). Occupational daydreams as predictors of vocational plans for college women. *Journal of Vocational Behavior, 10,* 156–166.

Tukey, J. W. (1985). Comment. *American Statistician, 39*(1), 12–14.

U.S. Department of Labor. (1977). *Dictionary of Occupational Titles* (4th ed.). Washington, DC: Government Printing Office.

Wallace, D. L. (1978). A validation study of the unisex form of the ACT Interest Inventory at the University of Southern Mississippi. *Dissertation Abstracts International, 39,* 5338-A. (University Microfilms No. 79-05154)

Walsh, W. B., & Betz, N. E. (1985). *Tests and assessment.* Englewood Cliffs, NJ: Prentice-Hall.

Watson, D., & Clark, L. A. (1984). Negative affectivity: The disposition to experience aversive emotional states. *Psychological Bulletin, 96,* 465–490.

Weiss, D. J. (Ed.). (1983). *New horizons in testing: Latent trait test theory and computerized adaptive testing.* New York: Academic.

What's next? Computer "explosion" in the schools. (1985, January 23). *USA Today,* p. 2B.

Wiener, Y., & Klein, K. L. (1978). The relationship between vocational interests and job satisfaction: Reconciliation of divergent results. *Journal of Vocational Behavior, 13,* 298–304.

Zajonc, R. B. (1980). Feeling and thinking: Preferences need no inferences. *American Psychologist, 35,* 151–175.

Zajonc, R. B. (1984). On the primacy of emotion. *American Psychologist, 39,* 117–123.

Zytowski, D. G. (1982). Assessment in the counseling process for the 1980s. *Measurement and Evaluation in Guidance, 15,* 15–21.

Zytowski, D. G. (1985). *Kuder Occupational Interest Survey manual supplement.* Chicago: Science Research Associates.

Zytowski, D. G., & Borgen, F. H. (1983). Assessment. In W. B. Walsh & S. H. Osipow (Eds.), *Handbook of vocational psychology: Vol. 2. Applications* (pp. 5–45). Hillsdale, NJ: Lawrence Erlbaum Associates.

Zytowski, D. G., & Warman, R. E. (1982). The changing use of tests in counseling. *Measurement and Evaluation in Guidance, 15,* 147–152.

5

Special Groups and the Beneficial Use of Vocational Interest Inventories

Linda S. Gottfredson
Center for Social Organization of Schools
Johns Hopkins University

RECENT CONCERNS ABOUT TEST USAGE
AND SPECIAL GROUPS

A dominant issue in vocational and counseling psychology since at least the 1970s has been whether or not traditional counseling methods are appropriate for women, minorities, and other special groups. The issue of appropriate treatment remains a lively one in many areas of social life, because large differences remain in education, occupation, and income by ethnic group, race, and sex, despite the elimination of most blatant forms of unfair discrimination.

Intensive efforts have been made to expunge potential sources of bias from counselor behavior and from the tools they use. Good rapport and effective interpersonal communication are generally understood to be essential for successful counseling and, not surprisingly, considerable attention has been given in the field to determining the effects on the counseling process of interracial or cross-gender counseling, counselor attitudes, counselee expectations, and cultural differences (Atkinson, Morten, & Sue, 1979; Casas, 1984; Schlossberg & Pietrofesa, 1978), and to developing guidelines for counseling women (Richardson & Johnson, 1984) and for becoming a "culturally skilled" counselor (Sue, 1981).

Counseling *tools*, as well as the counseling *process*, have also received considerable attention. Sexist language and stereotyped depictions of different ethnic groups, races, and sexes have been eliminated from informational booklets and materials. Assessment devices have been important tools in educational and career counseling, and so they too have been objects of scrutiny and controversy. Counselors use a variety of standardized assessments, including interest, aptitude, vocational maturity, and personality tests. Controversy over standardized

127

testing has engulfed the whole of psychology, but because vocational interest inventories have held an especially prominent place in the counselor's armamentarium, they have been the objects of most controversy in vocational and counseling psychology.

This chapter examines the appropriateness of interest inventories in counseling members of special groups and explores how interest inventories might be used beneficially in the career counseling of both minority and majority populations. These issues are pursued in three sections. The first section outlines recent concerns about special groups and the impact those concerns have had on the structure of interest inventories and on perceptions of the role interest inventories do or should play in the counseling process. Some parallels are shown between the controversy over interest inventories and the controversy over another frequent form of psychological assessment (intelligence testing) in educational and occupational settings. An examination of the special-groups literature then provides the backdrop for understanding past problems and future directions for interest measurement, particularly as it applies to disadvantaged social groups. The second section suggests that the use of any counseling tool, including inventories, can be improved by a more analytical understanding of the career choice problems that people have. Drawing on previous research and speculation, the author outlines the risk factors that predispose special groups toward higher rates of career choice problems, and then a problem analysis framework is presented that helps to clarify the problems any particular counselee may be facing, including those problems that may be generated by some special group status. The final section of the chapter proposes nine principles for the beneficial use of interest inventories for both minority and majority populations.

Impact of the Testing Controversy

Just as the concern for special groups in the field of counseling echoes wider social concerns of the last few decades, so too the controversy over interest measurement (Diamond, 1975; Tittle & Zytowski, 1978) can be seen as one manifestation of the larger movement questioning the fairness of psychological tests (Jensen, 1980; Samuda, 1975). The fairness of mental (e.g., intelligence) tests is both an older and more hotly debated topic than is the fairness of interest inventories, but the parallels between the two issues put the interest inventory controversy in a broader perspective.

Mental tests came under fire largely because they show large race differences in mental abilities. Likewise, interest inventories came under fire largely because they show sex differences in vocational interests. Not all measures that indicate race or sex differences are controversial, but mental tests and interest inventories are widely used, they measure traits that are important in life, and they frequently figure in educational and occupational decision making. The initial criticism of both types of test was that they may mismeasure the abilities or interests of some social groups and, specifically, that mental tests may be biased against blacks and other ethnic minorities, and that interest tests may be biased against women. Further criticisms of interest inventories were that fewer and lower status occupational scales were provided for women, and that interpretive materials were replete with sex stereotypes that might further constrict the vocational choices of females (Birk, 1975). Bias against the physically handicapped appears not to have been an issue, although special provisions are often made for testing the deaf, blind, and otherwise functionally impaired.

Criticisms of those tests have brought about changes in the tests themselves and in beliefs about how they should be used, if at all, under different circumstances. In the case of interest inventories, the criticisms led quickly to the production of guidelines for supposedly sex-fair measurement (Tittle & Zytowski, 1978, Appendix A) which, although not having the force of law, raised the specter of legal action against publishers who did not comply with those guidelines. Whether out of agreement with the guidelines or out of the fear of legal action, and probably for both reasons, publishers made numerous changes in the major inventories within a matter of a few years. The criticisms of established inventories also led to experimentation with new inventories, such as the Unisex Interest Inventory which utilizes more highly "sex-balanced" scales (Hanson & Rayman, 1976; Rayman, 1976). In regard to mental tests, criticisms have led to considerable legal and regulatory activity. Some states are now legally prohibited from using intelligence tests for some educational purposes (e.g., for assigning students to classes for the educable mentally retarded) and other states have voluntarily curtailed their use. Testing in employment settings has also declined, apparently in large part because of stricter and more costly validation standards (Tenopyr, 1981). Criticisms of mental tests have resulted in only occasional minor changes in the major tests, but have stimulated the development of new tests or testing systems such as The System of Multicultural Pluralistic Assessment (SOMPA; Mercer, 1979). There is considerable debate about whether the foregoing changes are beneficial or scientifically justified (Gordon, 1980a, 1980c; Schmidt & Hunter, 1981), but that there have been changes cannot be denied.

A frequent criticism has been that tests have been developed and standardized primarily with whites (for mental tests) and white males (for interest inventories). In response to this criticism, standardization samples for mental tests now include a representative proportion of minorities (Gordon & Rudert, 1979, p. 179) and parallel male and female standardization samples now are routinely sought for occupational scales in interest inventories (Campbell & Hansen, 1981).

Another criticism has been that test items themselves may be culture-bound. As a result, some items in the well established tests that appear on the surface to be biased have been eliminated—for example the ugliness item in some mental tests. In addition, all test items in the major mental tests produced today are submitted to panels of minority psychologists and other interested groups for scrutiny, and all items which those groups find offensive or otherwise questionable are eliminated (Educational Testing Service Board of Trustees, 1984; Jensen, 1980, p. 642). Similarly, all gender-specific titles in interest inventories have been changed to be gender-neutral (e.g., policeman to police officer). Another specific complaint regarding cultural bias has been that some types of test items presume that all people have had the same opportunity to exercise the interests and abilities being measured when, in fact, such opportunities may not have been equally accessible to all types of people. Attempts to characterize mental tests according to their culture fairness or culture "loadedness" (Jensen, 1980) reflect this concern. Responses to this issue with interest inventories have taken several forms. One widespread response has been to develop more "sex-balanced" scales, that is, to find items that men and women respond to at equal rates or to balance a female-favored item with a male-favored item in the same scale. It should be noted, however, that one eminent psychometrician (Cronbach, 1984) has criticized this response because it "falsifies the report of interests by refusing to count whatever part of the content domain is unappealing to females" (p. 440). A second approach has been to liberalize instructions so that one need not have had the opportunity to perform some activity but only be interested in trying the activity for an interest to be registered on the inventory.

Whether to norm, and how, has also been an issue. It is still generally considered inappropriate to norm mental tests separately for different social groups, although some of the newer mental tests nevertheless do so (Mercer, 1979). However, sex-specific or race-specific norms are sometimes employed when making decisions with mental test scores in educational and employment settings. For example, the frequently advocated practice of ranking minorities and whites separately by test scores and then selecting proportionately from both lists (one form of quotas) is tantamount to using separate norms in the first place to calculate the scores of minorities and whites. In contrast, separate norms by sex are now provided by most interest inventories. Both the Strong–Campbell Interest Inventory (SCII; Campbell & Hansen, 1981) and the Kuder Occupational Interest Survey (KOIS; Kuder & Diamond, 1979) provide occupational scale and general theme, or interest areas scores, on both the male and female norms for all test takers and, although Holland argues that raw scores are more appropriate for the scales of the Self-Directed Search (SDS), which is consistent with Cronbach's (1984, p. 422) endorsement of raw scores, the SDS manual provides the data by which counselors can use sex norms if they so desire (Holland, 1979a, Appendix C). The issue of norming is complex and differs for occupational versus basic theme scales, and it has been one of the most heated in the interest inventory controversy. Norming has generated much research but, in general, there is no solution to the norming problem that enjoys a consensus, so different inventories have tackled the matter differently.

Another issue has been whether all test takers should be given exactly the same test and, in this regard, more interest inventories have now become like current mental tests. Different test items are of necessity required for testing the mental capabilities of different age groups, but otherwise all test takers take exactly the same test and receive scores on the same scales. In the past, some major interest inventories such as the Strong Vocational Interest Blank (SVIB) had different forms for the two sexes (Campbell & Hansen, 1981), but it is now standard practice to provide the same assessment form and report scores on the same scales to all people taking an interest inventory. The only exceptions to this rule are the separate assessment procedures that have been established for the physically handicapped. For example, the SDS has a version for the sight-impaired (Holland, 1979a, p. 8). It also should be noted, however, that the male and female scales for the same occupation on the SCII are composed of some-what different items. Also, although Zytowski and Laing (1978) have provided evidence that scores on opposite-sex scales on the KOIS are valid, and although the *User's Guide* for the SCII (Hansen, 1984b) suggests techniques for interpreting opposite-sex occupational scales, earlier concerns about their interpretability (Johansson & Harmon, 1972; Lunneborg, 1975) linger. This, in turn, makes it relevant to note that a few occupations on recent versions of the SCII and Kuder have norms for only one sex (Campbell & Hansen, 1981; Kuder & Diamond, 1979), although the proportion of such occupations is small in the newly revised versions discussed in previous chapters of this book.

Finally, interpretive materials, which include the test manual as well as any reporting forms and accessory interpretive brochures, have been altered to avoid pigeonholing or stereotyping people because of their test scores or in other ways. Manuals and handbooks for mental tests (Matarazzo, 1972) are replete with admonitions to remember that test scores are not perfectly reliable, that people may change, and that many factors determine one's suitability for different kinds of employment. And interest inventory materials, for example, are now careful to point out that all jobs are suitable for all races and sexes and that stereotyping and past socialization should be considered in interpreting interest scores; they are also careful to present all races and sexes in an equally positive and non-stereotyped manner and to encourage exploration of diverse occupational alternatives.

Despite the recent changes in test content, standardization samples, and interpretive materials, sizeable race differences in responses to many test items and total scale scores remain on mental tests (Jensen, 1980) and sex differences remain on interest inventories (Campbell & Hansen, 1981; Holland, 1979a; Kuder & Diamond, 1979). For example, changes in the SDS to make its wording gender-neutral appear to have had little or no effect on item responses (Boyd, 1978). Extensively liberalized SDS instructions have produced only minor profile differences; they have failed to increase test-taker satisfaction; and they have failed to increase the number of options or the number of nontraditional options a college woman considers (Holland, 1979a, p. 54).

The failure of interest inventory modifications to change inventory outcomes is not surprising in view of the fact that *different* inventories all appear to have *equivalent* effects on test takers, despite those inventories' use of different norms, scaling procedures, and interpretive procedures (Holland, Magoon, & Spokane, 1981). The lack of effect of inventory modifications may also seem less surprising, in hindsight, by noting that vocational interests are quite stable at both the individual and aggregate levels: specifically, interests are quite stable after high school graduation and the interests of men-in-general and of women-in-general have changed little or not at all from 1930 to 1980 (Hansen, 1984a), 5 decades that span considerable social change. Sex differences in occupational values also seem to have remained quite stable during periods of social change (Herzog, 1982). And if social learning theories of vocational decision making (Mitchell & Krumboltz, 1984) are to be taken seriously, if the special-groups literature is correct that socialization to sex-typed vocational choices is essentially a pervasive, consistent, and enduring feature of people's environments, and if people continue to highly value and to try to implement their gender self-concepts in the occupational sphere (Gottfredson, 1981), then it seems unrealistic to have expected that recent changes in interest inventories would significantly diminish sex differences in occupational preferences (Boyd, 1978; Gottfredson, 1982).

Research findings about bias in mental tests and in interest inventories have also been parallel in some important respects. It is still widely believed that intelligence tests are culturally biased, but the research has shown conclusively that mental tests are not biased against blacks and other native-born English-speaking minorities. Similarly, many people assume that "it is probable that all existing career interest inventories are sex biased to some degree" (Fitzgerald & Crites, 1980, p. 51). Although the evidence regarding interest inventories is less extensive, and so less definitive, than that for mental tests, that research has also failed to confirm cultural or sex bias in major interest inventories such as the KOiS, the SDS, and the SCII. The SVIB, which was the forerunner of the SCII, may have been sex biased by definition, because it had separate forms for males and females that shared only 40% of their items in common, and because it reported scores on many fewer occupational scales for females than for males.

The research has also made clear that the superficial appearance of bias often has little relation to the real existence of bias (Gordon & Rudert, 1979). With regard to mental tests, for example, it had been widely assumed that culture-loaded or language-loaded mental tests are especially biased against blacks. However, culture-loaded mental tests have not been shown to be culturally biased, and black–white differences are no larger on such tests than they are on culture–reduced (e.g., performance) tests (Gordon, 1984, p. 467; Linn, 1982, p. 366). The evidence regarding interest inventories suggests that gender-specific items are not biased as had been widely assumed (Boyd, 1978; Gottfredson, 1976), although counselees and counselors alike rate less favorably the tests that include such items (Boyd, 1978). Similarly, the fact that test scores differ by social group is not by itself evidence that tests are biased.

The foregoing conclusions about lack of test bias are not universally accepted by any means, partly because many people are more concerned about test *fairness* than about test *bias* (Datta, 1978), the former referring to sociopolitical goals and the latter to the properties of a test. Bias in a test "refers to systematic errors in the *predictive validity* or the *construct validity* of test scores of individuals that are associated with the individual's group membership" (Jensen, 1980, p. 375). In contrast, *fairness* is often a term used to refer to equal distributions of outcomes across groups rather than (or in addition to) equal treatment or unbiased measurement.

Criteria used to assess test bias have been grouped under two general headings—internal and external validity. The former refers to the internal structure of a test and the latter to the relation of test scores to other performances that the test theoretically should predict. Research on internal validity shows that neither mental tests nor interest inventories are culturally or sexually biased. For example, the factor structure of mental tests is the same for blacks, Hispanics, Jews, white Gentiles, males, females, and different social classes (Gordon, 1984; Gordon & Rudert, 1979; Hennessy & Merrifield, 1976; Jensen, 1980, chapter 11), and the structure of interests is also largely the same by sex, race, social class, and language of inventory taken by bilingual persons (Cole, 1973; Fouad, Cudeck, & Hansen, 1984; Hansen, 1984a; Hanson & Cole, 1973; Harmon, 1975; Lamb, 1978; Smith, 1983; Weinrach, 1984).

Research on the external validity of mental tests also has failed to reveal bias. For example, extensive research shows that mental tests predict both educational and occupational performance equally well for blacks, Hispanics and whites (Gordon & Rudert, 1979; Hunter, Schmidt, & Rauschenberger, 1984; Jensen, 1980; Linn, 1982). The predictive bias that does exist stems largely from test unreliability and *favors* blacks when common regression equations are used (Hunter et al., 1984; Linn, 1982). External validity has been a more difficult criterion by which to assess the potential bias in interest inventories, because there is no longer a consensus about what an interest inventory should predict, if anything (Zytowski, 1978, p. 132; Tittle & Zytowski, 1978, p. xvii). Predictive validity has been a traditional criterion against which to assess inventories, but it is now rejected by people who argue that predictive validity places a premium on preserving the status quo.

This argument appears to have arisen because of the specific way in which predictive validity has been measured. Although the field has traditionally presumed that inventories ideally should predict vocational satisfaction and adjustment, which would seem to be appropriate goals for all test-takers, inventories have in practice usually been validated against the intermediate criteria of later entry, preparation for entry, or the desire for entry into a particular college major or type of work. It is really only the appropriateness of these latter intermediate criteria that is now called into question. In any case, evidence on the validity of the major interest inventories for predicting current or future choice indicates that it is similar for different minority groups (Borgen & Harper, 1973; Lamb, 1978) and for males and females (Hansen & Swanson, 1983; Harmon, 1969; Spokane, 1979; Zytowski, 1981, p. 32). Other external criteria have been sought by which to assess the fairness of interest inventories, for example, client satisfaction with the results of the inventory, number of options suggested, increased information seeking, reduction of indecision, and reduced need to see a counselor, but research on these criteria also suggests that inventories are equally beneficial for both sexes (Holland et al., 1981). Analyses of these types of criteria are usually referred to as *effects studies*, although the term *exploration validity* is sometimes used in reference to some of these external criteria.

The adequacy of mental tests and interest inventories for persons with handicaps has received little attention in the counseling literature. Special interest inventories have been developed for the mentally retarded (Power, 1984) and mental tests have long been used to help diagnose mental retardation (Gordon, 1980c). Research on the hospitalized physically disabled (Hershenson & Sloan, 1968) suggested indirectly that the SVIB is suitable for such persons. Holland (1979a, p. 8) summarized favorable evidence for the special form of the SDS for assessing the interests of the visually disabled. However, emotional disturbances appear to interfere with adequate assessment of both vocational interests (Hershenson & Sloan, 1968) and cognitive abilities (see Jensen's, 1980, discussion of the sources of large changes in tested intelligence). One recent text on vocational assessment in rehabilitation counseling (Power, 1984) described a wide variety of mental tests and interest inventories and, except for administrative constraints associated with visual or hearing handicaps, suggested that they both play an important role in counseling persons with handicaps. Interest testing of persons with spinal cord injuries (Rohe & Athelstan, 1982) illustrates how useful interest tests can be in treatment and rehabilitation.

The foregoing discussion does not constitute a blanket endorsement of either mental tests or interest inventories for all types of clients, because the research has dealt primarily with native-born English-speaking test takers. In the absence of clearcut evidence that tests are not biased for recent immigrants or for people who may speak little or no English, the tests cannot be assumed appropriate for these particular groups. At the same time, neither can the tests be assumed necessarily inappropriate. For example, research on the validity of English-language and translated versions of the VPI, SDS, and SVIB–SCII in other countries or for bilingual persons in this country has generally been positive (Hansen, 1984a; Hansen & Fouad, 1984; Holland, 1979a). Similarly, performance (i.e., nonverbal) tests developed for the United States or English populations (e.g., Raven's matrices [Raven, Court, & Raven, 1979]) appear to be equally appropriate for test takers unfamiliar with United States culture as well as for different groups within the United States population (Jensen, 1980); in fact, they are especially useful for "screening illiterate, semiliterate, bilingual, and otherwise educationally disadvantaged or socially depressed populations for potential academic talent" that might otherwise go undetected (Jensen, 1980, p. 648). To take another example, Japanese standardization of performance tests in the Wechsler Intelligence Scale for Children (WISC), which do not require translation, reveal a mean Japanese IQ of about 107—a result that would not be expected if such IQ tests did in fact require a knowledge of American culture (Gordon & Rudert, 1979; but see Flynn, 1984; Lynn, 1983; Stevenson & Azuma, 1983). In short, evidence to date suggests that the major mental tests and interest inventories in use in the United States today are equally valid for assessing different sexes and racial or ethnic groups, with the possible exception of recent immigrants or those who are not proficient in the language in which the test is administered.

Overall, then, the research on mental and interest tests has shown that the tests reflect real group differences. It does not necessarily follow, of course, that such group differences are desirable or unchangeable; that is a different issue.

The research indicating that the tests are not biased and that they reflect real differences among social groups has not quieted concerns about unfair testing so much as it has brought about a shift in the focus of concern. The testing controversy arose because tests showed group differences in *outcomes*. Therefore, as long as group differences in outcomes remain, so too will concerns about the *fairness* of the tests. Concern now focuses less on how tests should be constructed and more on how they should be used, if at all. One indication of this shift is reflected in Holland's recent proposals (1979a, p. 51; in press) that interest inventories be evaluated not only according to the traditional properties of reliability and validity, but also according to their usefulness and their effects on test takers.

A frequently expressed fear is that test results may only reinforce sex and race differences and leave potentials undeveloped unless the test results are interpreted and used properly (Birk, 1975; Samuda, 1975). Mental tests, for example, are sometimes seen as only reinforcing past race differences if they are not used for assessing problems and designing appropriate educational interventions for the test taker. Interest inventories have been defined as "sex-restrictive" simply if they suggest different distributions of occupations to men and women (Prediger & Hanson, 1974), and this is widely considered to be an undesirable feature of an inventory (Fitzgerald & Betz, 1983). There is, therefore, debate about whether interest inventories should merely reflect traits that may have resulted from past socialization or whether they should constitute a treatment designed to counteract or "upend" earlier socialization to stereotyped interests and social roles (Birk, 1975; Cole & Hanson, 1975; Datta, 1978; Holland, 1975). There has also been argument about whether tests can do much by themselves to counter many previous years of socialization and continuing reinforcement of resulting differences (Cole & Hanson, 1975; Holland, 1975) and about what kinds of supplementary interpretive procedures and materials can enhance the power of inventories to reduce sex differences in interests (Birk, 1975; Holland, 1975). But these are all issues about how tests should or can be *used* to benefit counselees, particularly those who are members of special groups.

Despite the rising interest in the issue of beneficial test usage, concrete and specific suggestions are as yet few for how tests should be properly used. For example, the National Research Council of the National Academy of Sciences (Wigdor & Garner, 1982) concluded that, although intelligence tests are not culturally biased, such tests could be used more wisely. However, that report provided little guidance for what would constitute beneficial test usage in different circumstances. Likewise, interest inventory manuals encourage counselors not to rely solely on interest inventory results, but to interpret them in the context of a wide variety of other information about the test taker (Campbell & Hansen, 1981; Holland, 1979a; Kuder & Diamond, 1979). However, manuals and reporting forms provide little explicit guidance to the counselor or the test taker about what that other information might be, how it might be obtained, or how it can be usefully integrated with inventory results. This is not said to criticize test developers and publishers, for they have been responsive to concerns about sex and race bias. It merely reflects the fact that the testing controversy has brought career counseling to the edge of a new frontier—the science and art of beneficial test usage.

Without explicit guidance on how to use the results of mental tests or interest inventories in the best interests of members of special groups, many educators and counselors appear reluctant to use tests at all. Although understandable, this reluctance is unfortunate, because it often means that counselors and test takers turn to less reliable and less objective information about capacities and interests. Counselors have been criticized in the past for channeling women and minorities into stereotyped jobs, and thus many are more comfortable with promoting vocational exploration than with the more traditional goal of promoting realism, because the latter smacks of restricting client opportunities (Birk, 1975). Although realism and exploration are not necessarily conflicting counseling goals (Gottfredson, 1985c), they are generally perceived as such, so this apparent dilemma leads some counselors to reject testing altogether.

Although there is little discussion about what constitutes beneficial test usage, and indeed the issue itself seems as yet to be largely implicit in the field, several types of literature provide clues as to what it might consist of. The remainder of this chapter is devoted to outlining what past research and speculation about special groups and career development suggests for a science of beneficial interest inventory usage, particularly for members of special groups.

The Special-Groups Literature

The term *special groups* is used most often in the vocational counseling literature to refer to social groups who are subject to social, political, and economic disadvantages or discrimination. The most commonly discussed groups include blacks, Hispanics, Asian-Americans, Native-Americans, and women (Atkinson et al., 1979; Brooks, 1984; Fitzgerald & Betz, 1983; Fitzgerald & Crites, 1980; Harmon, Birk, Fitzgerald, & Tanney, 1978; Jackson, 1981; Lazarus & Tobin, 1981; Picou & Campbell, 1975; Smith, 1983; Sue, 1981). Homosexuals, white ethnics, Jews, migratory workers, and delinquents are among the other social groups that are occasionally discussed as disadvantaged groups (Amos & Grambs, 1968; Brown, 1975; National Institute of Education, 1980), but they are generally accorded only passing mention. The deaf (Lacey, 1975), dyslexic (Gottfredson, Finucci, & Childs, 1984a), and other people suffering from physical, mental, or emotional handicaps (Overs, 1975) are rarely considered in either vocational psychology (Osipow, 1976) or the special-groups literature (see Picou & Campbell, 1975, for an exception) but have usually been discussed in the rehabilitation literature (Jaques & Kauppi, 1983). Although gifted students are often assumed to have some of the same problems as do other special groups (e.g., social isolation, under-achievement; Fields, 1984), they also appear to have been ignored in the special groups literature.

Although there is no consensus about what constitutes a special group or how many there are, the unifying theme of the literature is that many people have career problems because society is insensitive or unfair in its treatment of those people. This stance is evident in terms such as culturally disadvantaged or culturally oppressed which frequently are used to designate these groups. The literature focuses on the social groups most commonly presumed to be victims of discriminatory social processes, and in the last decade this literature has condemned deficit or social pathology (e.g., culture of poverty) models of race, sex, and ethnic differences, because such explanations of group difference are perceived to "blame the victim" (Smith, 1982) and to ignore the strengths of those groups (Casas, 1984; Richardson & Johnson, 1984; Samuda, 1975). Some attributes that are commonly viewed as dysfunctional may even, from another point of view, be perceived as strengths or adaptive behavior (Davidson, 1980, p. 130). It is further argued that it is more appropriate to view special groups as *different* in values than to view them as *deficient* in any regard (Sue, 1981, pp. 12–16).

The shunning of deficit models may account partly for why groups whose members are widely understood to have functional deficits or limitations (e.g., in hearing) tend to be ignored in the special-groups literature. Nevertheless, there is much more overlap between the problems of the physically, mentally, and emotionally handicapped and other special groups than is commonly recognized

(Hershenson & Sloan, 1968), and the former are considered special groups for the purposes of this chapter. The career problems of the blind, deaf, physically disabled, mentally ill, and dyslexic, for example, have been attributed not solely to their functional limitations, but also to insensitivities, stereotyping, and discriminatory social processes that are very much like those from which the members of other special groups are presumed to suffer (Gellman, 1959; Gottfredson, Finucci, & Childs, 1984b; Higgins, 1980; Jaques & Kauppi, 1983; Lacey, 1975; Osipow, 1976; Scott, 1969; Segal, 1978).

The more detailed discussions of the problems of special groups typically focus on one particular special group at a time and outline how that group differs from the majority society, the ways in which the group has been oppressed or otherwise disadvantaged in the United States, and the dilemmas and problems members of those groups face in pursuing success in a white male middle-class occupational world. The literature stresses that the problems these groups face are unique and have not been properly understood or appreciated in the counseling setting. It is frequently stated that vocational theories and assessments were developed from research on samples of white middle-class males and that they are therefore inadequate for understanding or aiding members of special groups. Some authors argue that different theories are necessary for special groups, and others argue that equal treatment in counseling may be discriminatory treatment for members of special groups (Sue, 1981, p. 107). It is frequently argued that it is destructive to emphasize changing the attributes of the victims rather than placing responsibility with society where it presumably more properly belongs. Therefore, there are frequent references to the need to teach respect for cultural differences, to the need to educate the members of special groups about the external sources of their problems, to the need to counteract negative stereotypes of special groups, and to the need for clients and counselors alike to challenge the status quo.

This literature has been useful because it has sensitized counselors to cultural and gender differences. Although there is still debate about whether research has demonstrated that counselors are, in fact, biased (Richardson & Johnson, 1984), the failure to understand or respect cultural and sex differences may have previously impaired counselor effectiveness and fairness in dealing with counselees from special groups. Perhaps a more important contribution of the special-groups literature in the present context is that it shifts attention to important career determinants that have tended to be ignored in current vocational theory. In particular, the special-groups literature has reinforced earlier occasional criticisms (Warnath, 1975) that vocational theory pays too much attention to the internal psychological sources of career development and it pays too little attention to external constraints (Atkinson et al., 1979; Brooks, 1984). It is stressed in the special-groups literature that members of special groups have been subject to societal restrictions and stereotypes that have severely limited the types of occupations available to them—constraints that do not exist for majority males.

The special-groups literature thus constitutes a challenge to current vocational theory and to the value of the tools and counseling interventions that the latter has fostered. These criticisms also echo the complaints of many sociologists that vocational psychology assumes free occupational choice, whereas the real world offers nothing of the sort for the bulk of our population.

The special groups literature has helped to generate more concern about the career development of special groups, but it has been of less use in providing guidance for acting on those concerns in career counseling settings (Casas, 1984; Holland, 1984). In particular, the literature has provided guidance for establishing rapport with people who are culturally different, but it has provided less guidance for what counselors should do after rapport is established to help members of special groups deal with the special problems they are assumed to have. One inadequacy of the literature in the present context is its failure to treat the problems of special groups in a sufficiently specific and analytic enough manner to aid counselors in their efforts with individual clients. Articles about special groups continue to provide additional detail on cultural differences and social oppression among a handful of special groups—primarily blacks, Hispanics, Asian-Americans, Native-Americans, and women—and, ironically, they continue to detail the very stereotypes they seek to destroy. However, they remain unclear about how these and other aspects of special-group status translate into the particular career problems that counselors are likely to see in their clients and be required to treat. For example, racism, discrimination, sexism, and stereotyping may all be undeniable social facts, at least at some point in the history of a special group, but they are ill-defined, all-embracing terms that are more emotionally evocative than scientifically descriptive. This issue can be clarified by noting that most of the problems associated with being a member of a special group that are discussed in the literature can be classified into four categories: societal reactions to special groups (e.g., slavery, immigration policy), mechanisms by which social and economic environments affect individuals (e.g., role modeling, restricted information), deleterious consequences for special groups as a whole (e.g., lower mean income, occupational segregation), and deleterious consequences for individuals' career development (e.g., unnecessarily constricted vocational choices). It would appear that the special-groups literature has given the most systematic attention to societal reactions to special groups and their deleterious consequences for those groups, whereas it has provided only a very ad hoc examination of the other two types of problem. The former group-level issues are useful for galvanizing concern for special groups and for designing social programs to aid whole social groups, but the latter individual-level issues are essential in diagnosing and treating clients in the traditional one-to-one or small group counseling settings.

A second limitation of the special-groups literature is its overemphasis on the uniqueness and externality of the problems special groups face. Such emphases are, once again, useful in galvanizing concern, but they may not be beneficial in the long run if they discourage comparative analyses of both internal and external barriers to career development. A similar observation by Jaques and Kauppi (1983) about the disabled is relevant to all special groups: "Often to compensate for the inattention given to the disabled those in the field come to emphasize their uniqueness or specialness. Although this can serve to mobilize certain resources of help, the focus on the differences rather than on the similarities of the disabled to people in general may ultimately serve to isolate the disabled even further from the general society" (p. 250). Each special group may indeed have its own values and unique history, and members of these special groups may be readily identifiable in social settings because of their physical features or behavior. Counseling psychology has stressed the uniqueness of all individuals, and it is equally true that each social group can be considered unique among all others. But this does not mean that the career development problems that members of special groups have are also unique. For example, the need to balance family and career goals is frequently presented as a unique problem of women. The problem may be more prevalent and severe for women, but it is also a problem that faces minorities who move into the majority culture. Nor can it be said to be a problem that all white middle-class males escape. To take another example, the stereotypes of different special groups differ from one group to another, but the negative effects of stereotyping are cited in discussions of all special groups (Atkinson et al., 1979, p. 18). Furthermore, the solutions proposed to the problems of special groups (e.g., expand vocational options) often sound like good advice with regard to any client (Crites, 1981, chap. 8; Fitzgerald & Crites, 1980, p. 56; Jackson, 1981). Direct and systematic comparisons of the problems of different special groups have not been made in the literature, but it would be beneficial to distill the mass of discussion on the problems of special groups into a smaller set of systematic and theoretically meaningful principles applicable to all groups that would be useful in counseling settings.

The special groups literature has been rather forceful, overall, in condemning majority groups for the problems special groups have and in rejecting explanations that partially locate the source of career problems within special groups themselves. Much of the blame placed on majority groups for the career problem of special groups may be well deserved, but the special groups literature, with some notable exceptions (Richardson & Johnson, 1984), seems to have adopted an unscientific stance toward the possible role that group differences in traits or social practices may play in hindering career development. For example, in discussing her thesis that race is a prepotent factor in career outcomes, Smith (1983) stated that "This situation occurs not because there are inherent differences among the various races in ability, subscription to success goals, or attitudes but rather because structural factors found in labor market dynamics, institutional practices, and the legacy of racism serve to perpetuate a differential career development among Americans of different racial backgrounds" (p. 166). Although stated as an apparent fact, this is actually a matter of scientific debate, particularly because racial differences in abilities (on unbiased tests) and in other career-relevant behaviors (e.g., fertility) have been well established.

Special groups are generally portrayed as different in social values and practices, differences that the literature argues should be more widely respected, but special groups are generally assumed *not* to differ in ways that could be taken as implying that one group is inherently different or in some way superior or inferior to another. Sex, race, and ethnic group differences in interests and abilities, for example, are usually discussed as products of socialization and of differential opportunity imposed by the majority culture, and authors who provide evidence suggesting otherwise (Benbow & Stanley, 1980; Jensen, 1969) are accused of being biased, racist, or sexist and of perpetuating negative, inaccurate, and destructive stereotypes. The stress on uniqueness has served to perpetuate an ad hoc and inconsistent approach to different special groups, and thus has continued to obscure rather than illuminate group differences in advantages and disadvantages that counselors should be aware of.

The rejection of possible group differences in capabilities or adaptive behavior (adaptive in American society) is clearly demonstrated by the efforts of some authors to counteract the *positive* stereotypes of Asian-Americans and to qualify their success (Sue & Kitano, 1979; Suzuki, 1977) and by claims that "the nature of stereotypes often seems to depend upon the moods or conditions of society rather than upon any real characteristics of the stereotyped group" (Sue & Kitano, 1979, p. 77). Group differences in values are sometimes used in explaining group differences in outcomes, but only in selected circumstances.

For example, the *lower*-than-average attainments of blacks, Hispanics, and Native-Americans are attributed to barriers imposed by the majority culture but the *higher*-than-average attainments of Asian-Americans and Jews are attributed to certain cultural values among the latter (Sue, 1979; Suzuki, 1977). Cultural values of special groups are generally rejected as explanations of lower-than-average attainments because they "blame the victim" (Suzuki, 1977, p. 27) and well documented group differences in abilities, (e.g., the superior science and math abilities of Asian-Americans) are seldom considered important in explaining either positive or negative group outcomes and are dismissed as stereotypes. It is not entirely clear how important group differences in abilities are, but it seems unwise to ignore them (Gottfredson, 1985b).

At the same time that the special-groups literature has maintained that deficit models ignore the strengths of a group, that literature itself has failed to describe those strengths or has dismissed putative career-related advantages (e.g., the conformity of Asian-Americans) as debilitating factors in other respects. Some of the putative advantages of majority males could similarly be redefined (e.g., high-level jobs are more stressful), but they never are in this literature. Discussions of Asian-Americans (who, in fact, achieve *higher* levels of education and occupation than do whites) leave the impression that to highlight the achievements or strengths of one group would be to weaken the claim that it—or any special group—merits particular concern (Gump & Rivers, 1975). Characterizations of Asian-Americans as a "model minority" are sometimes viewed as a "divisive concept used by the Establishment to pit one minority against another by holding one group up as an example to others" (Sue, 1981, p. 117).

In short, the heavy emphasis placed by the special-groups literature on external constraints has constituted a beneficial corrective to the overemphasis in vocational theory on the volitional aspects of career development. However, that literature has promoted an overly narrow conception of the problems some special groups may face, and it has failed to accord much significance to the strengths that some groups have. This literature still appears to be concerned primarily with mobilizing concern, whereas more effort might now be devoted to constructively channeling the concern that has already been aroused.

ANALYSIS AND COMPARISON
OF RISK FACTORS IN CAREER CHOICE

The foregoing discussion should not be construed as implying that members of special groups do not have problems that require special attention, or that research should not be devoted to special groups and their problems. What has been argued is that the special-groups literature has failed to take as broad a perspective as seems desirable, and that it has failed to examine the career problems of special groups systematically or analytically enough to provide much guidance to counselors in diagnosing and dealing with those problems at the level of the individual counselee.

The special-groups literature has dealt primarily with the problems that special groups face rather than with any strengths they may have; this chapter does also. This focus is not meant to imply that an analysis of a counselee's current or potential strengths is unimportant. On the contrary, such analyses are vital— especially for people who suffer from enduring handicaps. Gottfredson et al. (1984b) have argued, for example, that vocational counseling for the dyslexic *requires* a focus on developing compensatory strengths. Hershenson (1974) has pointed out that the focus on compensation in the rehabilitation literature is one that vocational psychology could profitably adopt. In short, compensatory strengths and strategies are important in career development, but it is beyond the scope of this chapter to deal with them.

The following discussion focuses on one aspect of career development that may recur throughout the life cycle—making occupational choices. Other tasks in career development are also important, but career choice is the task that traditionally has been of most concern in career counseling, so it is a particularly appropriate place to begin systematically outlining the career problems of special groups.

Fifteen social groups are systematically examined. These represent the groups that are most commonly researched or discussed, but they are not all that might be considered special groups. The object here is neither to advocate an unmanageable proliferation of special groups nor to denigrate or elevate the importance of any particular ones. Instead, the objective is to shift attention away from special group status and toward the problems that special group status actually poses for members of those groups. Thus, the groups used here should be considered as illustrative of analyses that could be performed with any special group. If white Protestant males are excluded, these groups represent at least 75% of the population.

The literature has dealt with several very different classes of problems. This chapter distinguishes among different types of individual-level problems: risk factors, underlying problems, symptoms (i.e., presenting problems), and criteria of successful development.

Risk Factors in Career Choice

It is useful to adopt the concept of risk factor in describing the career choice problems of special groups. Risk factors are attributes of the person or of the person's relation to the environment that are associated with a higher-than-average probability of experiencing the types of problems under consideration. A poor education is an example of a career risk factor because it does not bar one from succeeding occupationally, but it does decrease the *odds* of success; it is not a career problem itself, but it often contributes to such problems. For example, just as smoking increases one's chances of getting cancer, but by no means makes it a certainty, so too does being poorly educated decrease one's chances for succeeding occupationally.

This subsection of the chapter reviews the major career choice risk factors. The next subsection assesses how prevalent these risk factors may be in different segments of the population. What immediately follows is an attempt to organize diverse ideas and bits of information from many sources into a few analytically useful categories of risk. The list is only a starting point for more explicit and systematic discussion of the problems special groups face; it can no doubt be improved by others.

Twelve career choice risk factors are organized here according to whether they represent: (a) comparisons of the individual with the general population; (b) comparisons of the individual to other persons within the same social circle; or (c) family responsibilities. These risk factors appear to represent the major attributes and circumstances having a deleterious effect on career choice processes as identified by the special-groups literature, vocational development theory, and status attainment research in sociology.

Comparisons With the General Population: Low Intelligence, Poor Education, Poverty, Cultural Isolation, Low Self-esteem, and Functional Limita-

tion. Two decades of status attainment research in sociology (Blau & Duncan, 1967; Campbell, 1983; Duncan, Featherman, & Duncan, 1972; Jencks et al., 1972, 1979; Sewell & Hauser, 1975) have shown quite clearly that level of occupation aspired to and level actually attained are both influenced by differences in socioeconomic background, intelligence, and educational level attained. Since at least the time of the War on Poverty in the 1960s, these three variables have been perceived as keys to reducing inequalities between the less advantaged and the more advantaged segments of society. There continues to be debate about just how strong each of these influences is relative to the other and about why they are important (Campbell, 1983; Gottfredson, 1985a), but it is safe to say that higher intelligence (net of socioeconomic background) is predictive of getting better grades, doing better on standardized achievement tests, persisting in school and attaining higher levels of education, having higher educational and occupational aspirations, and performing better in training and on the job (Gottfredson, 1985a). Getting more education (net of ability) is associated with getting more prestigious and better paying jobs. More advantaged socioeconomic background, depending on how it is measured, predicts (net of ability) higher educational and occupational aspirations, getting more education, and (net of ability and education) higher income. Differences in socioeconomic background are usually interpreted as differences in economic resources, so coming from a poor family is listed here as a risk factor. Socioeconomic background actually can be decomposed theoretically into several components, and some of the other components (e.g., cultural isolation) are considered separately in the following.

Being culturally isolated or segregated and having low self-esteem have both been widely considered to be handicaps for minorities and women, although their actual relation to occupational attainment is not yet well understood. Low self-esteem is usually considered to be a separate problem from that of cultural isolation, but one which is likely to result from being a member of a culturally segregated group that is commonly viewed as being deviant or inferior. In a review of the literature on self-esteem, Gecas (1982) concluded that low self-esteem is associated with undesirable outcomes, including lower academic interests, aspirations, and achievements, but that it is not clear whether the converse is true, that is, that high self-esteem has favorable consequences. Some investigators have argued that a "medium" amount of self-esteem is optimal. Other aspects of self and self-concept are frequently invoked to explain the lower achievement levels of certain groups, but the most common have not stood up well to empirical test. For example, accumulated research questions the existence of fear of success as an enduring and stable personality trait and as a motive that characterizes primarily females (Minton & Schneider, 1980, p. 289); it also has been found that achievement motivation is not useful in predicting occupational attainment (Spenner & Featherman, 1978).

Cultural isolation refers to the common focus in the special-groups literature on the difficulties members of special groups have in fitting into and succeeding in a white man's occupational world. This term appears to encompass a variety of more specific problems that have been identified in the literature. For example, the apparent failure of many youngsters to identify with cross-race or cross-sex role models, presumably because of a sense of social distance or difference, may explain why the literature has placed so much stress on the detrimental effects of not having *same*-sex and *same*-race occupational role models. Cultural isolation also refers to not knowing the social behaviors appropriate in majority culture settings as well as to not being accepted as a member of the majority group (which is usually assumed to be white males) and not being accorded the same respect, understanding, and assistance (e.g., mentoring) as would a member of the majority group. For example, two arguments that have been put forward in favor of school desegregation have been that it might enable minority students to learn how to deal more effectively with whites, which presumably is necessary for their occupational success in a white occupational world, and that it might provide them access to useful informal networks (i.e., white networks) of information about job opportunities (Braddock, Crain, & McPartland, 1984).

Some individuals are at risk of having career problems because they have some unusual functional impairment or limitation such as dyslexia or the loss of hearing, sight, or use of limbs. These are deficits that can be considered the result of some genetic or environmental accident and as generally being outside the normal range of variation. Research has not made clear to what extent the occupational handicaps experienced by such people are due to the functional limitations themselves rather than to the social problems that generally accompany those limitations. However, it seems clear that many functional impairments can restrict the range of occupational alternatives, regardless of whatever secondary handicaps they may typically generate (Felton, Perkins, & Lewin, 1966; Ferron, 1981). Functional limitations obviously differ widely in type, severity, and social visibility (Hershenson, 1974). Career counselors may seldom see the most severely impaired (e.g., mentally retarded, schizophrenic, blind, deaf) because such cases usually are handled by more specialized service providers, but most counselors can expect to see some slightly to moderately dyslexic, hearing or speech impaired, physically handicapped, or otherwise functionally limited clients, because 17% of the population aged 18–64 in 1978 reported having some disability that limited the type or amount of work they could do (Lando, Cutler, & Gamber, 1982, Table 7). See Lando et al. (1982, Table 76) for the most common disabling conditions for different age groups and see Dearman and Plisko (1981, Table, 6.4) for the percentages of school students with different types of handicap.

Different Within Own Social Circle: Nontraditional Interests, Socially Isolated, Less Intelligent Than Family and Peers, and More Intelligent Than Family and Peers. The problems associated with having nontraditional interests are most commonly recognized in the literature on women's career development, but they are also a common theme in discussions of ethnic minorities. Rodriguez

(1979), for example, has discussed the family strains created by being a "scholarship boy"—that is, being upwardly mobile, entering a world alien to that of one's past, and thereby distancing or estranging oneself from childhood family and friends and from their values and expectations. A person may be a potential nontraditional in a variety of ways, including gender, social class, and ethnic group.

One need not be culturally different to be considered odd or different or to be cut off from the social interaction that most of us take for granted. Being *culturally* different means that one is segregated *together* with one's cultural group away from the rest of society. Being *socially* isolated refers here to being segregated, often as an individual, from the rest of one's own cultural group. This social isolation can occur because of societal reactions to unusual attributes of the person (such as blindness, disfigurement, or homosexuality) but also because some functional limitations (such as dyslexia or deafness) interfere with normal communication and thus with the everyday social learning and contact that it facilitates (see Lacey, 1975, on the deaf). The fairly new emphasis on mainstreaming handicapped school children and on creating a barrier-free environment for all physically disabled people appears partly to reflect a concern with decreasing the social isolation of the handicapped and its resultant disadvantages for them. Many of the arguments in favor of integrating handicapped with nonhandicapped populations parallel those given for integrating different racial/ethnic groups, including the increased capacity of the handicapped groups to function successfully in the majority society and increased acceptance and understanding across groups (Hanline & Murray, 1984).

As was noted earlier, *low social class* or *poor socioeconomic background* are broad terms that refer to a host of attributes that have been considered deleterious to career development. Lack of financial resources for pursuing a desirable education or occupation is one risk factor already noted. Another factor, discussed earlier, is segregation from the middle-class society which is commonly presumed to dominate cultural and economic affairs. But two other risk factors are evident if social classes are viewed as one way in which people define their own social circle. Considerably higher occupational attainment is required for youngsters from the higher social classes than from the lower social classes in order for those youngsters to equal the average level of attainment within their own social settings and thus to be considered successes in those settings. This is consistent with the fact that aspiration level is related to social class even after intelligence is controlled (Sewell & Shah, 1968). It is also well established that youngsters from the higher social classes tend to be more intelligent than youngsters from lower social classes, but that there is still much overlap in intelligence across the social classes and much variability within them (Sewell & Shah, 1968). Two types of youngsters appear to be at particular risk because of these circumstances. First, highly intelligent lower class youngsters may be likely to have unrealistically *low* aspirations, and less intelligent youngsters from the higher social classes may be likely to have unrealistically *high* aspirations (Gott-fredson, 1981). The gifted are a subgroup of all people with high intelligence compared to family and peers; not surprisingly, one career development problem often associated with giftedness is underachievement. The two risk factors just described seem to be a source of much of the unrealism that counselors encounter and so can be expected to be prevalent problems in any population.

Family Responsibilities: Primary Caregiver, Primary Economic Pro-vider.   Conflict between family and career is invariably discussed as one of the major problems women face, but two types of work–family conflict have actu-ally been identified in the special-groups literature, and they clearly are not restricted to being female. The first risk factor is that of being (or expecting to be) a primary caregiver. This refers to having major responsibility for the daily care of children, elderly parents, or other dependents. Not only is having chil-dren to care for a risk factor, but so too is bearing children at younger rather than older ages (Richardson & Johnson, 1984). The second risk factor is that of being (or expecting to be) a primary economic provider (i.e., having economic depen-dents). In discussions of the career problems of women, being an economic provider is usually seen as being consistent with having a career orientation and thus as not being a handicap in career development. However, the need to support a family can seriously impede optimal career development, if it means foregoing education or training for a more desirable job in order to make ends meet now. Newly divorced homemakers who reenter the job market and teenage parents both have been noted to face this family–career conflict. A similar, but perhaps less severe problem, is that of the youngster from a poor family who is expected to go to work as soon as possible to help support parents and siblings. It also is probably the case that many men who are primary economic providers may move into fields of work that do not particularly interest them in order to provide the income level or security that is desired or expected by the families they support (Gottfredson, 1981).

Differences in Risk Rates by Special Group

The foregoing risk factors are not restricted to any particular special group, nor even to special groups in general. They do, however, tend to be especially troublesome for some groups because the members of those groups have a higher than average probability of being at risk. Another useful step, then, in under-standing the career choice problems of special groups would be to outline the relative risk rates for different groups for each of the risk factors.

Relative risk rates are well known for some risk factors and for a few special groups; relevant data appear to be more scattered for additional risk factors and special groups; and data appear to be nonexistent for yet others. In short, some good data exist, but much less systematic information is available than would be desirable.

A synthesis of all the relevant data would require a review of diverse and scattered types of research, which is beyond the scope of this chapter. Table 5.1 constitutes an effort to begin such a task by compiling some of the data with which this author is most familiar. It provides estimates about whether the members in each special group in the table have a higher-than-average risk of being characterized by each of the twelve risk factors. The letters "X" and "x" represent estimates that the special group has an *unusually high risk*. The letters "O" and "o" represent estimates that the risk is *no more than average*. Some of the special groups actually are at *lower* risk than the population in general or than white males in particular, but this is noted only in the text. The uppercase letters (X and O) represent estimates based on high quality or extensive data. The text and Table 5.2 present some of the more illustrative data to support these estimates. Most of those data were obtained from government publications based on large surveys or censuses of the population. The lowercase letters (x and o) should be considered little more than the author's informed guesses, because they are estimates made with the benefit of little or no systematic relevant data. A blank means that no hypotheses are presented.

Several limitations of Table 5.1 should be noted. The first has already been discussed. Only a limited amount of good data is available. A second limitation is that the estimates apply to comparisons at the national level, and so are not necessarily applicable to the more restricted local populations with which counselors deal. Third, these estimates reflect differences in the *odds* that the members of different social groups are characterized by the various risk factors. The fact that one group has more affected members obviously does not mean that all, or even many, of the members of that same special group share the same handicapping attribute. There are many differences within social groups as well as between them. Fourth, both the risk factors and the special groups represent broad categories that obscure many detailed differences (as is illustrated by data presented later in Table 5.2). For example, there are many categories of Asian-Americans, and some groups often classified in that category (e.g., Native-Hawaiians) even appear to be more like non-Asian special groups (e.g., blacks) in some respects (e.g., achievement test scores, fertility) than they are like other Asian-American groups (e.g., Japanese-Americans). The foregoing limitations are, in fact, some of the reasons it is argued in a later section that, for most counseling purposes, individual counseless should be classified and treated according to the types of career development problems they have, rather than according to the special groups to which they belong.

The data on which the estimates in Table 5.1 are based are described in the following discussion and many are presented in Table 5.2. All hypotheses are for people in their teens and 20s, who are presumed here to be the major clientele of

TABLE 5.1
Special Groups Whose Members are Hypothesized to be at Higher-than-average Risk (X) Vs. not at Higher-than-average Risk (O) of Having Various Attributes that can Impede Optimal Career Development

Examples of Special Groups

Career Choice Risk Factors	Racial/Ethnic Group							Sex		Handicapped					
														Mentally	
	"WASP"	White ethnic	Black	Hispanic	Native Amer.	Asian Amer.	Jewish	Male	Female	Sight	Hearing	Use of Limbs	Dyslexic	Retarded	Ill
Different from general population															
Low intelligence	O		X	X	X	O	O	O	O					X	
Poor academic background	O		X	X	X	O	O	O	O[a]				X	X	
Comes from poor family	O		X	X	X	O	O	O	O				o	x	
Culturally isolated/segregated	o	x	x	x	x	x	x		x						
Functional limitation	O		X	X	X			O	O[b]	X	X	X	X	X	X
Low self-esteem	O		O					o	o						
Different within own social circle															
Potential non-traditional (i.e., has interests typical of a different sex, racial/ethnic group, or social class)	o								x						
Socially isolated/segregated									x	x	x	x	x		x
Low intelligence compared to family/peers															
High intelligence compared to family/peers														X	
Family responsibilities															
Probable/actual primary caregiver	OM		XF	XF				O	X					x	
Probable/actual primary economic provider			OM	XM				X	O						

Note: X = good evidence that at higher-than-average risk. x = author's estimate that at higher-than-average risk. O = good evidence that not at higher-than-average risk. o = author's estimate that not at higher-than-average risk. Blank = no hypothesis. M = males only. F = females only.

[a]See text for more detailed sex differences in education.

[b]There are sex differences for specific types of functional limitation.

TABLE 5.2
Indicators of the Relative Prevalence of Certain Career Development Risk Factors Among Young People

Indicators of Risk Factor	White		Black		Hispanic		Native-American		Asian-American		Total	
	M	F	M	F	M	F	M	F	M	F	M	F
Low Intelligence												
Standardized tests: high school sophomores, 1980 (means)[a]												
Vocabulary	52.0		42.4		44.2(Mex) 44.0(PR) 48.1(Cu)		45.0		51.6		50.0	
Math part 1	51.8		43.1		44.5(Mex) 43.9(PR) 48.0(Cu)		44.6		55.7		50.0	
Standardized tests: high school seniors, 1980 (means)[a]												
Vocabulary part 1	51.4		43.6		44.5(Mex) 44.3(PR) 48.5(Cu)		45.8		50.2		50.0	
Math part 1	51.5		42.8		43.8(Mex) 43.4(PR) 48.2(Cu)		45.2		54.2		50.0	
SAT scores, college-bound seniors, 1982 (means)[b]												
Verbal	444		341		379(Chic) 360(PR)		—		390		—	
Math	483		366		416(Chic) 403(PR)		—		513		—	

GRE combined quantitative and verbal, 1980/81 (means)[c]	1039	733	847(Mex) 801(PR)	925	1054	1015
GRE quantitative, % below score 500, 1980/81[d]	40.7	87.3	70.8(Mex) 74.0(PR)	59.8	26.5	44.2

Poor Educational Background

Years of education: 1980[e]

% with less than 12 years, aged 20–24	16.4 14.1	30.2 23.3	41.6 38.2	34.3 31.2	12.5 14.4	19.2 16.4
% with at least 16 years, aged 25–29	25.8 22.0	10.7 12.1	9.7 8.4	8.5 7.7	40.5 35.9	23.6 20.6

Representation among degree holders, 1978/79 or 1979/80: ratio of % of degrees to % of age-relevant population[f] (Numbers in parentheses are the ratio of % female of degree holders to % female of age-relevant population)

All fields: BA	1.11	0.51	0.62	0.57	1.13	— (0.99)
MA	1.10	0.58	0.36	0.66	1.05	— (0.98)
PhD	1.11	0.41	0.31	0.66	1.33	— (0.59)
Professional	1.14	0.35	0.45	0.50	0.95	— (0.54)
Quantitative fields: BA	1.13	0.32	0.55	0.43	1.93	— (0.50)
MA	1.12	0.21	0.29	0.50	2.79	— (0.36)
PhD	1.12	0.16	0.21	0.33	2.71	— (0.30)
Professional	1.12	0.35	0.47	0.50	1.58	— (0.50)

(Continued)

TABLE 5.2
(Continued)

Indicators of Risk Factor	White M	White F	Black M	Black F	Hispanic M	Hispanic F	Native-American M	Native-American F	Asian-American M	Asian-American F	Total M	Total F
Comes From Poor Family												
% of children below poverty level												
Below age 15, 1979[g]	12.4		40.8		27.6		n.a.		n.a.		16.8	
Aged 15–17, 1979[g]		8.6		42.3		21.8		n.a.		n.a.		13.6
Families & unrelated individuals, 1975[h]	9		28		24(Mex) 32(PR)		26		17(Ch) 7(Ja) 6(Ph)		n.a.	
Income, median household per capita, 1975[i]	4333		2263		2130(Mex) 2153(PR)		2453		3867(Ch) 6105(Ja) 3897(Ph)		n.a.	
Unemployment rate, aged 40–44, 1980 (a parental age group)[j]	3.7	4.4	7.8	6.8	6.0	8.0	9.7	9.2	2.5	4.4	4.1	4.8
Cultural Isolation or Segregation												
Limited or non-English speaking: elementary/secondary students, 1978[k]												
% of enrollment (of same race)	0.2		0.2		25.9		8.5		14.5		2.2	
*Occupations of workers aged 16 or over, 1980[l]												

% managerial or professional	24.4	22.0	10.8	15.4	11.4	11.8	13.8	16.9	32.9	23.2	22.5	20.7
Occupational prestige, aged 16–74, 1976 (mean)[m]	39.5	38.8	30.5	32.0	30.4 32.1	30.0(Mex) 32.9(PR)	33.9	33.5	43.9 40.8 37.0	38.3(Ch) 36.1(Ja) 40.3(Ph)	n.a.	
% of married women (husbands present) married to white men, 1970[n]												
aged 25–34	—	99.5	—	0.6	—	17.5	—	35.8	—	11.0(Ch) 30.6(Ja)	—	—
aged 35–44	—	99.7	—	0.6	—	15.0	—	35.2	—	6.9(Ch) 39.5(Ja)	—	—
aged 45–54	—	99.8	—	0.6	—	14.9	—	35.0	—	5.2(Ch) 14.9(Ja)	—	—
% of children living with mothers only, 1980[o]												
aged 15–17	14.4	46.8				20.9	n.a.	n.a.		n.a.	19.1	
Functional Limitation												
Work disability, aged 18–34, 1978[p]												
% disabled	5.5	6.2	10.2	7.3	2.3 5.6 5.4	12.2(Mex) 34.9(PR) 21.2(Other)	n.a.	n.a.	n.a.	n.a.	8.3	8.6
% severely disabled	1.8	1.9	3.6	3.5	1.4 5.5 4.8	4.8(Mex) 30.9(PR) 10.4(Other)	n.a.	n.a.	n.a.	n.a.	2.4	2.9

(Continued)

TABLE 5.2
(Continued)

Indicators of Risk Factor	White		Black		Hispanic		Native-American		Asian-American		Total	
	M	F	M	F	M	F	M	F	M	F	M	F
Primary Caregiver												
Number of live births per 1000 women, 1975[q]												
aged 10–14	—	0.6	—	5.1	—	n.a.	—	n.a.	—	n.a.	—	1.3
aged 15–17	—	28.3	—	86.6	—	n.a.	—	n.a.	—	n.a.	—	36.6
aged 18–19	—	74.4	—	156.0	—	n.a.	—	n.a.	—	n.a.	—	85.7
% of women still childless, 1982[r]												
aged 18–19	—	89.7	—	70.9	—	78.8	—	n.a.	—	n.a.	—	86.9
aged 20–24	—	69.4	—	48.9	—	51.1	—	n.a.	—	n.a.	—	66.6
aged 25–29	—	40.8	—	23.8	—	29.4	—	n.a.	—	n.a.	—	38.8
% of EVER MARRIED women still childless, 1970[s]												
aged 15–19	—	53.6	—	32.6	—	42.8(Mex) 35.2(PR) 42.5(Total)	—	42.5	—	55.3(Ch) 52.1(Ja) 48.1(Ph)	—	50.9
aged 20–24	—	37.4	—	20.6	—	22.0(Mex) 21.3(PR) 24.3(Total)	—	20.9	—	45.9(Ch) 46.1(Ja) 32.7(Ph)	—	35.6
aged 25–29	—	16.0	—	12.6	—	9.3(Mex) 9.6(PR) 11.3(Total)	—	9.6	—	32.3(Ch) 29.1(Ja) 21.7(Ph)	—	15.8
Number of children ever born per 1000 women, 1982[r]												
aged 18–19	—	118	—	370	—	264	—	n.a.	—	n.a.	—	156
aged 20–24	—	444	—	859	—	782	—	n.a.	—	n.a.	—	502
aged 25–29	—	1104	—	1668	—	1500	—	n.a.	—	n.a.	—	1176

154

Number of children ever born per 1000 women, 1970s

aged 15–19	—	70	118	—	111(Mex) 191(PR) 119(Total)	—	117	—	19(Ch) 27(Ja) 63(Ph)	—	76
aged 20–24	—	656	924	—	982(Mex) 1109(PR) 943(Total)	—	994	—	257(Ch) 279(Ja) 574(Ph)	—	686
aged 25–29	—	1713	2035	—	2226(Mex) 2133(PR) 2034(Total)	—	2330	—	1013(Ch) 1035(Ja) 1216(Ph)	—	1745

Primary Economic Provider

% still single (never married), 1982[t]

aged 18–19	94.2 (83.1)	98.7 (96.0)	87.8 (74.4)	n.a.	94.9 (84.9)
aged 20–24	70.1 (50.5)	82.3 (71.5)	65.6 (44.7)	n.a.	72.0 (53.4)
aged 25–29	34.1 (20.6)	48.3 (40.6)	31.1 (20.3)	n.a.	36.1 (23.4)

% married with spouse present, 1982[t]

aged 18–19	4.2 (14.1)	0.7 (2.7)	7.7 (20.1)	n.a.	3.7 (12.5)
aged 20–24	26.6 (41.7)	15.7 (22.3)	29.7 (44.7)	n.a.	24.9 (39.0)
aged 25–29	56.8 (65.6)	40.7 (39.7)	58.6 (63.1)	n.a.	54.7 (62.1)

Note: The Hispanic category cannot be presumed mutually exclusive with the other racial/ethnic groups unless indicated otherwise by an asterisk (*). Prior to 1980, the Census Bureau never singled out Spanish-origin persons as a mutually exclusive racial category. Instead, persons in the Spanish-origin category could be of any race. The practice in the other sources of data used here is unclear. Mex = Mexican. PR = Puerto Rican. Chic = Chicano. Cu = Cuban. Ch = Chinese. Ph = Philipino. Ja = Japanese.

[a]Dearman & Plisko (1981, Table 2.27, SD ≈ 10). [b]Berryman (1983, Table 2.27, SD ≈ 100). [c]Berryman (1983, Table 51). [d]Berryman (1983, Table 49). [e]U.S. Bureau of the Census (1984a, calculated from Table 262). [f]Berryman (1983, Tables 2, 5–7). [g]U.S. Bureau of the Census (1982, Table 48). [h]U.S. Commission on Civil Rights (1978, Table 4.6). [i]U.S. Bureau of the Census (1978, Table 4.2). [j]U.S. Bureau of the Census (1984a, Table 272). [k]Dearman & Plisko (1981, Table 2.11). [l]U.S. Bureau of the Census (1983b, Table 1). [m]U.S. Commission on Civil Rights (1978, Table 3.4). [n]U.S. Bureau of the Census (1973, calculated from Tables 10 & 11). [o]U.S. Bureau of the Census (1982, Table 23). [p]Lando, Cutler, & Gamber (1982, Table 7). [q]National Center for Health Statistics (1977, Table 1). [r]U.S. Bureau of the Census (1984b, Table 10). [s]U.S. Bureau of the Census (1973, Tables 8 & 13). [t]U.S. Bureau of the Census (1983c, Table 1).

most career counselors. Some indication is provided about how the hypotheses
may differ for older groups of people.

Low Intelligence. Eysenck (1984) has summarized the research on ra-
cial/ethnic differences in IQ. According to his review, "The highest IQs in
different parts of the world have been obtained by Mongoloid populations,
particularly the Japanese and Chinese, both in their own countries and in emigrated samples studied in the United States" (p. 260). The Japanese and Chinese
appear to score about a half a standard deviation above the white IQ mean on
nonverbal tests. Mongoloids "are followed by Caucasoid populations in North-
ern Europe or emigrated from there to the United States, Australia, and elsewhere. Caucasoid groups in Southern Europe come next, followed by Caucasoid
peoples in the Middle and Near East" (p. 260). In the IQ metric, the mean scores
of these Caucasoid groups range from about 100 to around 90. Eysenck's summary continues, "Amerinds [American-Indians] and Mexican-Americans come
next, followed by Afro-Americans, African Negroids, and Australoids" (p.
260). Mean IQs for the former groups range in the high 80s and mean IQs for the
latter groups nearer the low 80s. Data are sparser for some groups than for
others, but Eysenck notes that there have been hundreds of studies on blacks and
they "agree on the fact that the mean IQ of American blacks is approximately
85, and that they score somewhat higher on verbal than on nonverbal tests" (p.
258). Gordon (1980b) has also shown that the size of the black–white difference
in IQ has not changed since at least World War I. The foregoing data are
consistent with the fact that blacks are more than twice as likely as whites to be in
classes for the mentally retarded and Asian-Americans are more than twice as
likely as whites to be in programs for the gifted and talented (Dearman & Plisko,
1981, Tables 2.13 and 6.5). Eysenck (1984) also refers to the high IQ of British
Jews, which is consistent with the many studies of American Jews (Hennessy &
Merrifield, 1978). Whereas Mongoloids are particularly high on nonverbal IQ
tests, Jews are particularly high on verbal IQ tests—113 according to a review by
Gordon (1980b).

Table 5.2 shows aptitude and achievement test scores for American students
at different educational levels. The vocabulary test scores for high school sophomores and seniors, shown in Table 5.2, are good measures of *g* (general
intelligence), and they reveal the same ranking described above in Eysenck's
review of other sorts of data. Scores for these students on seven diverse tests
were reported (not shown here) and they all provide consistent evidence about
racial/ethnic differences in mental abilities: Asian-Americans score as well as or
better than whites on all tests; some Hispanic groups (Cubans) and American-
Indians score lower than whites on all tests (by about .2–.5 SDs), followed by
other Hispanic groups (Mexican-Americans and Puerto Ricans) and then by
blacks, who score close to one standard deviation below whites on most tests
(Dearman & Plisko, 1981, Table 2.27). Racial/ethnic differences in intelligence

may be somewhat smaller for particular educational groups than for the general population, because less intelligent people tend not to go as far in school as other people, but Table 5.2 shows that sizeable racial/ethnic differences in academic aptitude remain at all levels of education (see also Hennessy & Merrifield, 1978). Most of those racial/ethnic differences are found in the different individual fields of study as well (Berryman, 1983, Tables 50 & 51).

Profile differences by ethnic group among the high school students in Table 5.2 are also informative. In particular, mean scores of Asian-Americans equal those for whites on all tests except math, on which the former outperform whites by about .4 standard deviation. Data on spatial ability are available elsewhere for seniors (who are less representative of the general population than are sophomores) and they show that once again Asian-Americans outperform whites by about .4 standard deviation (Dearman & Plisko, 1981, Table 2.27). Table 5.2 shows that this strong quantitative ability profile for Asian-Americans is found among college-bound high school students (students taking the SAT) and among those seeking admission to graduate and professional schools (students taking the GRE). This elevated quantitative profile among Asian-Americans is interesting, because it is the typical profile among applicants to programs of study in engineering, mathematics, and the physical sciences (Berryman, 1983, Tables 35 & 36), and because Asian-Americans are in fact overrepresented in scientific and technical jobs.

Mental abilities are important for job performance in all jobs, but they are particularly important in high-level jobs (Gottfredson, 1985a). Nevertheless, it should be noted that they are not the only abilities that are important on some jobs and racial/ethnic groups appear to differ on these other capacities as well. In particular, psychomotor abilities are particularly important in some jobs, mostly low-level ones, and Asians-Americans, Hispanics, and Native-Americans have all been found to outperform whites on the psychomotor tests of the General Aptitude Test Battery (GATB), and blacks score only slightly lower than whites on such tests (Hunter, 1983).

Sex differences in mental abilities are small by comparison to racial/ethnic differences. There are no sex differences in mean intelligence, but there is evidence that females are less variable in general intelligence than are males, meaning that fewer of them are found at the high and low extremes of intelligence (Jensen, 1980, pp. 627–628). Males are higher on spatial visualization ability on the average (Jensen, 1980, pp. 626–627; Minton & Schneider, 1980, pp. 273–275), and there appear to be fewer females than males with extremely high math reasoning ability even after controlling for interest and prior coursework (Benbow & Stanley, 1980). Females do somewhat better than males on some measures of verbal aptitude, in particular, on tests of verbal fluency (Minton & Schneider, 1980, pp. 271–272). Females also appear to be somewhat superior to males in social sensitivity or insight as measured by the ability to judge emotions or states communicated by nonverbal cues (Minton & Schneider,

1980, p. 295). Finally, males surpass females in gross motor coordination, and the reverse is true for fine motor coordination (Minton & Schneider, 1980, p. 277).

This author knows of no evidence showing that the distributions of intelligence among the deaf, blind, dyslexic, and mentally ill differ from that of the general population, but there is some difficulty adequately assessing the intelligence of such groups. The mentally retarded are, by definition, of low intelligence.

There is no convincing evidence that younger cohorts are either more or less intelligent than older cohorts.

Poor Academic Background.   Table 5.2 provides data on educational attainment by sex and race for young people. (Cohorts born more recently are more highly educated than cohorts born earlier this century.) Females are less likely than males to drop out of high school, although the sex difference varies considerably by racial/ethnic group. Among persons aged 20–24, Hispanics are most likely to have dropped out of high school, followed by Native-Americans and then by blacks. Dropout rates for Asian-Americans are similar to those for whites. Whites are 2–3 times and Asian-Americans are about 4 times as likely to get 16 or more years of education as are Hispanics, blacks, and Native-Americans. Rates are approximately equal for males and females. Blacks, Hispanics, and Native-Americans are much less likely than whites to obtain a BA or higher degree; whites, Asian-Americans, males, and females are all about equally likely to get BAs or MAs, but Asian-Americans are *more* likely than whites to get PhDs and females are much *less* likely than males to get PhDs or professional degrees. Thus, males are more likely than females to be found at the extremes of educational attainment, both high and low, and the hypothesis of no sex difference in educational level shown in Table 5.1 should be understood to be an oversimplification of this more complex sex difference. Other data suggest that Jewish-Americans obtain more education than do either white Gentiles or Asian-Americans. For example, one follow-up of high school students, who were members of Jewish organizations, reported that 95% attended college (Swerdloff & Rosen, 1973).

Table 5.2 also provides some data on field of degree, which is an issue of particular concern in the special groups literature. Women, Native-Americans, and especially blacks and Hispanics are more underrepresented among people obtaining degrees in quantitative-based fields than in other fields. In contrast, Asian-Americans are 2–3 times as likely as whites to get degrees in quantitatively-based fields.

Work-disabled individuals tend to get less education than do the nondisabled. For example, Lando et al. (1982, Table 33) reported that 26% of work-disabled males aged 18–34 in 1978 had less than 12 years of education, and 14% had 16 or more years, as opposed to 17% and 21%, respectively for the nondisabled.

Percentages were 37% and 0.4% for the severely disabled males. Among females aged 18–34, percentages were 17% and 14% for the nondisabled, 30% and 10% for all disabled females, and 48% and 0.4% for the severely disabled. Although these data are not directly comparable to the data in Table 5.2, they suggest that the disabled resemble blacks and Hispanics in education more than they resemble whites, and that the severely disabled (especially women) fare worse than any of the racial/ethnic groups. Educational disadvantages could be expected to differ according to the type of disability in question and according to the severity of the functional limitation. For example, Gottfredson et al. (1984b) found that dyslexics obtain less education (particularly graduate and professional degrees) than would be expected on the basis of their intelligence and social class, and that severe dyslexics were at a greater disadvantage than mild dyslexics.

Comes From Poor Family.   Table 5.2 shows the percentage of *children* who live in families below the poverty line, the percentage of *households* below the poverty line, and the median household income per capita. These data show that black, Hispanic, and Native-American youngsters are probably much less likely than whites to have *family* financial resources at their disposal. Asian-Americans range from being somewhat less favored to considerably more favored than whites in this regard, depending on the particular Asian-American group in question. The same general trends are found for another indicator of family economic well-being—the unemployment rate among an age group that can be presumed to be parents of people in their teens and 20s.

Family poverty is presumed to be equal for male and female youth because they grow up in the same families. Although relevant data may exist for persons with handicaps, they were not located. Therefore, no hypotheses are presented for most of the handicapped groups. The mentally retarded may tend somewhat to come from somewhat poorer families, because *some* types of mental retardation run in families and mental retardation of parents can be presumed to adversely affect family economic well-being. There is some evidence that certain other handicapped groups such as dyslexics do *not* come from poorer families, but are fairly representative of all economic strata (Klasen, 1972, pp. 149, 169).

Cultural Isolation/Segregation.   It is not clear how to operationalize cultural isolation or segregation, but several relevant indices are shown in Table 5.2. If having limited proficiency in English is used as one indicator, it suggests that Hispanic children are most often isolated from the majority culture, followed by Asian-Americans, and then by Native-Americans. Essentially all whites and all blacks are English speakers. A different picture emerges if isolation is measured in terms of socioeconomic or occupational level of each racial/ethnic group as a whole, which might be considered an indicator of the occupational exposure youngsters receive. The two measures used here—mean occupational prestige level and percentage of workers who are professionals or managers—suggest that familiarity with high level jobs is likely to be at least as high for Asian-American youth as for white youth and to be considerably lower for blacks, Hispanics, and Native-Americans. Although comparable data are not available for white ethnics, some differences in occupational attainment are well documented. For example, Jews are greatly over represented in scientific and scholarly careers and among leading intellectuals in the United States, and Catholics are underrepresented in both areas (Hardy, 1974; Kadushin, 1972; Wuthnow, 1977). Rates of intermarriage with whites provide yet another pattern of isolation from the dominant culture. Among married women with husbands present, only about 1 in 200 blacks is married to a white man versus 1 in 3 for most age groups of Japanese- or Native-American women. Rates for Hispanics and Chinese are intermediate.

The data presented here suggest that different racial/ethnic groups probably differ considerably in their isolation from the white majority culture depending on the particular indicator in question and that they are isolated according to some indicators but not others. This is consistent with data on racial segregation; for example, black–white segregation is high in housing, lower in schooling, and yet lower in employment (Becker, 1981). It is assumed here that, overall, all racial/ethnic groups are somewhat culturally isolated and segregated.

It is also assumed that men and women are culturally isolated from each other to some degree, but this assumption reflects a common belief more than any particular empirical evidence. To the extent that women are culturally isolated, it might be expected that children living only with their mothers might also be somewhat isolated. Table 5.2 shows that in 1980, 47% of black teenagers and 21% of Hispanics versus only 14% of whites were somewhat isolated according to this criterion. Comparable data for children were not available for the other racial/ethnic groups, but related data (U.S. Bureau of the Census, 1983a, calculated from Tables 121, 161) on the percentage of families that are female-headed (no husband present) show that Native-American families in 1980 were about twice as likely as white families to be female-headed (23% vs. 11%). Among Asian-Americans, Japanese and Philipino families were equally likely (12%) and Chinese families were less likely (8%) than white families to be female-headed. People with handicaps are presumed to be no more and no less *culturally* isolated than the nonhandicapped members of their social groups.

Functional Limitation. Approximately one third of adults aged 20–34 in 1972 (not shown in Table 5.2) reported some chronic health problem, and about 7% reported that they were disabled to the extent that their condition limited the type or amount of work they could do; 2% reported being severely disabled (Krute & Burdette, 1981, Table J). By age 55–64, $\frac{2}{3}$ of adults reported some chronic condition, and 29% reported being work disabled (18% severely so). Some conditions are more prevalent among whites than nonwhites (e.g., respiratory or digestive problems, neoplasms), but others are more prevalent among nonwhites (e.g., cardiovascular, mental, and urogenital problems; Krute & Burdette, 1981, Table I). However, nonwhites are more often disabled by their conditions; among adults aged 20–64 in 1972, about 14% of whites were disabled, but 19% of nonwhites were. A slightly larger proportion of women than men had some chronic condition (51% vs. 46%) and were disabled (15% vs. 14%; Krute & Burdette, 1981, Table F). As with race, the sex differences vary according to the specific condition in question. A few specific examples illustrate this variability. The percentages of men, women, whites, and nonwhites who were disabled because of the following conditions are, respectively, 0.8, 0.5, 0.7, and 0.3 for hearing problems; 0.8, 0.8, 0.8, and 1.1 for visual impairments; 2.5, 3.2, 2.6, and 5.3 for mental problems; and 0.8, 1.4, 1.2, and 0.4 for nonrespiratory allergies (Krute & Burdette, 1981, Tables F and H). Detailed data for different nonwhite categories are sparse, but they suggest that racial/ethnic groups cannot be assumed to have the same types or numbers of disabilities. Although the data for some Hispanic groups seem suspect, Table 5.2 shows data for the percentages of people aged 18–34 in 1978 in different racial/ethnic groups who reported having a disability that limited the type or amount of work they do. The handicapped groups listed in Table 5.1 of course have at least one functional limitation by definition.

Self-esteem.   Low self-esteem has commonly been attributed to all groups that have been subject to discrimination and negative stereotyping, but empirical research appears to contradict this assumption. Reviewers outside the special-groups literature have repeatedly concluded from the extensive body of research on self-esteem that general self-esteem among blacks is equal to or greater than that of whites (Gecas, 1982; Gerard, 1983) and that males and females report similar levels of self-esteem from the early school years through adulthood (Minton & Schneider, 1980, p. 315). Differences in self-esteem by social class are negligible (Gecas, 1982). Thus, it cannot be assumed a priori that any racial/ethnic or other special group is at particular risk of low self-esteem. There is some suggestion, however, that racial desegregation can damage the self-esteem of the less successful group (Gecas, 1982; Gerard, 1983). There is also some evidence that the self-esteem of functionally handicapped groups suffers in nonhandicapped settings. For example, the self-esteem of the educable mentally retarded is higher in handicapped as opposed to nonhandicapped settings, unless the nonhandicapped setting is specifically structured to prevent or obscure the unfavorable social comparisons that normally occur (Madden & Slavin, 1983). Several studies reviewed by MacMillan (1977, pp. 257–258) showed that self-concepts became more favorable when children were placed in classes for the educable mentally retarded; and self-concepts became less favorable when the children were returned to regular classes, probably because of changes in referent group. To some extent, social or cultural isolation may actually protect self-esteem when social comparison processes (Gecas, 1982) in more integrated settings are likely to be unfavorable.

Authors in the special-groups literature generally cite studies that apparently support the contention that there are race and sex differences in general self-esteem (Fitzgerald & Betz, 1983), so there is some inconsistency here that must be resolved. Table 5.1 relies on the conclusions of experts on self-esteem outside the special-groups literature (Wylie, 1984).

There is, however, more consensus that specific components of self-esteem differ by race and sex. For example, self-efficacy, self-confidence, locus of control, and related perceptions of competence (as opposed to self-worth) appear to differ by race, sex, and power relations in specific circumstances (Betz & Hackett, 1981; Gecas, 1982; Minton & Schneider, 1980, pp. 286–288, 450). Research that controls for the actual differences in competence described above (Betz & Hackett, 1981) suggests that concepts of self-efficacy may be more useful than concepts of self-worth for explaining the career choices of some special groups.

Different Within Own Social Circle: Nontraditional Interests, Social Isolation/Segregation, Low Intelligence Compared to Family and Peers, and High Intelligence Compared to Family and Peers.   The author knows of no evidence concerning rates for nontraditional interest, but it is assumed here that majority whites are traditional and that females are now more likely to have nontraditional interests than are males.

There is no reason to presume that individuals of any particular racial/ethnic group or sex are especially likely to be isolated within their own social groups. Handicapped individuals can be presumed to be, but most evidence is anecdotal. Measures of psychological social distance suggest that some disabled groups (e.g., mentally ill, mentally retarded, alcoholic) are much more isolated by negative social reactions than are others (e.g., diabetic, amputee, blind; Tringo, 1970).

The mentally retarded are undoubtedly of lower intelligence than many or most of the people in their own social circles, but there seems no reason to expect members of any other special group listed in Table 5.1 to be especially likely to be at either the extreme low or high ends of the intelligence distribution of their family and peers.

Primary Caregiver.   If the presence of children is taken as an indication that a person is a primary caregiver, fertility data provide some evidence concerning race and sex differences in this risk factor. (It is assumed here that being a mother is much more demanding of caregiving and a more serious family–work conflict than is being a wife, and fertility data are provided for all women whether mrried or not.) Table 5.2 shows that among women aged 18–19 in 1982, 86.9% were still childless, that two-thirds of 20–24 year olds were childless, and that the percentage dropped to about 40 by ages 25–29. If it is presumed that fathers are not primary caregivers when mothers are present in the household, then only a tiny fraction of males at these same ages have day-to-day responsibility for children or other dependents because only 3–4% maintain families without a wife (calculated from data in U.S. Department of Labor, 1980, Table 79).

Racial differences among women are also evident in Table 5.2. At all ages shown, black and Hispanic women are considerably less likely than whites to be childless (ignoring marital status), and both of these groups have borne twice as many children as have whites. The differences are especially striking for the high school and college ages, where birthrates are at least two to three times as high for blacks and Hispanics as for whites, and the highest birthrates are found for blacks. For example, whereas only about 10% of 18–19-year-old white women in 1982 had at least one child, more than 20% of Hispanic women and almost 30% of black women had at least one child. Although life-time expectancies for childbearing are similar across the three racial/ethnic groups (U.S. Bureau of the Census, 1984b, Table 2), it is apparent that Hispanic women tend to bear their first children at younger ages than do whites, and blacks bear children at still younger ages. These differences would seem to be extremely important, but they have been totally ignored in the special-groups literature.

Comparable fertility data are not available for recent years for Asian-Americans, Native-Americans, or the handicapped. Data for all racial/ethnic groups listed in Table 5.2 are available for 1970, however. (Percent still childless is available only for the subset of women who were *ever married* by that time.) Those data, shown in Table 5.2, suggest that fertility rates among Native-Americans are high and similar to those among blacks; in contrast, rates for the different Asian-American groups are usually lower than those for whites. Comparable data from 1960 show the same pattern (Bogue, 1969, Table 18–20).

Primary Economic Provider. This risk factor refers here to having at least one financial dependent for whom one is largely responsible. Good data are not available, but some indication is provided by assuming that all married males with a wife present and all women with children under age 18 but without husbands present are primary economic providers, and that the percentage of men who are single (never married) is an estimate of the number of men *without* financial responsibility for other people. Table 5.2 shows that only 5% of males aged 18–19 in 1982 had ever married. The percentages rise to 28 among men aged 20–24 and to 64 among men aged 25–29. (Data for females are shown for purposes of comparison, but they are not considered relevant in this context.) At each age, men are less likely to have married than women are to have had at least one child; this suggests that women tend to become primary caregivers at younger ages than men become economic providers. This sex difference in family responsibilities is even more pronounced when only married men with wives present are considered. Among women aged 16–44, 26% have children under 18 but no husband present (calculated from data in U.S. Bureau of the Census, 1983d, Table 23).

Racial/ethnic differences are also evident in Table 5.2. At all ages Hispanic men are somewhat more likely than whites to be married with a spouse present, and black men are considerably less likely to be primary economic providers according to this criterion. On the other hand, black *women* may be more likely than white women to be primary economic providers (Gump & Rivers, 1975).

Individuals with handicaps are assumed less likely than nonhandicapped individuals to be either primary caregivers or primary economic providers, because fewer disabled than nondisabled marry (Lando et al., 1982, Table 17). Some handicapped groups, particularly the mentally retarded and the severely physically disabled, may be more likely to be dependents themselves, but the author has no data to support that assumption.

The analysis of risk factors and relative risk rates seems useful in several ways. It indicates in more specific and more meaningful terms some of the conditions implied by general concepts such as racism and stereotyping. For example, cultural isolation, poverty, and low self-esteem are some of the marks that racist practices are assumed to leave on affected individuals. In addition, Table 5.1 shows that each special group shares some of the same risks as do some other special groups. For example, higher rates of risk for low intelligence, little education, and few financial resources are shared by a few of the racial/ethnic groups; cultural isolation or segregation is probably shared by all racial/ethnic groups; and isolation of some sort is shared by most or all types of special groups. Systematic differences among the special groups are also evident, but the differences are more a matter of degree of overlap in disadvantages than lack of overlap altogether. The handicapped and the two sexes tend to face different types of risks than do the different racial/ethnic groups.

Table 5.1 also illustrates how a common list of risk factors compiled from studies of different individual special groups can help focus attention on risk factors that are important for some social groups but that are often ignored. For example, being a primary caregiver is typically assumed to be a career development problem for women, but the data in Table 5.2 are a reminder that this problem is much more prevalent among women in some racial/ethnic groups than in others. Likewise, although males generally are perceived not to be subject to any special risk factors, this assumption may be incorrect. Males tend to bear the economic burdens of supporting a family, and this responsibility can impede optimal career development. This burden also varies by racial/ethnic group, although not in the same way as do the racial/ethnic differences in being a primary caregiver.

The list of risk factors generated from groups that have already been studied is useful for understanding the problems of groups that have not been studied. For example, the list provides a way of thinking about the career problems of reentry women, displaced workers, homosexuals, the aged, delinquents, and many other special populations.

A more general implication of Table 5.1 is that members of *any* group, whether "special" or not, can be afflicted by any of the risk factors. Listing the problems of special groups in an analytical manner, but without reference to special group status per se, helps the counselor to be alert to problems a counselee may have that are *not* typical for that type of person. In other words, the entries in Table 5.1 indicate what risk factors are most likely for different types of people, but the list of risk factors in Table 5.1 provides a more comprehensive list of problems that should be kept in mind for all people.

Finally, by relying primarily on empirical evidence rather than on common beliefs, the entries in Tables 5.1 and 5.2 illustrate that many common assumptions about special groups are false. For example, it is well established in the psychological literature that special groups are much more similar in self-esteem and much less similar in cognitive abilities than is commonly asserted.

CAREER CHOICE PROBLEMS AND THEIR DIAGNOSIS

It is not sufficient for counseling purposes to know only what the risk factors are that can lead to career choice problems. Counselors typically deal with counselees who *already* have problems that require diagnosis and treatment. Counselors are not concerned solely with the treatment of career and other problems, nor are they unconcerned with the prevention of those problems. However, counselors function more like physicians than like public health officers in the sense that they have traditionally specialized more in responding to the problems individuals bring to them than in designing group-level interventions to prevent the sorts of problems they treat. A knowledge of group differences, such as those described in the previous section, is valuable to counselors, as are in-depth descriptions of particular special groups and the atypical circumstances they often face. However, it has not been clear how counselors should use such group-differences data when dealing with individuals who may or may not be typical of their groups.

This section outlines a framework for classifying and diagnosing career choice problems that links the information gained from group-level analyses to the individual-level approach of traditional career counseling. More specifically, it represents an attempt to organize much of what has been said in the literature about special groups in a way that illustrates the linkage of those data and hypotheses to common career counseling issues such as indecision, realism, and exploration in vocational choice and in a way that provides a better understanding of how interest inventories may be most useful in the overall career counseling process. This diagnostic framework focuses on the external and internal barriers commonly associated with special group status and so only partially overlaps diagnostic or theoretical systems with a psychodynamic or developmental orientation (Knefelkamp & Slepitza, 1978).

Diagnosis refers to having a systematic way of recognizing and classifying problems, and it is often considered useful, if not essential, for determining effective treatment. Stated more simply, it helps to have a good idea what the problem is before trying to treat it. A variety of diagnostic schemes have been developed for classifying career development problems (Bordin, 1946; Campbell & Cellini, 1981; Crites, 1969, 1981; Pepinsky, 1948; Rounds & Tinsley, 1984; Williamson, 1939), but none has attracted much interest on the part of researchers or practitioners (Rounds & Tinsley, 1984)—a situation that suggests that none has been found particularly useful. It seems imperative, however, to continue the search for better ways by which counselors can identify and analyze the career choice problems of counselees (Osipow, 1982; Rounds & Tinsley, 1984), particularly for those counselees at special risk.

The problem framework described here uses four categories of problem: risk factor, underlying problem, symptom (presenting problem), and assessment criterion. Twelve risk factors have already been described. Each of the three other categories is briefly described before showing the relations among them and their implications for beneficial test usage.

Distinction Between Assessment Criteria, Presenting Problems, and Underlying Problems

Although it may be a laudable goal to help people solve most or all of their problems, the limited resources of both counselors and clients make it more realistic and efficient to focus on those problems that significantly impede successful development. This makes it especially useful to have in mind what the features of *successful* development are when trying to assess and rank the major problems counselees have. These criteria of successful career choice development are referred to as *assessment criteria*. Five major assessment criteria are proposed in Table 5.3: (a) has the counselee identified one or more educational/occupational alternatives? (b) are the counselee's chosen educational/occupational alternatives realistic in light of his or her interests and abilities? (c) is the counselee happy and comfortable with the alternatives he or she has identified? (d) has the counselee unnecessarily restricted his or her alternatives? and (e) is the counselee aware of and realistic about obstacles and opportunities for implementing his or her educational/occupational plans?

As indicated in Table 5.3, the criteria are applied sequentially, for reasons of both logic and efficiency, although in practice criteria 2–4 can be considered simultaneously to some extent. These criteria are consistent with other diagnostic schemes that emphasize indecision and unrealism about suitability of choice (e.g., Crites, 1981, and the other "descriptive" classifications discussed by

TABLE 5.3
Outline of a System for Assessing Career Choice Problems

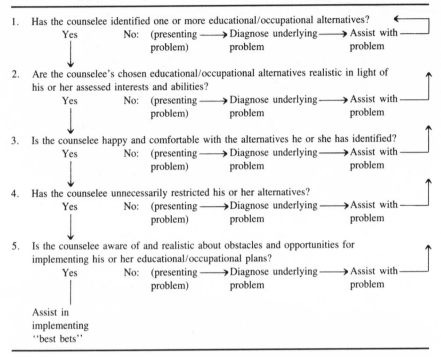

1. Has the counselee identified one or more educational/occupational alternatives?
   Yes   No: (presenting ──→ Diagnose underlying ──→ Assist with ──┐
                        problem)   problem   problem

2. Are the counselee's chosen educational/occupational alternatives realistic in light of his or her assessed interests and abilities?
   Yes   No: (presenting ──→ Diagnose underlying ──→ Assist with ──┘
                        problem)   problem   problem

3. Is the counselee happy and comfortable with the alternatives he or she has identified?
   Yes   No: (presenting ──→ Diagnose underlying ──→ Assist with ──┘
                        problem)   problem   problem

4. Has the counselee unnecessarily restricted his or her alternatives?
   Yes   No: (presenting ──→ Diagnose underlying ──→ Assist with ──┘
                        problem)   problem   problem

5. Is the counselee aware of and realistic about obstacles and opportunities for implementing his or her educational/occupational plans?
   Yes   No: (presenting ──→ Diagnose underlying ──→ Assist with ──┘
                        problem)   problem   problem

Assist in
implementing
"best bets"

Rounds & Tinsley, 1984), but they include two criteria that are not considered in many schemes—counselee comfort with the choice(s) and counselee realism about the accessibility (as opposed to the suitability) of the choice(s). Providing information about job openings and training requirements has been a major activity in guidance and career counseling, of course, but diagnostic schemes usually stop short of assessing counselees' realism about their prospects and plans for actually implementing their choices. This last criterion may be an especially important one when aiding members of special groups because they are generally presumed to have to cope with diverse barriers. The five assessment criteria listed in Table 5.3 are not the only ones that might be proposed, and there are difficulties in determining whether counselees have met them (Hewer, 1966), but they seem consistent with two prominent goals in career counseling— ensuring opportunity while at the same time encouraging wise choice. The five criteria should be considered guides for promoting successful development, not absolute nor necessarily even consistent goals. Circumstances may be such that individuals may not be able to pursue occupations that are optimal in terms of interests and abilities or they may choose, for good reasons, not to pursue such occupations.

If the counselor determines that the counselee meets an assessment criterion, then the next assessment criterion is considered. However, if the counselee fails to meet the criterion, then the problems underlying that failure are sought before going on to the next criterion. Certain *presenting problems* (e.g., anxiety, academic failure) may be typically associated with different types of developmental failure, but they are of limited value in diagnosing and treating the counselee's career choice problems. They are merely symptoms in this context, and so are not discussed further.

Four classes of *underlying problems* are described next: (a) lack of self-knowledge; (b) having life goals and values that conflict with one another (internal conflict); (c) having goals and values that conflict with those of important people in one's life (external conflict); and (d) perceived barriers and opportunities. These four general underlying problems can be conceptualized as ranging from "inner" to "outer" in terms of whether the problem relates to the person's knowledge of and reactions to self, to family and friends, or to institutions of education and employment. The specific problems that underlie failures to meet the five different assessment criteria differ from one criterion to another, as detailed later, but these same general types of problems may be responsible for failure to meet any of the developmental criteria. These four categories of underlying problem appear to provide a useful way of organizing the many specific problems that have been identified by research, theory, and clinical experience, but they also serve as a stimulus for identifying other problems that may be seldom, if ever, discussed in the counseling literature. The underlying problems discussed here are similar to the problems included in diagnostic schemes designed to illuminate the etiology of vocational problems (e.g., Bordin, 1946; see also the Rounds & Tinsley, 1984, review of "psychodynamic" classifications of vocational problems).

A Problem Analysis Framework

Table 5.4 illustrates a framework for analyzing career choice problems. Examples of specific problems that can underlie failure to meet each of the assessment criteria are shown for each of those five criteria. These examples are illustrative, not exhaustive. The individuals presumed to be at most risk of having the specific underlying problems are listed opposite those problems. The individuals at most risk are those people who are characterized by the risk factors shown in Table 5.1. The last column of Table 5.4 thereby provides a way to trace the consequences of special group status to failures in career choice. Although the table is based on a reading of the literature, it should be considered a synthesis more of hypotheses than of findings in the field.

The following discussion illustrates the types of details that are provided in Table 5.4 for each of the five assessment criteria.

TABLE 5.4

A Problem Analysis Framework for Career Choice Problems: Five Assessment Criteria and Their Related Presenting Problems, Possible Underlying Problems, and Individuals Most at Risk

Assessment criterion	Presenting problem(s)	Possible underlying problems	Individuals most at risk (risk factor)
1. Has the counselee identified one or more educational/occupational alternatives?	No: Undecided	*Lack of self-knowledge*	
Yes (go to next criterion)		uncertain identity	
		--does not know own interests, personality, strengths and weaknesses	functional limitation
			low self-esteem
		--interests/abilities not well developed	culturally isolated/segregated
			socially isolated/segregated
		Internal conflict	
		cannot reconcile own incompatible life goals	
		--interesting work is too low in pay or prestige	a potential (social class) nontraditional
			primary economic provider
		--interesting work is wrong sextype	a potential (gender) nontraditional
		--job preferences conflict with family life	primary caregiver
		External conflict	
		goals conflict with family's wishes	primary caregiver
			primary economic provider
			a potential nontraditional (any type)
		friends have different goals	a potential nontraditional (any type)
		Perceived barriers and opportunities	
		perceived barriers to preferred work	
		--thinks preferred job(s) not available	
		--training is expensive	poor family
		--lacks necessary ability	poor academic background

(Continued)

TABLE 5.4
(Continued)

Assessment criterion	Presenting problem(s)	Possible underlying problems	Individuals most at risk (risk factor)
		--expects bias in hiring	low intelligence low intelligence compared to family/peers functional limitation ⎤ a potential nontraditional (any type) culturally isolated/segregated socially isolated/segregated functional limitation
2. Are the counselee's chosen educational/occupational alternatives realistic in light of his or her interests and abilities (i.e., are interests and abilities sufficient)? Yes (go to next criterion) No: may be no presenting problem and may be happy with choice lack of interest or motivation academic difficulties depression anxiety		*Lack of self-knowledge* --has overestimated own ability or special talents --mistaken about own interests	low intelligence socially isolated/segregated a potential (gender) nontraditional
		Internal conflict own life goals are incompatible --has sacrificed interests for pay or prestige --has sacrificed interests for sextype or family responsibilities --ignores lack of ability in order to pursue pay or prestige *External conflict* following course expected by parents,	a potential (social class) nontraditional primary economic provider a potential (gender) nontraditional primary caregiver low intelligence compared to family/peers

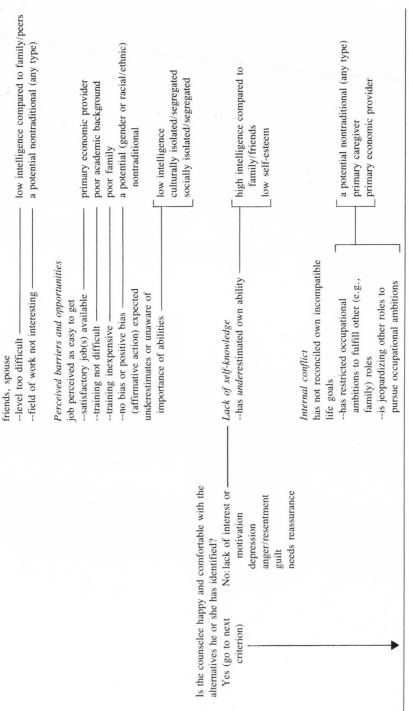

friends, spouse
--level too difficult ————— low intelligence compared to family/peers
--field of work not interesting ————— a potential nontraditional (any type)

Perceived barriers and opportunities
job perceived as easy to get
--satisfactory job(s) available ————— primary economic provider
--training not difficult ————— poor academic background
--training inexpensive ————— poor family
--no bias or positive bias ————— a potential (gender or racial/ethnic)
(affirmative action) expected   nontraditional
underestimates or unaware of
importance of abilities ————— ⎡ low intelligence
                              ⎢ culturally isolated/segregated
                              ⎣ socially isolated/segregated

Lack of self-knowledge
--has *under*estimated own ability ————— ⎡ high intelligence compared to
                                          ⎢ family/friends
                                          ⎣ low self-esteem

Internal conflict
has not reconciled own incompatible life goals
--has restricted occupational ambitions to fulfill other (e.g., family) roles
--is jeopardizing other roles to pursue occupational ambitions ————— ⎡ a potential nontraditional (any type)
                                                                      ⎢ primary caregiver
                                                                      ⎣ primary economic provider

3. Is the counselee happy and comfortable with the alternatives he or she has identified?
Yes (go to next criterion)
No: lack of interest or motivation
    depression
    anger/resentment
    guilt
    needs reassurance

(Continued)

171

TABLE 5.4
(Continued)

Assessment criterion	Presenting problem(s)	Possible underlying problems	Individuals most at risk (risk factor)
		External conflict has accommodated to family and peer expectations --has restricted his or her ambitions --has restricted locale of training or employment	a potential nontraditional (any type) primary economic provider primary caregiver
		Perceived barriers and opportunities preferred job perceived as difficult to get --jobs(s) not available --training for more preferred job is too expensive or lengthy --lacks ability for more preferred job	poor family primary economic provider poor academic background low intelligence compared to family/peers functional limitation
		--expects bias in hiring	functional limitation a potential (gender or racial/ethnic) nontraditional culturally isolated/segregated socially isolated/segregated
4. Has the counselee unnecessarily restricted his or her alternatives? Yes (go to next criterion)	No: may be no presenting problem and may be happy with choice wants training information wants job information wants job search training	*Lack of self-knowledge* --has underestimated abilities	low self-esteem functional limitation
		--has never considered possibility of self in other roles (e.g., lacks role models)	socially isolated/segregated culturally isolated/segregated poor family primary caregiver

172

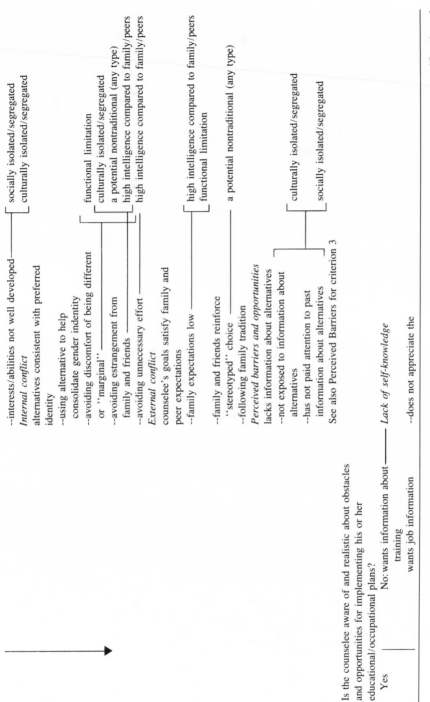

--interests/abilities not well developed —— socially isolated/segregated
  culturally isolated/segregated

Internal conflict
alternatives consistent with preferred identity

--using alternative to help consolidate gender indentity

--avoiding discomfort of being different or "marginal" —— functional limitation
  culturally isolated/segregated
  a potential nontraditional (any type)
  high intelligence compared to family/peers

--avoiding estrangement from family and friends —— high intelligence compared to family/peers

--avoiding unnecessary effort

External conflict
counselee's goals satisfy family and peer expectations

--family expectations low —— high intelligence compared to family/peers
  functional limitation

--family and friends reinforce "stereotyped" choice —— a potential nontraditional (any type)

--following family tradition

Perceived barriers and opportunities
lacks information about alternatives

--not exposed to information about alternatives

--has not paid attention to past information about alternatives —— culturally isolated/segregated
  socially isolated/segregated

See also Perceived Barriers for criterion 3

5. Is the counselee aware of and realistic about obstacles and opportunities for implementing his or her educational/occupational plans?

  Yes

  No: wants information about —— *Lack of self-knowledge*
    training
    wants job information —— --does not appreciate the

(Continued)

173

TABLE 5.4
(Continued)

Assessment criterion	Presenting problems(s)	Possible underlying problems	Individuals most at risk (risk factor)
	wants job search training discouraged about plans resisting or denying need to adjust goals	effort or motivation that will have to expend	
		Internal conflict	
		--not willing to consider need to adjust goals	
		External conflict	
		--would be embarrassed to change plans	
		Perceived barriers and opportunities	
		--not exposed to enough information about job requirements	socially isolated/segregated
Assist counselee in gathering information and in implementing "best bets."		--has not taken full advantage of information and opportunities in own social environment (e.g., friends and relatives)	culturally isolated/segregated
		--has not made much effort to gather information	socially isolated/segregated

Assessment Criterion 1: Counselee is Able to Voice a Choice.   This criterion refers specifically to being able to name one or a small number of occupations as viable alternatives. It does not refer to being undecided about which of those particular options is best. That final narrowing of one's choices to a single title need not, and probably should not, be done until after people have investigated the accessibility of various alternatives, how to make themselves more competitive, and developed back-up alternatives. In short, this criterion is somewhat different from the concept of being "undecided."

Not knowing one's own interests and abilities or not even having any well-developed interests and abilities both represent a lack of knowledge about oneself. A lack of knowledge about one's own interests and aptitudes obviously makes it difficult to identify occupations that might be consistent with those interests and abilities, so it can result in the inability to voice a choice at all. Although lack of self-knowledge probably occurs for a variety of reasons and in all populations, certain risk factors identified earlier show how special group status can be implicated in this type of indecision. Although the deaf, minorities, and women have all been thought, at least by some authors, to be handicapped more often than other groups by lack of self-knowledge, it is probably not these statuses per se that suppress the development of self-knowledge. That suppression can more likely be traced to the social and cultural isolation that often accompanies those statuses, because isolation or segregation can restrict a person's experiences and opportunities for developing and testing one's interests and competencies.

An inability to reconcile one's own incompatible life goals can also paralyze career decision making. For example, a primary economic provider may be unable to identify an occupation that will simultaneously meet his or her economic goals (e.g., economic security) and vocational interests (e.g., art). Two other examples are the mechanically inclined woman (a potential gender non-traditional) who may be unwilling to consider a masculine job, and the mother or single parent (i.e., a primary caregiver) who is unable to identify occupations that will allow that person to fulfill interests and family responsibilities at the same time.

The foregoing conflicts in goals are internal because they involve career and life goals and values held by counselees themselves. But goal conflict can also be more external. To illustrate, some people might like to follow their nontraditional interests, but are hesitant to do so because family and friends encourage them to do otherwise (e.g., a woman interested in firefighting or a man interested in nursing).

Finally, some people may be unable to voice a choice because they see their preferred occupation(s) as inaccessible to them. For example, a person from a poor family may perceive the necessary training for a preferred occupation as too expensive; people with nontraditional interests or physical limitations may expect bias against people like themselves; or persons handicapped by low intelligence, poor academic background, or a functional limitation may assume that they lack the necessary ability for getting and keeping the preferred job. Whether accurate or not, such perceptions of inaccessibility can lead to the inability to state and pursue an occupational preference.

In short, a wide variety of underlying problems may lead to the inability to state an occupational choice. The risk factors to which these problems can be traced often differ, but it should be noted that all but one of the risk factors is represented for this assessment criterion and that some members of all special groups, including white males, can thereby be expected to be at risk in some way of being unable to voice a career choice.

Assessment Criterion 2: Interests and Abilities Are Adequate for Occupation(s) Chosen.   The same four general underlying problems can lead to the failure to meet this second criterion, but their specific manifestations and the risk factors with which they are associated are often different. Overestimating one's abilities and being mistaken about one's interests both represent a lack of knowledge about oneself that can lead to making choices that are unrealistically high or out of touch with the kinds of activities one really enjoys most. Overestimating one's abilities may be associated, for example, with low intelligence, and being mistaken about one's interests may stem from being a potential nontraditional (e.g., a woman automatically assuming that she shares typically feminine interests).

It was noted earlier that internal and external conflict of goals can lead to indecision, but they can also lead to unsuitable choices. For example, both primary economic providers and primary caregivers may sacrifice, sometimes unnecessarily, their interests for their family responsibilities, the former by opting for higher pay regardless of interests, and the latter opting for a job with flexible scheduling and easy reentry regardless of interests or pay. Other people—particularly those who are significantly less intelligent than family and friends, but who wish to meet the same standards of success—may ignore their low abilities or work especially hard in order to pursue jobs beyond some particular level of pay or prestige. This type of person may even realize that the chosen occupation is too difficult but may still pursue it because of family pressure. Many potential nontraditionals may also pursue occupations for which they are unsuited because family and friends expect them to do what is typical for their sex, race, ethnic group, social class, or particular family tradition.

Many individuals may pursue jobs of little interest to them simply because those jobs are perceived as readily available. For example, they may perceive the training as easy or inexpensive, that many such jobs are available, or they may expect that the employers for those jobs will be especially favorable to hiring someone like themselves (i.e., of their race or sex). People who feel at some disadvantage in the labor market (e.g., have a poor academic background or a functional limitation) or who feel that they need to find employment in a hurry (e.g., a primary economic provider) may be drawn by the accessibility of a job rather than by the opportunity to use their interests and abilities. To take a more specific example, Hershenson (1974) has noted that there are special opportunities for people with certain types of handicap (e.g., newstands for the blind) and that certain handicaps actually represent a competitive advantage in some jobs (e.g., deafness in noxiously noisy jobs). These and other such opportunities for the handicapped are desirable, but they can be a two-edged sword if they divert individuals from searching for jobs more suitable to their interests. Yet other individuals may pursue jobs that are quite difficult in view of their abilities because they are unaware of or underestimate the ability requirements of those jobs. People at particular risk may be those who tend to have little information about occupations and would include people of low intelligence and people who have been culturally or socially isolated.

Assessment Criterion 3: Counselee Is Satisfied With Choice. Not only should a choice seem appropriate to the counselor, but it also should be congenial to the counselee. It may not be possible to find an occupational alternative that is both realistic and satisfying to the counselee, but a lack of enthusiasm may indicate some underlying problem that *is* remediable and that in turn may allow the identification of a more satisfying choice.

People may have chosen unchallenging and unsatisfying occupations because they have underestimated their own abilities. People at particular risk would seem to include those with low self-esteem or the more talented people in a social setting who assume they are no more able than their less talented peers to pursue jobs requiring high-level abilities.

People may also be dissatisfied with their choices, although their abilities and interests are adequate for those occupations, because they have not reconciled incompatible life goals. Potential nontraditionals and primary caregivers may have knowingly restricted their occupational ambitions in order to fulfill other (e.g., family) roles, so that they are left unenthusiastic about their career choices. But it is also the case that some people will be uncomfortable precisely because they *do* decide to pursue their career ambitions and thereby jeopardize valued noncareer roles. Accommodating to family and peer expectations can also result in dissatisfying occupational choices. For example, both primary economic providers and primary caregivers may restrict the types of training or employment they will consider in order to minimize financial or other costs to their families.

Perceived barriers to obtaining one's most preferred occupation may also lead people to voice choices about which they are not enthusiastic. The desired jobs simply may not exist in that locality, or training may be too expensive (e.g., for poorer youngsters) or too lengthy (e.g., for primary economic providers or primary caregivers). The person may lack the qualifications required for the more preferred job because of poor education, low intelligence, or physical limitations; potential gender or racial/ethnic nontraditionals and the physically impaired, among others, may also expect bias in hiring that can destroy their chances of employment in the preferred job. Once again, those perceptions may or may not be accurate, but they can still affect decision making.

Assessment Criterion 4: Choices Are Not Unnecessarily Restricted. A chosen occupation may be entirely within one's range of interests and capabilities, but not represent as full a utilization of one's talents and interests as might be possible. The concern here is not with ensuring that counselees seek the ideal choice for them, but that they seek a fulfilling one. This issue of unnecessary restriction of choice is probably the developmental criterion that has drawn the most concern in discussions of special groups. It is not necessarily the case, however, that counselees themselves, including white males, are dissatisfied with overly restricted occupational choices, even with choices that hold little promise of actually satisfying them later on.

Lack of self-knowledge can lead to unnecessary restriction of choice. Individuals who have been culturally or socially isolated may not have well developed interests, and others (e.g., people with low self-esteem or physical impairments) may have underestimated their abilities. Many people probably restrict their choices simply because they have never considered many alternatives; the restriction results not so much from rejecting alternatives as it does from never even having entertained them in the first place. Role models may be important partly for this reason. Even though people may have some knowledge about potential occupations, they may need a stimulus to think of the occupations in question as alternatives for someone like themselves. Social or cultural isolation and being a primary caregiver may lead to restriction in choice partly for this reason.

A number of internal conflicts can also lead to unnecessary restriction of choice. Some males and females may express sex-stereotyped choices partly in an effort to consolidate their gender identities. Potential nontraditionals may choose occupations typical of people like themselves in order to avoid the discomfort of being different or estranging themselves from their family and friends. Some individuals who are considerably more intelligent than most people in their social surroundings simply may be unwilling to seek more challenging jobs when they can easily meet the less challenging standards of success in their own social circles.

The expectations of other people who are important in one's life (e.g., parents) can also lead to restriction of choice. For example, potential nontraditionals may occasionally mention nontraditional options for which they receive no encouragement, and they may receive much unsolicited encouragement for pursuits typical for their sex, race, or social class.

Finally, socially or culturally isolated people may be especially likely to be unaware of or to have little information about all the alternatives that are actually realistic for them, so they may be unable—not just disinclined—to even consider those options. Other people may be uninformed because they have never paid attention to available information about the alternatives they have assumed are inappropriate for them. As discussed elsewhere (Gottfredson, 1981), it is costly in time and effort to actively seek out information about jobs, meaning that people know most about the jobs to which they have been exposed. But for the same reason, people cannot be expected to even pay attention to, and mentally process, all occupational information to which they are exposed, and instead they can be expected to attend to and remember only that which is most salient to them at the time.

Assessment Criterion 5: Counselee Is Realistic About Accessibility of Chosen Occupation(s).   An occupation may be optimal in terms of one's interests and abilities and yet be unrealistic because it simply is unavailable. It may also be a poor bet because of the obstacles (e.g., intense competition) to actually obtaining that kind of work. This does not mean that the choice necessarily should be discouraged, but it does mean that counselees should be aware of what they are up against to be better prepared to pursue their goals more effectively. In addition, disillusionment and wasted time, money, and effort often result from ignorance of barriers and opportunities.

The fifth assessment criterion is now a neglected issue in the literature on career development as well as in the literature on special groups, so there are few hypotheses to list in Table 5.4. More attention to this issue would seem to be desirable in the future.

Perhaps the biggest underlying problem for special groups with regard to meeting this criterion of development is lack of information about, or misperceptions of, barriers and opportunities. Socially or culturally isolated people may now be aware of more occupational alternatives than they were routinely exposed to in the past, but they may not have developed a comparable awareness of the effort, abilities, interests, and qualifications that are required in those occupations. Having focused on the importance of race and sex in explaining race and sex differences in employment patterns, some women and minorities may overestimate the opportunities that have recently opened up to them, and they may underestimate the attributes that are important—even for white males—for entering and succeeding in different occupations. Being a white male may have been necessary in some jobs in the past, but it has rarely been sufficient. It is probably realistic for nontraditionals to still expect to be treated somewhat differently on most jobs, but it is important for them to realize that they can expect problems, barriers, and opportunities that have little or nothing to do with their special group status. Some problems are just part of "the natural struggle of getting to the top" (Rogan, 1984, p. 59).

Other counselees may not be aware of or may discount barriers that are realistic for them to expect. For example, persons with physical handicaps must be realistic about the prejudices and inconveniences typical for their handicaps in testing, interviewing, and mobility or other incidental activities in different educational and work environments. Careful planning and strategies for overcoming those prejudices and complications are required for optimal career development. Similar statements could be made with regard to women and their family goals and responsibilities.

SOME PRINCIPLES
OF BENEFICIAL TEST USAGE

The testing controversy, the special-groups literature, and the analysis of career choice problems just presented all help to put vocational interest testing in broader perspective and to suggest how those inventories might be used in a beneficial manner. Many of the principles presented next are restatements or elaborations of principles already reflected implicitly or explicitly in the counseling literature. The following list is not complete; it consists largely of principles either suggested by or concerned with the problems of special groups, but at the same time, many of these principles apply to any person or group.

Principal 1

Inventories should be viewed as treatments. The testing controversy and the concern about the welfare of special groups together have transformed perceptions of the purposes of interest measurement. Interest measurement is less often conceived of now simply as measurement or information gathering, and the provision of test results is no longer seen only as providing information. Interest inventories are now seen less as diagnostic tools for the counselor and more as treatments that can either support or counteract the status quo. For example, in the context of discussing how inventories might stimulate career exploration, Cole and Hanson (1975) argued that "interest inventories should no longer be merely reported or interpreted. They should change behavior" (p. 12). Just 3 years later, Zytowski (1978) stated that "interest inventories have become an instrument of social change" (p. 129). This transformation of perceptions is also evidenced by the fact that interest tests have traditionally been evaluated for their accuracy but only more recently for their effects on test takers (Holland, in press). Similarly, in their discussion of intervention studies, Rounds and Tinsley (1984) noted that "the active ingredients of several vocational intervention procedures are assumed to be the assessment process itself" (p. 130). If interest inventory results are reported to test takers, it seems best to conceptualize inventories as treatments—perhaps not necessarily effective or beneficial ones, but treatments nonetheless (Gottfredson & Holland, 1978; Holland, in press).

Principal 2

Interest inventories and their interpretive materials constitute packages of interventions, the specific packages differing somewhat from one inventory to an-

other. Interest inventories tend to be discussed as discrete and unitary entities but, in reality, they have evolved into more complex conglomerations of treatments or "programmed learning experiences" (Holland, 1979a, p. 2). The heart of an inventory is the set of items that constitute the interest and related scales, but an inventory generally includes some auxiliary materials that always accompany the inventory (e.g., the *Occupations Finder* of the SDS) and other interpretive materials that are optional (e.g., the booklet *Understanding Yourself and Your Career* for the SDS and the occupational codes in the appendices to the *User's Guide to the SVIB-SCII*, Hansen, 1984b). Specific components of an inventory, other than the test scales, often include: instructions for how to interpret the scores, suggestions for what other information about self and jobs the test taker should consider when making a vocational choice, classificatory schemes for how to organize and think about similarities and differences among occupations, instructions designed to counter common misperceptions and stereotypes about employment, information about what contributes to job satisfaction and performance, lists of occupations that the test taker previously may have been unaware of or uninformed about, information about what people in different jobs are like, and information about how similar the test taker is to people in some jobs versus others. One trend in interest inventory development and revision has been the progressive addition and elaboration of such components in the accompanying manual and other interpretive materials. This trend reflects an effort by test developers and publishers to be responsive to concerns about test fairness; many revisions have involved interpretive material rather than test items or scoring procedures. But it also appears to represent a trend toward making interest inventories more comprehensive simulations of the counseling experience and to incorporate a wider range of counseling treatments into the inventory package.

It may seem obvious that interest inventories can be decomposed into different treatment components, as indeed some researchers have tried to do in evaluation studies (Holland et al., 1981), but this perspective also helps to clarify the controversy about interest tests in the special groups literature and how inventories can be utilized. In particular, this perspective shows not only how the same interest inventory can serve many different purposes or treatment goals (Gottfredson & Holland, 1978), but also how an inventory can simultaneously serve what have often been perceived (Zytowski & Borgen, 1983) as inconsistent goals—realistic assessment and exploration. For example, it has frequently been debated whether inventories should reflect past development, which represents the status quo, or whether they should promote exploration and change. A specific manifestation of this debate has been the controversy over whether an inventory should produce the same distributions of scores for women and for men (which presumably promotes more exploration for women) or whether it should be allowed to show sex differences in interests (differences which are generally attributed to previous socialization). Although it may be true that an inventory cannot be *scored* to both assess past development as well as to stimulate changes in future development, different *components* of an inventory can be directed toward the two different goals. In fact, a good inventory probably does both—providing a good assessment of the person's current interests and competencies (via the inventory scales and their scoring and interpretation) and promoting exploration, partly by stimulating (via educational interpretive materials) the test taker to think about the origins of those interests and how they might investigate other undeveloped interests and partly by providing an efficient way of examining more alternatives (via an occupational classification) than the test taker would have otherwise.

Inventories can be seen as somewhat *flexible* arrangements of treatments, some components perhaps being more effective than others and some which the counselor may wish to replace or augment with more potent treatments as needs and goals dictate. For example, interest inventories help to focus exploration and perhaps make it more effective by helping test takers to better understand their current orientations. But they are neither necessary nor probably adequate for effective exploration of nontraditional options, which may be better achieved by embedding an interest inventory within a group exercise or in a broader system of treatment such as the Vocational Exploration and Insight Kit (VEIK; Holland, 1979b).

In short, interest inventories may serve many purposes, but they may not serve all of them equally well nor should they necessarily be expected to do so as long as it is clear what they do well and what they do not. The extensive construct validity for the major inventories (Campbell, 1971; Holland, 1985) suggests that they serve the purposes of assessment well and do so fairly. How well they accomplish other goals is not clear, because so little research has yet been done to evaluate their effects, and because few past evaluations have been analytical enough to determine which components of the inventories in question are responsible for any effects the inventory has (Holland et al., 1981).

The general point is that inventories can be expanded, elaborated, and embedded in larger systems of treatment to fulfill many different purposes, but there is no reason to expect the inventory items and scoring methods themselves to always be harnassed to those purposes. For example, one concern in the past has been that inventories do not measure a person's potential or undeveloped capacities and interests, a failure which, it is claimed, may make them unfair in the sense that they merely reinforce the ways in which women's interests have been artificially channeled by society. One response to this concern was the liberalization of test-taking instructions on some inventories which, as was discussed earlier, turned out not to have an appreciable effect on sex differences in test outcomes. Having few interests or a flat profile may reflect a lack of development or a diffuse identity, but no one has advocated changing interest inventory items or scoring procedures to reveal the latent interests or identities of people with such profiles. It is recognized, as with inconsistent profiles, that such people need to expose themselves to more or new experiences so that their interests can more fully develop (Campbell & Hansen, 1981, p. 95; Kuder & Diamond, 1979, p. 12; Weinrach, 1984). Interpretive materials can advocate such experiences and other interventions such as Job Experience Kits (Krumboltz, 1970) can provide them, but interest inventories as currently structured assess only developed interests. Furthermore, they appear to be the best available means of meeting this very useful goal.

Principle 3

Interest inventories are most useful when embedded within a broader career counseling process that recognizes the constraints on career choice. This principle seems always to have been a basic precept in the use of interest inventories. What has changed over time are the views of what the major constraints on career choice are and thus what the broader vocational counseling process should consist of. The developmental literature (Super, 1984) has broadened the early guidance models, which focused on matching interests and abilities to occupational requirements, to emphasize the integration of diverse career and life goals throughout the whole life. The special groups literature has brought about a different kind of change. It has shifted attention toward the social and economic barriers that can thwart the implementation of interests and abilities in work and that can perhaps even channel those interests and abilities in particular directions. Both approaches would deny that interests and abilities are sufficient information for adequate career counseling—the first primarily because other life goals are important and the latter because social and economic barriers may prevent their implementation. Both are also consistent with the view that vocational choice is a compromise process and that an understanding of other major constraints, of both an internal and an external nature, is required for optimizing career development (Gottfredson, 1981). The special-groups literature has argued that current vocational theories and counseling methods may be inappropriate for members of special groups because they were developed from samples of white middle-class males. The fact that those theories and methods may be less useful than desired may be more the result of idealized views of career development even for white middle-class males. The special-groups literature makes obvious the constraints on free choice that certain sorts of people face, but probably not even the most advantaged individuals have unconstrained choice of occupation.

   The fact that vocational interests may not play as important a role in career choice as was once assumed and that they may be more readily sacrificed than other aspects of one's social self (e.g., status, gender role) when compromises are required (Gottfredson, 1981) does not mean that inventories should no longer have a prominent place in the career counseling process. It means that interest inventories probably have not been fully utilized when they are used and that some other types of information have been too little used by comparison. This chapter has tried to show how counselors might more systematically assess the constraints and conflicts that may be impeding the career development of their individual counselees. Interest inventories can be utilized not only in assessing interests but also in diagnosing other constraints on career choice and in identifying alternative courses of action when compromise is required. Some counselors consider the interpretation of interest inventories to be a mechanical, routine, and uninteresting task. In contrast, if inventories are interpreted not in isolation but in relation to other preferences and social pressures, they can be a key to understanding more general complaints and anxieties and to predicting the compromises counselees will probably have to consider. Such use of interest assessments requires clinical judgment because there are no guidelines for such activities and because situations vary considerably from one counselee to another.

Principal 4

Treatment should be tied to goals. Test usage in the counseling setting, like any treatment, should be guided by specific goals. This chapter specified five criteria or goals for career choice. By structuring the search for career choice problems according to whether or not counselees meet these criteria, diagnosis and treatment may become more efficient and effective, particularly in view of the time constraints imposed on the counseling process. Other goals for career choice have been advocated in the literature—for example, proficiency at the general process of decision making (Mitchell & Krumboltz, 1984; Tiedeman & Miller-Tiedeman, 1984; see Osipow, 1982, for a list of possible outcome criteria). However, the goals proposed here seem consistent with the emphasis of many diagnostic schemes on indecision and unrealism. They also are consistent with the newer concern that the career alternatives of special groups not be restricted because of special group status. Structuring the analysis of career choice problems according to the five criteria ensures that both counselors and counselees confront and deal with career choices that may be less than optimal.

The special-groups literature has been particularly concerned that the aims, and not just the methods, of career guidance may not have been beneficial to members of special groups, a criticism that has sometimes been voiced about psychotherapy in general. The concern about how to avoid structuring counseling according to the cultural values of the counselor may have led some practitioners to avoid taking a stand on what healthy development is. But perhaps a more useful professional response is to make the goals of counseling and of interest inventories more explicit. Such a response would be consistent with the trend of making interest inventories more accessible and understandable to test takers (Holland, in press).

Principal 5

Goals for the counseling process, including interest inventories, should relate to the adjustment and welfare of the individual rather than to the social groups of which the individual may be a member. Improving the life circumstances and career development of special groups is a desirable social goal, and the profession has taken responsibility for establishing programs targeted to various special groups. However, the goal of any counselee–counselor encounter is to aid the particular counselee in that encounter. The goal should not be to promote any particular group outcome such as to reduce sex or race differences in career outcomes, although such group outcomes may generally be desired by the community at large, because that goal may or may not accord with the counselee's own particular needs and wishes or special characteristics. It is an unspoken covenant of the counseling relationship that the needs of the counselee take precedence over those of the counselor, of the institutions with which either the counselor or counselee is associated, or of any particular social group. Trust on the part of the counselee is essential to a good counseling relationship, and it has frequently been noted that members of special groups often are distrustful of counseling (Sue, 1981). Using counselees as vehicles to promote social goals, which are distinct from the welfare of the individual counselee, may only further erode trust in the profession, no matter how well intentioned the profession may be (e.g., see Brooks, 1978, on the need for "non-ideological" services for reentry women). Consequently, this chapter has focused on goals for personal development (e.g., suitable, satisfying, unrestricted, and accessible careers) and on the problems from which individual people may suffer and that may interfere with optimal personal development (e.g., lack of knowledge about self and jobs, internal and external conflicts), although special groups were of particular concern.

Efforts to promote social change are a legitimate activity, but probably not within the counseling setting unless they coincide with the needs and desires of the counselee. This statement is equally applicable to any counseling tool such as interest inventories. Counseling tools should not be designed to promote social change, except via improving the adjustment and welfare of the *individuals* subjected to them, unless other goals are clearly stated to both counselors and counselee. This interpretation questions the advisability of frequent recommendations to norm interest inventories so that they "produce approximately equal distributions of scores for men and women throughout the full range of possible general scale and occupational scale scores" (Cole & Hanson, 1975, p. 13). Although the goal of *widening* the options that individuals consider is now widely accepted, there is no clear relation between this individual-level goal and the group-level goal of producing *equal* distributions of interests for men and women. There is no evidence to suggest that a society that provides opportunities for fully developing and utilizing everyone's potentialities will produce distributions of occupational choices or employment that are identical, or even similar, across all social groups.

Principal 6

Career counseling strategies, including the use of interest inventories, should be targeted to counselees' career development problems rather than to counselees' special group statuses unless there is a compelling reason to do otherwise. The members of some special groups appear to have an elevated risk of certain problems, but group status is too weak a predictor of career choice problems to be used to assign treatments to individuals. Treating clients according to their special group status is tantamount to stereotyping them rather than to treating them as individuals. The knowledge that some special groups are more likely to suffer from certain problems is useful knowledge, because it suggests what services will be most in demand in different client populations. But even in counseling programs that are targeted to particular special groups, it is useful to remember that those special programs themselves are probably more effective in reducing career development problems to the extent that they actually focus on those career development problems rather than being more diffuse examinations of special group status. Special group status is also an important piece of information in the process of diagnosing a counselee's problems, but treatment should follow from the problems that are actually identified. At this time, it seems most beneficial for counselors to assume that *any* type of counselee can have *any* type of career choice problem, and that no type of person is certain to have any particular problem.

Principal 7

Interest inventory scores are useful in diagnosing whether career choice is proceeding satisfactorily and why it may not be if it is not. Specifically, inventoried interests are integral to assessing whether the counselee has been successful in meeting two criteria discussed earlier (i.e., whether choices are suitable and fulfilling in terms of interests and abilities). This use of inventories is probably a common one. However, inventoried interests can also be used in diagnosing the particular problems underlying the failure to meet any of the first four of the five criteria for successful career choice when those interests are used in conjunction with other data about the individual. For example, lack of self-knowledge, which can lead to indecision as well as to unrealistic or unfulfilling choices, may be revealed by comparing a counselee's interest scores to his or her self assessment. And interest inventory manuals note that a flat profile may indicate undeveloped interests. It has been found that inventoried interests are more useful in predicting later occupation chosen or entered if they are consistent with expressed choices (Holland, 1979a, p. 15). But it is also useful to look at *disagreements* between inventoried and expressed interests as a useful strategy for diagnosing problems that appear to disrupt optimal development (Hansen, 1984a; Holland, 1979a, p. 5). In particular, interest inventory results can be used

to probe for internal or external conflicts, problems that can also lead to indecision or to unrealistic or unfulfilling choices. For example, if expressed choices
(i.e., occupational aspirations) differ from assessed interests, additional questioning may reveal that the individual has compromised or ignored vocational
interests in favor of an alternative that is of higher pay or status, or that is more
consistent with family responsibilities or the gender identity the counselee wishes
to project. It may also reveal conflicts between the wishes of the counselee and
the expectations of the counselee's family or friends. The potential value of
interest inventories in diagnosing the problems underlying failures in development seems not to be fully appreciated, perhaps because the constraints on career
development themselves have not been fully appreciated.

Principal 8

*Interpretive materials that accompany interest inventories can be valuable in
exposing and treating some underlying problems in career choice.* Improving
self-knowledge has been the traditional treatment goal for interest inventories.
Improved self-knowledge reassures counselees who have already made suitable
choices (criterion 3) and helps others to ascertain what a suitable choice might be
if they have either been unable to identify a choice (criterion 1) or have identified
an unsuitable one (criterion 2).

More recently, many people have argued that interest inventories should
promote the exploration of alternatives because some counselees have a very
restricted view of their alternatives (criterion 4). Some arguments about how
interest inventories should be normed, and thus how scores are to be calculated
and reported, seem to stem partly from the belief that exploration can be promoted by altering scoring procedures. It is debatable whether interest inventories
scores themselves should be used to challenge people's images of themselves,
even if those images are "stereotyped," in order to promote exploration (Gottfredson, 1982). However, most inventories are now being structured via their
interpretive materials to promote exploration in other ways. Most importantly,
classifications that group occupations according to interest type provide a way
for test takers to peruse a wider variety of occupations than they might otherwise,
but in an economical and understandable way.

For example, the current *Occupations Finder* for the SDS and VPI lists 500
occupations by interest profile, the forthcoming revision of the *Occupations
Finder* will list more than 1,000 titles (Holland, personal communication,
November 16, 1984), and the *Dictionary of Holland Occupational Codes* (Gottfredson, Holland, & Ogawa, 1982) provides Holland codes for all 12,099 job
titles in the *Dictionary of Occupational Titles* (U.S. Department of Labor, 1977).
SCII results are similarly linked to most occupations in the United States econo-
my by virtue of the SCII now providing scores on Holland interest themes
(Campbell & Hansen, 1981).

This type of interpretive material may be most useful in overcoming restriction due to lack of knowledge about occupations that limits perceptions of opportunities, but other interpretive materials could be envisaged to counter other sources of restriction of choice. For example, interpretive materials could have counselees explore internal and external conflicts that might explain why their inventoried interests do not agree with their expressed interests, if that is indeed the case. The exercise of exploring goal conflicts may in itself help promote a deeper examination and a prioritization of one's life choices. Although this process is one that the counselor could stimulate and guide, there seems to be no reason that interpretive materials could not be expanded to mimic more of the career counseling process and the treatment it provides.

Principal 9

Interest inventories are useful in developing next-best alternatives when compromises are necessary. Not all conflicts are solvable or all barriers surmountable. Compromises are usually necessary even for the most advantaged people, because either internal or external barriers may block the fulfillment of one's major vocational interests. It is highly likely that vocational interests often are not of highest priority when people have to make compromises (Gottfredson, 1981). This means that the five criteria should be viewed as idealized goals rather than as necessarily fully attainable ones. But it also means that interest inventory results are useful in identifying "next best" alternatives, which is always a desirable practice anyway. They can also be used in helping people to identify nonoccupational outlets for their vocational interests when occupational ones are not accessible. The point here is not that counselors should reconcile clients to the barriers they face, but that they should help counselees to recognize those barriers, deal with them, and if necessary work around them as much as possible.

CONCLUSION

Psychological tests have been under fire for over a decade now, and interest inventories are no exception. Research has failed to show that current major mental tests or interest inventories mismeasure (i.e., provide biased measurement of) the traits of women or minorities in the United States, but questions of *fairness* remain. The concern has become, "What role do or should tests play in a society where social groups differ substantially in both the types and levels of careers they enter, and even in the careers they say they prefer?" This concern is often posed as a choice between measuring the effects of past development and changing the course of future development.

The special-groups literature in counseling psychology has made a good case that counselors cannot confine themselves to measuring and interpreting psychological traits, such as interests and aptitudes, in isolation from the social factors that impinge on the life chances of their counselees. The controversy over interest measurement is a specific example of the concerns raised in the special-groups literature, because it has drawn heavily on discussions in that literature on the barriers that people face as a result of discrimination and stereotyping. In addition, efforts to improve the fairness of inventories and their use represent one concrete way in which the profession has grappled with these issues to improve current counseling practice. Both external and internalized barriers have been a focus of concern, which has led to inventory changes designed to educate people about the barriers they may face and to changes designed to reveal interests that may have been suppressed by differential opportunities and socialization processes. Although there is no consensus about the proper construction and use of interest inventories, the controversy has led to the promulgation of standards for test construction and interpretation.

The interest inventory controversy has been confined almost exclusively to one special group—women. This is true despite the fact that the social practices that have been claimed to have created the barriers faced by women, minorities, and the handicapped are essentially the same (e.g., discrimination and stereotyping), that those processes are presumed to create both internal and external barriers for all special groups, that the consequences of those barriers are apparently much the same for all social groups (e.g., lower income, occupational segregation, and lack of fulfillment), and that the general solutions offered are often much the same as well (e.g., challenge the status quo, promote exploration). Having focused on women alone, the interest inventory controversy has given counselors little guidance for the use of inventories with minorities, persons with handicaps, and other special groups. Neither has the special-groups literature itself provided much guidance to counselors, because it has focused more on arousing concern and improving rapport with counselees than on showing what a concerned and sensitive counselor might do. Furthermore, speculation has outrun and often ignored the empirical evidence about special groups and their problems.

This chapter outlined and compared the problems that special groups face. It indicated that there are systematic similarities and differences among different special groups, both in the types of risk factors they typically face and in the incidence of those factors within groups. That review of career choice risk factors provides several types of information to counselors. It provides concrete data about group differences that have often been ignored or misrepresented in the special-groups literature. It illustrates that a single theory or framework for evaluating the problems of special groups is not only possible but is also desirable. A more analytical account of the career choice problems of special groups also suggests that counselors should start with the assumption that *all* people face barriers and conflicts, that no one—not even advantaged white males—have unconstrainted choice of occupation. Thus, a focus on the problems of special groups stimulates more useful theory and practice for all counselees.

Although it is useful, knowledge about group differences is not sufficient for the counseling of individuals, who may or may not be typical of their groups and who may be members of several. The problem for counselors is how to use information about groups to help individuals without stereotyping them according to their special group statuses. A diagnostic framework was presented that links the risk factors especially prevalent in some social groups (e.g., poverty, cultural isolation, family responsibilities) to the developmental outcomes that have been of concern in the counseling process (e.g., indecision, realism, and unrestricted choice). With this linkage, it is possible to see more clearly what the role of interest inventories has been and might be in counseling members of special groups.

Two main conclusions emerge from that linkage of group problems with individual-level career development criteria. First, it reinforces the growing view that vocational interests are not as powerful an influence on career choice, even for advantaged individuals, as has commonly been assumed in the past. The inadequacies and modifications of interest inventories that have been debated so heatedly in the field pale by comparison to the career-related obstacles posed by parental objections, childcare responsibilities, and perceptions of discrimination in the labor market—obstacles that people face regardless of how their interests are assessed. This in no way means that the fulfillment of interests is unimportant; it means only that fulfillment is often difficult to achieve and may be considered secondary to other personal goals when compromises are required.

The second conclusion is that interest assessment can play a role in opening opportunities and counteracting internal and external barriers, but not in the way usually discussed. There is no inherent dilemma between valid assessment and removing barriers to optimal development, as is assumed so frequently in the interest measurement literature. It is important to have a valid assessment of a person's current vocational interests, even when those interests may be partly the result of cultural restrictions the person has faced. Those interests reflect people's conceptions of who they are—conceptions that are often resistant to change. Whether the goal is to fulfill those interests or to change them, it is helpful to know what they are, because they influence career attitudes and behavior. Although not generally perceived as such, promoting exploration or change is a separate issue in the construction and use of interest inventories. Interpretive materials can be designed to promote exploration, and change in self-conceptions too if that is desired by the counselee, without compromising the assessment function of an inventory. Perhaps the most overlooked potential use of inventories in career counseling is as tools for diagnosing some of the constraints people face that may impede career development in general and the fulfillment of vocational interests in particular. By juxtaposing interest inventory results to other client goals and constraints, those results can be used to help expose, reassess, and more effectively deal with impediments to successful career development that clients may not have fully recognized earlier.

To summarize, the interest inventory issue regarding special groups is not one of assessment *or* social change. Rather, it is assessment *and* exploration of opportunities and constraints. Whether these two activities are accomplished by an inventory alone or by an inventory supplemented by other materials, beneficial test usage requires both. Beneficial usage may lead to the reduction of group differences, but that should not be its objective; the objective is to help individual test takers better fulfill their potentials, whatever they are.

REFERENCES

Amos, W. E., & Grambs, J. D. (Eds.). (1968). *Counseling the disadvantaged youth.* Englewood Cliffs, NJ: Prentice–Hall.

Atkinson, D. R., Morten, G., & Sue, D. W. (Eds.). (1979). *Counseling American minorities: A cross-cultural perspective.* Dubuque, IA: Wm. C. Brown.

Becker, H. J. (1981). *City correlates of segregation: Percent black and racial segregation.* (Desegregation Program report). Baltimore, MD: The Johns Hopkins University, Center for Social Organization of Schools.

Benbow, C. P., & Stanley, J. C. (1980). Sex differences in mathematical ability: Fact or artifact? *Science, 210,* 1262–1264.

Berryman, S. E. (1983). *Who will do science?* New York: Rockefeller Foundation.

Betz, N. E., & Hackett, G. (1981). The relationship of career-related self-efficacy expectations to perceived career options in women and men. *Journal of Counseling Psychology, 28,* 399–410.

Birk, J. M. (1975). Reducing sex bias: Factors affecting the client's view of the use of career interest inventories. In E. E. Diamond (Ed.), *Issues of sex bias and sex fairness in career interest measurement* (pp. 101–122). Washington, DC: Department of Health, Education, and Welfare, National Institute of Education, Career Education Program.

Blau, P. M., & Duncan, O. D. (1967). *The American occupational structure.* New York: Wiley.

Bogue, D. J. (1969). *Principles of demography.* New York: Wiley.

Bordin, E. S. (1946). Diagnosis in counseling and psychotherapy. *Educational and Psychological Measurement, 6,* 169–184.

Borgen, F. H., & Harper, G. T. (1973). Predictive validity of measured vocational interests with black and white college men. *Measurement and Evaluation in Guidance, 6,* 19–27.

Boyd, V. S. (1978). Neutralizing sexist titles in Holland's Self Directed Search: What difference does it make? In C. K. Tittle & D. G. Zytowski (Eds.), *Sex-fair interest measurement: Research and implications* (pp. 21–25). Washington, DC: National Institute of Education.

Braddock, J. H. B., II, Crain, R. L., & McPartland, J. M. (1984). A long-term view of school desegregation: Some recent studies of graduates and adults. *Phi Delta Kappan, 66,* 259–264.

Brooks, L. (1978). Supermoms shift gears: Re-entry women. In L. W. Harmon, J. M. Birk, L. E. Fitzgerald, & M. F. Tanney (Eds.), *Counseling women* (pp. 218–229). Monterey, CA: Brooks/Cole.

Brooks, L. (1984). Counseling special groups: Women and ethnic minorities. In D. Brown & L. Brooks (Eds.), *Career choice and development* (pp. 355–368). San Francisco: Jossey-Bass.

Brown, D. A. (1975). Career counseling for the homosexual. In R. Reardon & H. Burck (Eds.), *Facilitating career development: Strategies for counselors* (pp. 234–247). Springfield, IL: C. C. Thomas.

Campbell, D. P. (1971). *Handbook for the Strong Vocational Interest Blank.* Stanford, CA: Stanford University Press.

Campbell, D. P., & Hansen, J. C. (1981). *Manual for the Strong-Campbell Interest Inventory* (3rd ed.). Stanford, CA: Stanford University Press.

Campbell, R. E., & Cellini, J. V. (1981). A diagnostic taxonomy of adult career problems. *Journal of Vocational Behavior, 19,* 175–190.

Campbell, R. T. (1983). Status attainment research: End of the beginning or beginning of the end? *Sociology of Education, 56,* 47–62.

Casas, J. M. (1984). Policy, training, and research in counseling psychology: The racial/ethnic minority perspective. In S. D. Brown & R. W. Lent (Eds.), *Handbook of counseling psychology* (pp. 785–831). New York: Wiley.

Cole, N. S. (1973). On measuring the vocational interests of women. *Journal of Counseling Psychology, 20,* 105–112.

Cole, N. S., & Hanson, G. R. (1975). Impact of interest inventories on career choice. In E. E. Diamond (Ed.), *Issues of sex bias and sex fairness in career interest measurement* (pp. 1–17). Washington, DC: Department of Health, Education, and Welfare, National Institute of Education, Career Education Program.

Crites, J. O. (1969). *Vocational psychology.* New York: McGraw–Hill.

Crites, J. O. (1981). *Career counseling.* New York: McGraw–Hill.

Cronbach, L. J. (1984). *Essentials of psychological testing* (4th ed.). New York: Harper & Row.

Datta, L. E. (1978). Foreword. In C. K. Tittle & D. G. Zytowski (Eds.), *Sex-fair interest measurement: Research and implications* (pp. ix–xi). Washington, DC: National Institute of Education.

Davidson, J. P. (1980). Urban black youth and career development. *Journal of Non-White Concerns, 8,* 119–140.

Dearman, N. B., & Plisko, V. W. (1981). *The condition of education, 1981 edition.* Washington, DC: National Center for Education Statistics.

Diamond, E. E. (Ed.). (1975). *Issues of sex bias and sex fairness in career interest measurement.* Washington, DC: Department of Health, Education, and Welfare, National Institute of Education, Career Education Program.

Duncan, O. D., Featherman, D. L., & Duncan, B. (1972). *Socioeconomic background and achievement.* New York: Seminar.

Educational Testing Service Board of Trustees. (1984). *Trustees' public accountability report.* Princeton, NJ: Educational Testing Service.

Eysenck, H. J. (1984). The effect of race on human abilities and mental test scores. In C. R. Reynolds & R. T. Brown (Eds.), *Perspectives on bias in mental testing* (pp. 249–292). New York: Plenum.

Felton, J. S., Perkins, D. C., & Lewin, M. (1966). *A survey of medicine and medical practice for the rehabilitation counselor.* Washington, DC: U.S. Department of Health, Education, and Welfare, Vocational Rehabilitation Administration.

Ferron, D. T. (Ed.). (1981). *Disability survey 72: Disabled and nondisabled adults.* Washington, DC: Department of Health and Human Services, Social Security Administration.

Fields, C. M. (1984, September 5). Problems of the gifted get too little notice, psychologists say. *Chronicle of Higher Education, 29,* 1, 8.

Fitzgerald, L. F., & Betz, N. E. (1983). Issues in the vocational psychology of women. In W. B. Walsh & S. H. Osipow (Eds.), *Handbook of vocational psychology, Vol. 1: Foundations* (pp. 83–159). Hillsdale, NJ: Lawrence Erlbaum Associates.

Fitzgerald, L. F., & Crites, J. O. (1980). Toward a career psychology of women: What do we know? What do we need to know? *Journal of Counseling Psychology, 27,* 44–62.

Flynn, J. R. (1984). Japanese IQ. *Nature, 308*(5956), 222.

Fouad, N. A., Cudeck, R., & Hansen, J. C. (1984). Convergent validity of the Spanish and English forms of the Strong-Campbell Interest Inventory for bilingual Hispanic high school students. *Journal of Counseling Psychology, 31,* 339–348.

Gecas, V. (1982). The self-concept. *Annual Review of Sociology, 8,* 1–33.

Gellman, W. (1959). Roots of prejudice against the handicapped. *Journal of Rehabilitation, Jan–Feb*, 4–6, 25.

Gerard, H. B. (1983). School desegregation: The social science role. *American Psychologist, 38*, 869–877.

Gordon, R. A. (1980a). Examining labelling theory: The case of mental retardation. In W. R. Gove (Ed.), *The labelling of deviance: Evaluating a perspective* (2nd ed., pp. 111–173). Beverly Hills, CA: Sage.

Gordon, R. A. (1980b). Implications of valid (and stubborn) IQ differences: An unstatesmanlike view. *Behavioral and Brain Sciences, 3*(3), 343–344.

Gordon, R. A. (1980c). Labelling theory, mental retardation, and public policy: Larry P. and other developments since 1974. In W. R. Gove (Ed.), *The labelling of deviance: Evaluating a perspective* (2nd ed., pp. 175–225). Beverly Hills, CA: Sage.

Gordon, R. A. (1984). Digits backward and the Mercer-Kamin law: An empirical response to Mercer's treatment of internal validity of IQ tests. In C. R. Reynolds & R. T. Brown (Eds.), *Perspectives on bias in mental testing* (pp. 357–506). New York: Plenum.

Gordon, R. A., & Rudert, E. E. (1979). Bad news concerning IQ tests. *Sociology of Education, 52*, 174–190.

Gottfredson, G. D. (1976). A note on sexist wording in interest measurement. *Measurement and Evaluation in Guidance, 8*, 221–223.

Gottfredson, G. D., & Holland, J. L. (1978). Toward beneficial resolution of the interest inventory controversy. In C. K. Tittle & D. Zytowski (Eds.), *Sex-fair interest measurement: Research and implications* (pp. 43–51). Washington, DC: National Institute of Education.

Gottfredson, G. D., Holland, J. L., & Ogawa, D. K. (1982). *Dictionary of Holland occupational codes*. Palo Alto, CA: Consulting Psychologists.

Gottfredson, L. S. (1981). Circumscription and compromise: A developmental theory of occupational aspirations [Monograph]. *Journal of Counseling Psychology, 28*, 545–579.

Gottfredson, L. S. (1982). The sex fairness of unnormed interest inventories. *Vocational Guidance Quarterly, 31*, 128–132.

Gottfredson, L. S. (1985a). Education as a valid but fallible signal of worker quality: Reorienting an old debate about the functional basis of the occupational hierarchy. In A. C. Kerckhoff (Ed.), *Research in sociology of education and socialization* (Vol. 5, pp. 123–169). Greenwich, CT: JAI.

Gottfredson, L. S. (1985b, October). *Societal consequences of the g factor in employment*. Paper presented at the fall conference of the Personnel Testing Council of Southern California, Newport Beach, CA.

Gottfredson, L. S. (1985c, August). *Vocational exploration and realism: Promoting both simultaneously*. Paper presented at the annual meeting of the American Psychological Association, Los Angeles, CA.

Gottfredson, L. S., Finucci, J. M., & Childs, B. (1984a). Explaining the adult careers of dyslexic boys: Variations in critical skills for high-level jobs. *Journal of Vocational Behavior, 24*, 355–373.

Gottfredson, L. S., Finucci, J. M., & Childs, B. (1984b). *The adult occupations of dyslexic boys: Results of long-term follow-up and implications for research and counseling* (Education and Work Program report). Baltimore, MD: The Johns Hopkins University, Center for Social Organization of Schools.

Gump, J. P., & Rivers, L. W. (1975). A consideration of race in efforts to end sex bias. In E. E. Diamond (Ed.), *Issues of sex bias and sex fairness in career interest measurement* (pp. 123–140). Washington, DC: Department of Health, Education, and Welfare, National Institute of Education, Career Education Program.

Hanline, M. F., & Murray, C. (1984). Integrating severely handicapped children into regular public schools. *Phi Delta Kappan, 66*, 273–276.

Hansen, J. C. (1984a). The measurement of vocational interests: Issues and future directions. In S. D. Brown & R. W. Lent (Eds.), *Handbook of counseling psychology* (pp. 99–136). New York: Wiley.

Hansen, J. C. (1984b). *User's guide for the SVIB-SCII*. Stanford, CA: Stanford University Press.

Hansen, J. C., & Fouad, N. A. (1984). Translation and validation of the Spanish form of the Strong-Campbell Interest Inventory. *Measurement and Evaluation in Guidance, 16*, 192–197.

Hansen, J. C., & Swanson, J. L. (1983). Stability of interests and the predictive and concurrent validity of the 1981 SCII for college majors. *Journal of Counseling Psychology, 30*, 194–201.

Hanson, G. R., & Cole, N. S. (Eds.). (1973). *The vocational interests of young adults* (monograph 11). Iowa City: ACT Publications.

Hanson, G. R., & Rayman, J. (1976). Validity of sex-balanced interest inventory scales. *Journal of Vocational Behavior, 9*, 279–291.

Hardy, K. R. (1974). Social origins of American scientists and scholars. *Science, 185*(4150), 497–506.

Harmon, L. W. (1969). The predictive power over 10 years of measured social service and scientific interests among college women. *Journal of Applied Psychology, 53*, 193–198.

Harmon, L. W. (1975). Technical aspects: Problems of scale development, norms, item differences by sex, and the rate of change in occupational group characteristics—I. In E. E. Diamond (Ed.), *Issues of sex bias and sex fairness in career interest measurement* (pp. 45–64). Washington, DC: Department of Health, Education, and Welfare, National Institute of Education, Career Education Program.

Harmon, L. W., Birk, J. M., Fitzgerald, L. E., & Tanney, M. F. (Eds.). (1978). *Counseling women*. Monterey, CA: Brooks/Cole.

Hennessy, J. J., & Merrifield, P. R. (1976). A comparison of the factor structures of mental abilities in four ethnic groups. *Journal of Educational Psychology, 68*, 754–659.

Hennessy, J. J., & Merrifield, P. R. (1978). Ethnicity and sex distinctions in patterns of aptitude factor scores in a sample of urban high school seniors. *American Educational Research Journal, 15*(3), 385–389.

Hershenson, D. B. (1974). Vocational guidance and the handicapped. In E. L. Herr (Ed.), *Vocational guidance and human development* (pp. 478–501). Boston: Houghton Mifflin.

Hershenson, D. B., & Sloan, C. M. (1968). Recent studies using the SVIB with the physically, emotionally, and culturally handicapped. *Rehabilitation Counseling Bulletin, 12*, 23–28.

Herzog, A. R. (1982). High school seniors' occupational plans and values: Trends in sex differences 1976 through 1980. *Sociology of Education, 55*, 1–13.

Hewer, V. H. (1966). Evaluation of a criterion: Realism of vocational choice. *Journal of Counseling Psychology, 13*, 289–294.

Higgins, P. C. (1980). *Outsiders in a hearing world*. Beverly Hills, CA: Sage.

Holland, J. L. (1975). The use and evaluation of interest inventories and simulations. In E. E. Diamond (Ed.), *Issues of sex bias and sex fairness in career interest measurement* (pp. 19–44). Washington, DC: Department of Health, Education, and Welfare, National Institute of Education, Career Education Program.

Holland, J. L. (1979a). *The Self-Directed Search: Professional manual*. Palo Alto, CA: Consulting Psychologists.

Holland, J. L. (1979b). *The Vocational Exploration and Insight Kit*. Palo Alto, CA: Consulting Psychologists.

Holland, J. L. (1984). A celebration of the career development view [Review of *Handbook of vocational psychology, Vol. 1: Foundations* and *Vol. 2: Applications*]. *Contemporary Psychology, 29*, 862–864.

Holland, J. L. (1985). *Making vocational choices: A theory of vocational personalities and work environments*. Englewood Cliffs, NJ: Prentice-Hall.

Holland, J. L. (in press). New directions for interest testing. In B. Blake & J. C. Witt (Eds.), *The future of testing*. Hillsdale, NJ: Lawrence Erlbaum Associates.

Holland, J. L., Magoon, T. M., & Spokane, A. R. (1981). Counseling psychology: Career interventions, research, and theory. *Annual Review of Psychology, 32*, 279–305.

Hunter, J. E. (1983). *Fairness of the General Aptitude Test Battery: Ability differences and their impact on minority hiring rates*. (USES test research report No. 46). Washington, DC: U.S. Department of Labor, Employment & Training Administration.

Hunter, J. E., Schmidt, F. L., & Rauschenberger, J. (1984). Methodological, statistical, and ethical issues in the study of bias in psychological tests. In C. R. Reynolds & R. T. Brown (Eds.), *Perspectives on bias in mental testing* (pp. 41–99). New York: Plenum.

Jackson, A. L. (1981). Career counseling for minority persons. In D. H. Montross & C. J. Shinkman (Eds.), *Career development in the 1980s: Theory and practice* (pp. 233–238). Springfield, IL: Charles C Thomas.

Jaques, M. E., & Kauppi, D. R. (1983). Vocational rehabilitation and its relationship to vocational psychology. In W. B. Walsh & S. H. Osipow (Eds.), *Handbook of vocational psychology, Vol. 2: Applications* (pp. 207–258). Hillsdale, NJ: Lawrence Erlbaum Associates.

Jencks, C., Smith, M., Acland, H., Bane, M., Cohen, D., Gintis, H., Heyns, B., & Michelson, S. (1972). *Inequality: A reassessment of the effect of family and schooling in America*. New York: Harper Colophon.

Jencks, C., Bartlett, S., Corcoran, M., Crouse, J., Eaglesfield, D., Jackson, G., McClelland, K., Mueser, P., Olneck, M., Schwartz, J., Ward, S., & Williams, J. (1979). *Who gets ahead? The determinants of economic success in America*. New York: Basic Books.

Jensen, A. R. (1969). How much can we boost IQ and scholastic achievement? *Harvard Educational Review, 39*, 1–123.

Jensen, A. R. (1980). *Bias in mental testing*. New York: Free Press.

Johansson, C. B., & Harmon, L. W. (1972). Strong Vocational Interest Blank: One form or two? *Journal of Counseling Psychology, 19*, 404–410.

Kadushin, C. (1972). Who are the elite intellectuals? *The Public Interest, (29)*, 109–125.

Klasen, E. (1972). *The syndrome of dyslexia: With special consideration of its psychological, psychopathological, testpsychological, and social correlates*. Baltimore: University Park.

Knefelkamp, L. L., & Slepitza, R. (1978). A cognitive-developmental model of career development—An adaptation of the Perry scheme. In J. M. Whiteley & A. Resnikoff (Eds.), *Career counseling* (pp. 232–246). Monterey, CA: Brooks/Cole.

Krumboltz, J. D. (1970). *Job experience kits*. Chicago: Science Research.

Krute, A., & Burdette, M. E. (1981). Prevalence of chronic disease, injury, and work disability. In D. T. Ferron (Ed.), *Disability survey 72: Disabled and nondisabled adults* (pp. 47–65). Washington, DC: Department of Health and Human Services, Social Security Administration.

Kuder, F., & Diamond, E. E. (1979). *Kuder DD Occupational Interest Survey general manual*, (2nd ed.). Chicago: Science Research.

Lacey, D. (1975). Career behavior of deaf persons: Current status and future trends. In J. S. Picou & R. E. Campbell (Eds.), *Career behavior of special groups* (pp. 297–328). Columbus, OH: Charles E. Merrill.

Lamb, R. R. (1978). Validity of the ACT Interest Inventory for minority group members. In C. K. Tittle & D. G. Zytowski (Eds.), *Sex-fair interest measurement: Research and implications* (pp. 113–119). Washington, DC: National Institute of Education.

Lando, M. E., Cutler, R. R., & Gamber, E. (Eds.). (1982). *1978 survey of disability and work*. Washington, DC: U.S. Department of Health and Human Services, Social Security Administration.

Lazarus, B. B., & Tobin, N. (1981). Helping women to make freer choices. In D. H. Montross & C. J. Shinkman (Eds.), *Career development in the 1980s: Theory and practice* (pp. 210–232). Springfield, IL: Charles C Thomas.

Linn, R. (1982). Ability testing: Individual differences, prediction, and differential prediction. In A. K. Wigdor & W. R. Garner (Eds.), *Ability testing: Uses, consequences, and controversies. Part II: Documentation section* (pp. 335–388). Washington, DC: National Academy Press.

Lunneborg, P. W. (1975). Interpreting other-sex scores on the Strong-Campbell Interest Inventory. *Journal of Counseling Psychology, 22,* 494–499.

Lynn, R. (1983). Lynn replies. *Nature, 306*(5940), 292.

MacMillan, D. L. (1977). *Mental retardation in school and society.* Boston: Little, Brown.

Madden, N. A., & Slavin, R. E. (1983). Mainstreaming students with mild handicaps: Academic and social outcomes. *Review of Educational Research, 53,* 519–569.

Matarazzo, J. D. (1972). *Wechsler's measurement and appraisal of adult intelligence* (5th ed.). Baltimore: Williams & Wilkins.

Mercer, J. R. (1979). *SOMPA: Technical manual.* New York: The Psychological Corporation.

Minton, H. L., & Schneider, F. W. (1980). *Differential psychology.* Monterey, CA: Brooks/Cole.

Mitchell, L. K., & Krumboltz, J. D. (1984). Social learning approach to career decision making: Krumboltz's theory. In D. Brown & L. Brooks (Eds.), *Career choice and development* (pp. 235–280). San Francisco: Jossey-Bass.

National Center for Health Statistics. (1977). Teenage childbearing: United States, 1966–75. *Monthly Vital Statistics Report, Natality Statistics, 26*(5), (Supplement, September 8). 1–15.

National Institute of Education. (1980). *Conference on the educational and occupational needs of white ethnic women.* Washington, DC: U.S. Department of Education.

Osipow, S. H. (1976). Vocational development problems of the handicapped. In R. Rusalem & D. Malikan (Eds.), *Contemporary vocational rehabilitation* (pp. 51–61). New York: New York University Press.

Osipow, S. H. (1982). Research in career counseling: An analysis of issues and problems. *The Counseling Psychologist, 10,* 27–34.

Overs, R. P. (1975). Career behavior of the physically and mentally handicapped. In J. S. Picou & R. E. Campbell (Eds.), *Career behavior of special groups* (pp. 177–198). Columbus, OH: Charles E. Merrill.

Pepinsky, H. B. (1948). The selection and use of diagnostic categories in clinical counseling. *Applied Psychology Monographs, 15.*

Picou, J. S., & Campbell, R. E. (Eds.). (1975). *Career behavior of special groups.* Columbus, OH: Charles E. Merrill.

Power, P. W. (1984). *A guide to vocational assessment.* Baltimore, MD: University Park.

Prediger, D. J., & Hanson, G. R. (1974). The distinction between sex restrictiveness and sex bias in interest inventories. *Measurement and Evaluation in Guidance, 7,* 96–104.

Raven, J. C., Court, J. H., & Raven, J. (1979). *Manual for Raven's progressive matrices and vocabulary scales. Section 1: General overview.* London: H. K. Lewis.

Rayman, J. R. (1976). Sex and the single interest inventory: The empirical validation of sex-balanced interest inventory items. *Journal of Counseling Psychology, 23,* 239–246.

Richardson, M. S., & Johnson, M. (1984). Counseling women. In S. D. Brown & R. W. Lent (Eds.), *Handbook of counseling psychology* (pp. 832–877). New York: Wiley.

Rodriguez, R. (1979). Going home again: The new American scholarship boy. In D. R. Atkinson, G. Morten, & D. W. Sue (Eds.), *Counseling American minorities: A cross-cultural perspective* (pp. 149–158). Dubuque, IA: Wm. C. Brown.

Rogan, H. (1984, October 29). Women executives feel that men both aid and hinder their careers. *Wall Street Journal,* pp. 35, 59.

Rohe, D. E., & Athelstan, G. T. (1982). Vocational interests of persons with spinal cord injury. *Journal of Counseling Psychology, 29,* 283–291.

Rounds, J. B., Jr., & Tinsley, H. E. A. (1984). Diagnosis and treatment of vocational problems. In S. D. Brown & R. W. Lent (Eds.), *Handbook of counseling psychology* (pp. 137–177). New York: Wiley.

Samuda, R. J. (1975). *Psychological testing of American minorities: Issues and consequences.* New York: Dodd, Mead.

Schlossberg, N. K., & Pietrofesa, J. J. (1978). Perspectives on counselor bias: Implications for counselor education. In L. W. Harmon, J. M. Birk, L. E. Fitzgerald, & M. F. Tanney (Eds.), *Counseling women* (pp. 59–74). Monterey, CA: Brooks/Cole.

Schmidt, F. L., & Hunter, J. E. (1981). Employment testing: Old theories and new research findings. *American Psychologist, 36,* 1128–1137.

Scott, R. A. (1969). *The making of blind men.* New York: Russell Sage Foundation.

Segal, S. P. (1978). Attitudes toward the mentally ill: A review. *Social Work, 23,* 211–217.

Sewell, W. H., & Hauser, R. M. (1975). *Education, occupation, and earnings.* New York: Academic.

Sewell, W. H., & Shah, V. P. (1968). Social class, parental encouragement, and educational aspirations. *American Journal of sociology, 73,* 559–572.

Smith, E. J. (1982). Counseling psychology in the marketplace: The status of ethnic minorities. *The Counseling Psychologist, 10,* 61–68.

Smith, E. J. (1983). Issues in racial minorities' career behavior. In W. B. Walsh & S. H. Osipow (Eds.), *Handbook of vocational psychology, vol. 1: Foundations* (pp. 161–222). Hillsdale, NJ: Lawrence Erlbaum Associates.

Spenner, K. I., & Featherman, D. L. (1978). Ambition. *Annual Review of Sociology, 4,* 373–420.

Spokane, A. R. (1979). Occupational preference and the validity of the Strong-Campbell Interest Inventory for college women and men. *Journal of Counseling Psychology, 26,* 312–318.

Stevenson, H. W., & Azuma, H. (1983). IQ in Japan and the United States. *Nature, 306*(5940), 291–292.

Sue, D. W. (1979). Ethnic identity: The impact of two cultures on the psychological development of Asians in America. In D. R. Atkinson, G. Morten, & D. W. Sue (Eds.), *Counseling American minorities: A cross-cultural perspective* (pp. 83–94). Dubuque, IA: Wm. C. Brown.

Sue, D. W. (1981). *Counseling the culturally different.* New York: Wiley.

Sue, S., & Kitano, H. H. L. (1979). Stereotypes as a measure of success. In D. R. Atkinson, G. Morten, & D. W. Sue (Eds.), *Counseling American minorities: A cross-cultural perspective* (pp. 69–82). Dubuque, IA: Wm. C. Brown.

Super, D. E. (1984). Career and life development. In D. Brown & L. Brooks (Eds.), *Career choice and development* (pp. 192–234). San Francisco: Jossey-Bass.

Suzuki, B. H. (1977). Education and the socialization of Asian Americans: A revisionist analysis of the "model minority" thesis. *Amerasia, 4,* 23–51.

Swerdloff, S., & Rosen, H. (1973). *Eight years later: Education and careers of young Jewish adults.* Washington, DC: B'nai B'rith Career and Counseling Services.

Tenopyr, M. L. (1981). The realities of employment testing. *American Psychologist, 36,* 1120–1127.

Tiedeman, D. V., & Miller-Tiedeman, A. (1984). Career decision making: An individualistic perspective. In D. Brown & L. Brooks (Eds.), *Career choice and development* (pp. 281–310). San Francisco: Jossey-Bass.

Tittle, C. K., & Zytowski, D. G. (Eds.). (1978). *Sex-fair interest measurement: Research and implications.* Washington, DC: National Institute of Education.

Tringo, J. L. (1970). The hierarchy of preference toward disability groups. *The Journal of Special Education, 4,* 295–306.

U.S. Bureau of the Census. (1973). *Census of Population: 1970. Subject reports. Final report PC(2)-3A. Women by number of children ever born.* Washington, DC: U.S. Government Printing Office.

U.S. Bureau of the Census. (1982). *Characteristics of American children and youth: 1980.* (Current Population Reports, P-23, No. 114.) Washington, DC: U.S. Government Printing Office.

U.S. Bureau of the Census. (1983a). *1980 Census of the population. Vol. 1, Characteristics of the population, Chapter C: General social and economic characteristics, U.S. summary. PC80-1-C1*. Washington, DC: U.S. Government Printing Office.

U.S. Bureau of the Census. (1983b). *Detailed occupation and years of school completed by age, for the civilian labor force by sex, race, and Spanish origin: 1980. PC80-S1-8*. Washington, DC: U.S. Government Printing Office.

U.S. Bureau of the Census. (1983c). *Marital status and living arrangements: March 1982*. (Current Population Reports, P-20, No. 380). Washington, DC: U.S. Government Printing Office.

U.S. Bureau of the Census. (1983d). *Population profile of the United States: 1982*. (Current Population Reports, P-23, No. 130). Washington, DC: U.S. Government Printing Office.

U.S. Bureau of the Census. (1984a). *1980 Census of population. Vol. 1, Characteristics of the population: Detailed population characteristics, Part 1, United States Summary. PC80-1-D1-A*. Washington, DC: U.S. Government Printing Office.

U.S. Bureau of the Census. (1984b). *Fertility of American women: June 1982*. (Current Population Reports, P-20, No. 387). Washington, DC: U.S. Government Printing Office.

U.S. Commission on Civil Rights. (1978). *Social indicators of equality for minorities and women*. Washington, DC: U.S. Commission on Civil Rights.

U.S. Department of Labor. (1977). *Dictionary of occupational titles* (4th ed.). Washington, DC: U.S. Government Printing Office.

U.S. Department of Labor. (1980). *Perspectives on working women: A data-book*. Washington, DC: U.S. Government Printing Office.

Warnath, C. G. (1975). Vocational theories: Direction to nowhere. *Personnel and Guidance Journal, 53*, 422-428.

Weinrach, S. G. (1984). Determinants of vocational choice: Holland's theory. In D. Brown & L. Brooks (Eds.), *Career choice and development* (pp. 61-93). San Francisco: Jossey-Bass.

Wigdor, A. K., & Garner, W. R. (1982). *Ability testing: Uses, consequences, and controversies. Part 1: Report of the committee*. Washington, DC: National Academy Press.

Williamson, E. G. (1939). *How to counsel students*. New York: McGraw-Hill.

Wuthnow, R. (1977). Is there an academic melting pot? *Sociology of Education, 50*, 7-15.

Wylie, R. C. (1984). Self-concept. In R. J. Corsini (Ed.), *Encyclopedia of psychology: Vol. 3* (pp. 282-285). New York: Wiley.

Zytowski, D. G. (1978). Implications for counselors of research on sex-fairness in interest measurement. In C. K. Tittle & D. G. Zytowski (Eds.), *Sex-fair interest measurement: Research and implications* (pp. 129-133). Washington, DC: National Institute of Education.

Zytowski, D. G. (1981). *Counseling with the Kuder Occupational Interest Survey Form DD*. Chicago: Science Research.

Zytowski, D. G., & Borgen, F. H. (1983). Assessment. In W. B. Walsh & S. H. Osipow (Eds.), *Handbook of vocational psychology, Vol. 2: Applications* (pp. 5-40). Hillsdale, NJ: Lawrence Erlbaum Associates.

Zytowski, D. G., & Laing, J. (1978). Validity of other-gender-normed scales on the Kuder Occupational Interest Survey. *Journal of Counseling Psychology, 25*, 205-209.

Author Index

Subject Index